BORDERLANDS
Riding the Slipstream

A COLLECTION OF AUSTRALIAN STORIES,
POETRY AND ARTWORK

Edited by
Paul Collins

FORD ST

Also edited by Paul Collins

Metaworlds

Dream Weavers

Strange Fruit

The MUP Encyclopaedia of Australian Science Fiction and Fantasy

Fantastic Worlds

Spinouts (co-editor Meredith Costain)

Tales from the Wasteland

Trust Me!

Trust Me Too

Rich & Rare

BORDERLANDS
Riding the Slipstream

Paul Collins has edited numerous anthologies – including Australia's first fantasy collection, *Dream Weavers* – along with *Fantastic Worlds*, *Rich & Rare* and *Trust Me Too*, and together with Meredith Costain, sixty short anthologies in the *Spinouts* and *Thrillogies* series. During his career, he has received the A Bertram Chandler, Peter McNamara and Aurealis awards for his writing and editing work. In 2021 he was awarded the Leila St John citation and medal by the Children's Book Council of Australia for services to children's literature. Paul is also a small press publisher of books for young readers and the author of over 250 books and short stories.

FORD ST

*With thanks to Savannah, Analena, Palmina,
Kristina, Gemma and Grazia for those extra eyes*

First published by Ford Street Publishing, Melbourne,
Victoria, Australia

2 4 6 8 10 9 7 5 3 1

This publication is copyright. Apart from any use
as permitted under the Copyright Act 1968, no part
may be reproduced by any process without prior written
permission from the publisher. Requests and enquiries
concerning reproduction should be addressed to

Ford Street Publishing Pty Ltd,

162 Hoddle Street, Abbotsford, Vic 3067, Australia

ISBN 9781922696403

Ford Street website: www.fordstreetpublishing.com

First published 2024

Target audience: For upper primary/lower secondary
school age

Subjects: Short stories, Australian.

Australian poetry.

Other creators/Contributors: Collins, Paul, 1954– editor

© this collection Paul Collins 2024

© cover illustration and design Shaun Tan

© illustrations Anne Ryan

Cover credit note: 'On My Way to Paradise' originally
published in *Creature*, Windy Hollow Books, 2022

© in individual text/illustrations remains with each
contributor

Printed in China by Tingleman Pty Ltd

Contents

Foreword ix
Isobelle Carmody

Fantasy
Shaun Tan
The Bird King 1

Cecilia Dart-Thornton
The Churchyard Yarrow 12

Justin D'Ath
Kaspar 32

Pamela Freeman
Ancestral Trees 56

Science Fiction
Ian Irvine
Uncertainty 72

Paul Collins
The Immortality Backup 84

John Larkin
The Way up to Heaven 103

Contemporary
Bill Condon
A Dog of His Own 111

Dianne Wolfer
Shifting Edges 119

Michael Earp
Message Me — 135

Susanne Gervay
Faith and the Elephant God — 145

Tony Thompson
The Knight — 155

David Metzenthen
Rabbit Life — 167

Deborah Abela
Into the Wild — 179

Sean McMullen
Three Days and Three Nights — 188

Kirsty Murray
Trick or Treat or Death — 199

Adventure
Sue Bursztynski
The Trail of Gold — 215

Crime
Lucy Sussex
The Barefoot Thieftaker — 230

Romance
Janeen Brian
Take It on the Cheek — 249

Scot Gardner
Safety Second — 261

Oliver Phommavanh
She's All Chat — 279

Ghost
George Ivanoff
Ghost Ship — 285

Juliet Marillier
The Audition — 303

Michael Pryor
Ghost Bait — 317

Sean Williams
The Tragedy of Evely Vyle — 341

Horror
Sophie Masson
Awakening — 372

Trinity Ryan
The Clockmaker's Cat — 383

Historical
Gary Crew
To Go On — 403

Simon Higgins
The Cabin Boy and the Creature — 416

James Phelan
Tale of Two Times — 437

Pamela Rushby
The Karoola Quarantine — 452

Humour

Barry Jonsberg
*Mr Postlethwaite's Class of Exceptionally
  Gifted Children*   474

Elizabeth Fensham
*Good Fences Make Good Neighbours –
  a Fowl Story*   486

Victor Kelleher
The Wannabe Genie   509

Graphic
Leigh Hobbs
Old Tom's Room   527

Poetry
Harry Laing
The Story of My Life   530

Lorraine Marwood
Raid   532

Meredith Costain
Waiting . . .   536

Sherryl Clark
How to Catch a Shadow   538

Steven Herrick
A Tattoo   540

Ursula Dubosarsky
Willy Wagtail   542

About the Contributors   544

Foreword

Isobelle Carmody

I have always been drawn to writing that carried me far from my own unloved and mundane backyard.

As a child, I was drawn to worlds that were new and strange to me, adventures that happened in places I had never been, stories about experiences that didn't belong to the world I inhabited. Some would call this reading escapism, and perhaps I was escaping the powerlessness of childhood in my reading.

But I was also escaping the limitations of the adult lives I saw unfolding around me, and the specific misery of being a kid who does not fit into her own world for reasons she doesn't understand.

The label of escapism is problematic, however. It suggests a fleeting holiday from reality in a fun park where the true difficulties of existence and striving of the human condition are absent, and all problems are easily resolved, leading to an inevitable and eternal happy ever after. In fact, such stories weren't satisfying to me.

I need to see the struggles and confusions of life in my reading because it makes stories feel real and true. The attraction of genre fiction is that the stories are both an escape from a world of ordinary concerns to a world where a writer and/or their characters seek answers to deeper questions, meaning and purpose.

I find myself and my deepest questions in these stories. And then – and this is the most important thing – I return to reality stronger, braver, wiser, inspired, and more resilient.

I love genre stories, and good realism, but best of all, I love stories that straddle the wall built by criticism and marketing between those forms of writing, and tales that set up shop right alongside the border. I have come to define these sorts of stories as slipstream. That term was coined by author Bruce Sterling, who uses it to define books and stories that are neither realism or genre, but something slippery that moves between and around these terms. You will find in this anthology some gems belonging to this sub-genre.

This brings me to the stories in this unique collection. *Borderlands: Riding the Slipstream* contains stories that are not only individually great reads, but when read as a collection, they have been chosen and arranged to carry readers back and forth across the borderland between realism and the fantastic. This allows an exploration of the ways in which writers use genre tools to ask and shape answers to their questions.

This collection – with its fabulous evocative cover from Shaun Tan – will sharpen a sense of form and an awareness of genre tools in both students and teachers of literature.

What I love about the stories here is my feeling that they were written without constraining definition, because writers often think they know where a story is going, and then have that delicious experience of the story taking over. Good stories have their own engines and the ideas and questions must make their own journey. Sometimes, as a writer, if you are brave enough and the idea is strong enough, you become a passenger along for the ride.

Herein, a reader can travel from the humorous realism of Barry Jonsberg's 'Mr Postlethwaite's Class of Exceptionally Gifted Children' to the alarming ineptitude displayed by Victor Kelleher's 'Junior Genie', and to the purity of hope in Bill Condon's 'A Dog of His Own', or, they can move through the eeriness of Cecilia Dart-

Thornton's 'The Churchyard Yarrow', and Sophie Masson's 'Awakening' to the lovely whimsy of David Metzenthen's 'Rabbit Life'. Then on to history with Gary Crew's 'To Go On' which begins with a real boy who ran away to sea, or Lucy Sussex's 'The Barefoot Thieftaker' set in the time before detectives. George Ivanoff's 'Ghost Ship' will carry a reader out into space with pirates and Justin D'Ath will bring us back to reality via a very grounded fantasy in 'Kaspar', from where we might travel on to an unsettling future in which people are transformed by downloading the lives of dogs into their brains, in Paul Collins' 'The Immortality Backup'.

There is also diversity of form with wonderful poetry such as Harry Laing's 'The Story of My Life' and Steven Herrick's 'A Tattoo', not to mention beautiful poetic writing from Shaun Tan in writer mode with his strange and lovely 'The Bird King'.

On a journey through this anthology you will find stories that take your breath away, like Pamela Freeman's 'Ancestral Trees' and Juliet Marillier's exquisitely-written 'The Audition', offering two realities, and Michael Earp's 'Message Me', which plays with the mind, to debut author Trinity

Ryan's 'The Clockmaker's Cat', which defies categorisation.

Enlivened by Anne Ryan's wonderful artwork, each of the stories in this book allows a profound individual journey, but collectively, the stories allow young readers to explore the many ways we can ask questions about the real world in which we all live.

This is a very special collection because it allows readers to explore the many forms of creative writing that make up a thrilling borderland between realism and genre.

Isobelle Carmody
Melbourne 2024

The Bird King

Shaun Tan

A long time ago there were no clocks or maps or ordinary things, and everything was covered in silence and dust. But somehow, there were always birds. Small, wingless and blind, but birds nonetheless, making their dusty nests, laying their tiny eggs, and singing. In darkness they sang, quietly at first, but louder as their numbers grew, eventually loud enough to wake the sun. That great solar eye peered across a strange and ancient landscape, its enormous wings opening to a new blue day. The birds could feel its warmth, grew eyes to see its light, and wings to lift themselves up in that blue. Below them the earth gave birth to a great family of wondrous creatures, all crawling, floating, slithering, swimming or walking about, each with their own daily business. For all this, we owe the birds.

Among them lived a king. Not the kind that lives in a castle, sits on thrones or makes laws, for this was very, very long ago when such things did not yet exist. This king looked much like other animals, walking comfortably on all fours, wandering the landscape, fascinated by the smallest detail of everything he saw and always finding some new inspiration each day. His mind roamed as much as his hands and feet. The other animals loved him very much, and he loved them too.

In the evenings, all would gather in the shadows of hills to hear the king reflect upon his long walks. He would describe things he had seen, things that he might have seen, and things that he had not seen at all, only imagined. The last of these entertained his audience most of all, as there seemed no limit to the king's inventiveness. Every day ended the same way, the animals returned to their burrows, nests, lairs and hives, the sun slowly folded its wings and the grass whispered quietly to itself. The birds, as always, looked on.

One morning the king wandered further than he had ever done before, drawn to something glinting in the distance. He came across a kind of animal he had never seen before, an old woman, kneeling by the shore of a black lake. A light breeze carried away small pieces of her once beautiful robes, and her face seemed made of ash, lines carved into her cheeks by the long passage of tears. But what struck the king's eye most of all was a golden crown atop her bowed head, shining bright against the greyness of this mysterious scene.

'Who are you?' he asked.

'I don't know,' she uttered in a voice like sliding stone, a small plume of dust leaving her barely moving lips. Puzzled, the king asked about her crown, as he could not draw his eyes from it.

'A wonderful and cursed thing,' whispered the despondent figure. 'It knows every dream of the wearer and brings it forth into the world.'

Compelled by a powerful and nameless desire, the king asked the woman to let him place the crown upon his own head, if only for a moment. She turned away. 'If I remove the crown, I will surely die. I have worn it so long, become so consumed by its promise as to have forgotten all else. I cannot even remember myself – all the things that made me who I am. I exist now only because I imagine myself so, upon seeing my reflection in this pool.'

Bewildered, the king left the old woman alone and continued his wanderings. Yet he

could not stop thinking about the crown, and walked by the woman each day – even though she was too absorbed in her own reflection to pay him any notice. And each day a single tear ran down her face, fell into the pool and broke that visage into a hundred ripples. Thereupon her already faded figure would fade a little more, and the wind would pluck more pieces from her ragged gowns. This continued until one day there was nothing more than a pile of ash where she once knelt, and on top of it the golden crown.

Seeing his chance, the king hurried down to the shore and took it.

As soon as he placed the crown upon his head, he knew the old woman's words were indeed true. Marvellous creatures of his imagination emerged from the Earth and walked about as if alive, much to his astonishment. Later that evening, as the king revealed this new magical object to all the animals that had gathered by the hills, they were together overcome by laughter, joy and wonder that continued well into the night. Even the sun woke briefly at this noisy jubilation, but soon closed its great eye again, and none saw the tear that fell beyond the horizon.

The next day, everyone returned to their

usual occupations, crawling, swimming, flying and so on – all except the king. He was content to sit upon a hill all day, imagining one fanciful thing after another and watching them climb out of the earth as the sun looked on without comment. So it was that he spent more and more days alone working on his own creations, and less time wandering the land or communing with the other animals. He became obsessed with creating new things, each more elaborate, more beautiful, more impressive than the last. At the same time, the other animals grew less and less interested in these inventions. 'They move and speak, but are not truly alive,' they complained. 'They come from the Earth but do not belong to it.'

The king grew angry at this. 'You are stupid animals!' he cried, and he stood up tall on two legs to show how different he was from lowly creatures. 'You know nothing!'

And with that he imagined a huge tower in which he could create without criticism. He imagined bigger and more beautiful animals than those he had known, animals that would work for him without question, admire his achievements and tell him how great a king he was. The place around the tower became a kingdom, and that kingdom grew, drawing all that it needed from the earth to build a vast domain of marvellous creation, leaving great craters and tracts of lifeless dust in its wake. The king's ingenuity and ambition seemed to know no bounds, even though it was always surrounded by a high wall, erected to silence the lament of other animals.

One day a single bird from beyond the kingdom managed to breach the wall and fly all the way to the king's tower. The king had become so absorbed in his own world that he didn't recognise the animal that now flew through his window until it began to talk. It told of the origin of all things, the land he had left behind, and how it was disappearing as more and more earth was consumed to build what had now become a sprawling folly.

This news was so unsettling that the king could not bear to hear it. Without thinking, he imagined something to eat the bird, and the messenger was promptly devoured by a pouncing beast. Despairing at what he had done, he imagined another creature to sweep up the scattered feathers into the darkest corner of the tower's keep, and so it was done.

Many more birds came to visit the king

over the years, but none returned to report what they had seen. Eventually, there were so few birds in the land that they could no longer wake the sun, and everything fell to darkness once again. This did not concern the king too much, however, for he simply imagined a sun of his own, one that hung above his kingdom like a glowing silver ball. Having been away from the world for so long, however, he could no longer imagine all the colours that had once captivated him, and the kingdom was illuminated by a cold and unchanging light.

Further years passed, countless in number – for the sun was gone and time had lost its meaning. As memory and inspiration dwindled, the king's subjects became increasingly monotonous copies of each other, a dull parade that praised his genius in a single droning voice. That they built great statues in honour of their master only added to his misery.

Alone, bitter and frustrated, he began to despise everything he had made. In a dark rage, he imagined a monstrous dragon that would consume everything. No sooner had the thought crossed his mind than a fire-blackened creature crept forth from the ground with a terrible moan, billowing cinders and clawing its way through the kingdom. Startled by the power of his own deep despair, the king could not imagine how to quell it. The dragon twisted and turned, devouring the kingdom's buildings and animals by the thousands. It chased the king himself and he imagined higher and higher towers in a desperate bid to escape. When the dragon began to gnaw on the foundations of the final tower, the king crawled into the furthest, darkest corner of the keep, cowering hopelessly.

There he noticed a single feather that had been swept aside so long ago. It was the most beautiful thing he could ever recall having seen, and as he held it between his fingers, he remembered the form of a bird, and suddenly great feathery wings began to unfold from his back. The walls around him cracked and split; the dragon thundered and the tower began to fall, but the king leapt through the nearest window, spread his wings, and narrowly escaped fiery snapping jaws.

He flew across the dark sky for what seemed an eternity, far beyond his kingdom's ruins, and when he could no longer imagine his own passage, he fell to the dark desert below. There were no hills or forests anymore, only dusty holes from which the material of his kingdom had been mined, and only a handful of pale and sightless birds nested, singing their weak chorus, forever trying to raise the sun. They paused in their labours, sensing the strange thing that had landed before them. The king had been gone for so long that none would have even remembered him, had they eyes to see.

But the song of these sorry creatures awakened some faint spark of feeling in the king, something at once old and new, and he looked upon them in the pale starlight. He could see their beaks and feathers and small trembling bodies, their reality so startling and inspiring that he himself became a bird completely. His feathered head forgot all else, and being too small to support a crown, was finally free of it: the cursed thing rolled away into the darkness. And so a new bird began to sing, its body weak but its voice strong with renewed spirit, and it lifted the chorus. The sun was roused and peered its sleepy eye once again over a distant horizon, opening its own great blue wings once again. Plants began to grow, flowers bloomed, insects came, and other animals too; forests spread and rivers resumed their ancient course, carrying all that remained of a once mighty kingdom to the sea. The birds – including the one that forever forgot it was once a king – rejoiced. And so the world went on living and dying, shifting and changing, remembering and forgetting, to this very day.

And what became of the crown? Such powerful things will never vanish from the world so long as there are those who so desire them. Many came to wear it, enjoy its rapture and suffer its curse, and many will continue to do so. And the dragon? It too comes and goes as the ages pass, wreaking mindless havoc, undoing all things bad and good. You can sometimes hear it on a windless night, thrashing and writhing in the unseen distance, waiting to be summoned by a lost and weary heart.

The Churchyard Yarrow

Cecilia Dart-Thornton

Rose wrapped her shawl close around her and passed through the village, carrying a bundle under one arm. The low stone cottages scattered along the road up and down the hill were thatched with heather and turf. Young and agile, Rose moved swiftly past the Rafferty place. Around at the side, a little girl was throwing out

scraps for the chickens. She bobbed a curtsy to Rose, who smiled in acknowledgement.

The sky was overcast and a metallic tang in the air threatened thunder. As she left the village outskirts, Rose could hear it dimly rumbling, away in the west, like a cauldron simmering. Down along the floor of the vale the ground became boggy. A narrow footpath descended rapidly towards a stone bridge crossing over the stream, before mounting the steep incline on the other side.

Wild-haired children were playing by the stream. One of them had made himself a whistle out of a dead-nettle stalk, and was piping eerie and tuneless air. Rose called out to the children and waved, and they returned her salute. She left them behind and – lifting her skirts to avoid stepping on the hems – climbed towards the McGintys' place which was nestled in a hollow beneath Madigan's Leap.

The interior of the McGintys' cottage was redolent with mingled scents of herbs, tallow and tanned leather. Through the open door at the rear could be glimpsed the narrow chamber that was Flynn's workroom. Hides, thongs and implements of the cobbler's trade hung from hooks hammered into the walls.

In the main room, bunches of dried leaves swung from the exposed roof beams. Among them, yarrow, wood sage, dandelion, mallow, lemon balm and hart's tongue fern. Some strings of onions dangled there also, and a small leg of ham the McGintys were saving for special occasions. On top of the rafters sat a row of four hens, and a sheepdog was curled up under a settle. In the corner stood an old spinning wheel, its distaff wound with lint. A single rush light – like a yellow hound's tooth – burned at the centre of the table. The dancing flame duplicated itself in Ilvenna McGinty's eyes and caressed the curves of her young face as she listened to Rose telling her story. She was clad in drab woollen skirts, with a knitted shawl draped about her shoulders.

A goat's head poked in at the window and emitted a rude bleat. Ilvenna stood up and flapped her pinafore at it. The head withdrew hurriedly and there was a scuffling sound of hoofs on stones as the goat moved away.

'Ma! Gallytrot's after gettin' into the garden again!' Ilvenna shouted out the back door. Then she came and seated herself at the table as before, opposite her visitor.

'Sure,' she said, 'ye're axin' a very barrelful o' questions, Miss Rose. 'Tis more than a simple love-divination ye're after.' She scratched her head thoughtfully. 'I never did anyt'ing like this before, seekin' a body you've only ever dreamed of.'

'I know it is a lot to ask,' said Rose. 'But even if you could just find out whether he is real or not, that would be enough.'

'Would it?' Ilvenna fixed her eyes on Rose.

'Well, no,' Rose admitted, 'but it would be better than nothing.'

Ilvenna scratched her head once more. 'I'll have to t'ink about this.'

'I can tell you more about the dreams,' said Rose helpfully.

'Go on.'

Beyond the window a goat bleated. There was a clang, as if someone had dropped a wooden pail with an iron handle, and an old woman's voice shouted, 'Get out of here, yer great baraille ramhar!'

The two girls in the cottage continued conversing, oblivious to these diversions.

'I dreamed that there was a band of tinkers,' said Rose, 'and they were gathered in a lane deeply bordered with flowering hawthorn and elder. And they had a horse which was so old and worn out that it had fallen to its knees and could not get up. But the tinkers were cursing the horse and whipping it, because they wanted it to get up and pull their wagon. The horse was incapable of moving, but they dug a hole beneath its ribs and lit a fire.'

'Sweet Jesus,' said Ilvenna, her face grey as ash.

'And then he was there,' said Rose, 'and it was the wrath of Solomon coming down on the tinkers. First, he stamped out the fire, kicking the flaming sticks in the faces of those who had lit it. Then he was on them like the Furies, knocking them this way and that with his staff, and although he was greatly outnumbered, they were caught off guard, and seeing the rage burning in his eyes they must have thought him a madman. They ran off, in fear of their lives, and when they were gone, he knelt down beside the poor old horse. He stroked its head and said something in its ear, softly, gently. Then he pulled out his knife and he did something very quick. From that very moment the horse was free from all suffering. My boy cleaned his knife on the grass and rose to his feet, casting one sad look at the dead beast. Then he glanced up and beheld me. He took one step towards me, but then I saw him and the flowery lane no more.'

With a swift movement, Ilvenna wiped her eyes with the back of her hand. "Tis a dramatic life he's leadin', this young man,' she observed drily.

'Not so dramatic, I think,' replied Rose. 'I have only told you some of the dreams that affected me most. But it is not all danger and fighting. There have been times when I've witnessed him playing a fast and furious game of hurling, and his team winning. And I have glimpsed him in a large and firelit room, surrounded by talk and song and laughter, holding a tankard brimming with black stout.'

'And is it always in the night-time you're seein' him?'

'No – sometimes I have seen him during my waking hours. A daydream, I suppose they call it. But, when I lie in my bed at night,' Rose went on softly, 'I have dreamed I am floating above his bed, looking down and watching him sleep. He opens his eyes and sees me. Then he smiles and reaches out. I reach too, but we can never quite touch each other, and after a while the dream fades.'

Ilvenna sniffed. 'There's much to be done,' she said, somewhat hoarsely, 'if we are to find this lad. D'ye love him?' she added abruptly.

A look of shock crossed Rose's features. 'I never thought about it,' she answered. 'Honestly, I do not know! I only know that he's has been part of my life ever since I can remember. When I see a face that resembles his, a pang goes through my heart. I catch myself searching for him around every corner, in every crowd. But do I love him? If a fierce longing to touch someone is love, then I do. If a sense of terrible desolation every time the dreams are snatched away is love, then I do. If the certainty that he is part of you, like your own blood, and that he is necessary for life, like breathing – if that is love, then I do love him.'

'Right,' said Ilvenna, 'that's important, because we cannot do anything wit' ye if ye don't love him, whateffer.' She pushed her stool back, stood up and paced the floor restlessly. 'There's many a way of divinin' love,' she said, as if thinking aloud. 'There's ways o' gettin' a vision o' your future husband, not that you're needin' any more visions. There's ways o' findin' out the first letter o' his name – and if you already have a sweetheart, there's ways o' findin' out whether he is faithful – or whether he'll leave ye for another. But there's only one way I know to tell if your true love lives or not. And for that ye must wait till Midsummer's Day.'

'That's months away. I cannot wait any longer!' exclaimed Rose with impatience. 'Can you not simply give me a way of getting some wishes so that I can wish for him to be here beside me?'

'No!' Ilvenna whirled on her heel. 'Now listen to me, Miss Rose, you don't go wishin' for things like that, not until we know for sure if he's livin' or not. D'ye want to be haunted by a ghost for the rest o' yer days?'

Rose smiled. 'Yes. If it were he, yes.'

'Ach! Hold yer nonsense,' scoffed Ilvenna. 'You do not know what ye're sayin'. You must never speak lightly o' such matters. Now Rose, if ye're after bein' foolish, I will not help you.'

'I'm sorry,' said Rose meekly, knowing that her friend meant to carry out her threat.

Ilvenna was mollified. 'On Midsummer's Eve,' she said, 'you must pick two flowers o' orpine. Name one of them Rose, and the other one Rose's Sweetheart. Stick them in two empty cotton reels and leave them beside your bed when you go to sleep. In the mornin', look at them as soon as you waken. If the one that stands for your sweetheart has shrivelled and died, then you'll know he is no livin' man. If it has wilted and bends away from the other flower, you'll know he lives but loves you not. If the two flowers are bent towards each other, then he lives and loves ye. But when ye're pickin' the flowers, ye must say the words I will teach you, otherwise the whole t'ing will never work.'

As Ilvenna was speaking, Ma McGinty appeared outside the door. She kicked off her muddy wooden clogs and left them on the threshold, then came inside, stooping to avoid the low lintel. 'Good mornin' to you, Miss Rose,' she said, putting down a pail of water and wiping her large, ruddy hands on her apron. Her brow was shiny with perspiration and her gown had been mended in many places.

'Good morning, Mrs McGinty. I hope you're well. I wish't Mama had let us send for you or Ilvenna when she was ill abed with the consumption.'

Ma McGinty nodded understandingly. 'There are folk that will never come to us. They have their reasons, so they do. We might have helped your ma, wit' dandelion roots and leaves of fairy thimble, and mullein and yarrow – we might indeed. 'Tis a shame and I'm sorry for ye.'

Rose indicated the wrapped bundle she had placed on the table. 'I have brought the embroideries so that Flynn can take them with him on his next trip to market.'

Mrs McGinty nodded dismissively. She said, 'Just now I heard my daughter tellin' ye how to find out if a man is livin'.'

'Yes,' said Rose.

'That should be worth a bit to ye, eh? More than a sack o' meal. Maybe a haunch o' mutton from one o' the farms, or a flitch o' bacon? We're savin' the ham up there for Pentecost.' She poked her chin at the rafters overhead. 'I cannot tell ye how long it is since I last tasted meat.'

'Ma, we have already agreed on the

fee . . .' Ilvenna's voice trailed off.

Ma McGinty had always driven a keen bargain. It was only to be expected. She was accustomed to working hard for every mouthful of food, and she expected value for value. Planting work-roughened hands on her broad hips, she stood looking at Rose. Her eyes were sunk between folds of freckled skin and her once copper hair was white as lightning. Somehow, she seemed a formidable adversary.

'Mrs McGinty,' said Rose, calmly meeting her gaze, 'if I can find out by St Valentine's Day whether this man lives, I will bring you anything you want.'

'It cannot be done! It is impossible!' expostulated Ilvenna. 'Anyway, why the haste, Miss Rose? You've waited all your life . . .'

'Hush now,' her mother said firmly. 'If that's what Miss Rose wants, we can provide.'

She lowered herself onto a three-legged stool.

'But Ma –'

'Sit you down, mo cailin, and you will be learnin' something this morning,' said Ma McGinty, waving a hand at her daughter. Rolling her eyes towards the ceiling, Ilvenna acquiesced.

'Listen well, Miss Rose,' said Ma McGinty. 'I have not taught this to Ilvenna because there's a mite o' peril in it, but not if you use the brains God gave you. This is what you must do . . .'

On St Valentine's Eve, after the rest of the household was abed, Rose crept from the house and climbed the hill to where the Catholic church stood in its grove of yew trees. It was close to midnight. High overhead, the moon was a polished sickle. Ragged clouds blew across its face, but there was enough light to see by as Rose entered the churchyard. She knelt beside the grave of a young man who had died ten years earlier, and her lips began to move in silent prayer. The wind was in the north, blowing from the direction of Charter Hall. It carried with it the faint sound of a clock striking twelve. As the chimes rang, Rose plucked nine leaves of yarrow that were growing on the grave, and as she picked, she said:

'Yarrow, yarrow, I seek thee yarrow,
And now thee I have found.
I pray to the good Lord Jesus
As I pluck thee from the ground.'

Hastily tucking the leaves inside her

shawl, she turned and hurried home.

When she entered the bedchamber she shared with her sister, Lizzie, she put seven of the yarrow leaves in her right stocking and tied it to her left leg, but saved two leaves, one of which she put under her pillow. The other, she folded and placed inside the small, curled shell of her left nostril. Then she whispered, without waking her sister:

'Green yarrow, green yarrow, you wear a white flower,
If my love lives, my nose will bleed sure;
If my love don't live, it won't bleed a drop,
If my love do live, 'twill bleed every drop.'

And as she laid her head on the pillow she murmured:

'Good night, pretty yarrow,
I pray thee sweet yarrow,
Tell me by the morrow,
If my true love lives.'

As Rose began to fall asleep, she found herself reflecting that Ma McGinty's spells and potions did not always work; a fact the wise woman fiercely contended. The thought presently evaporated and her mind drifted. Beyond the walls the west wind carried on its back the crashing roar of the surf at the foot of Madigan's Leap, and the cry of a bittern winging through the night.

At the dawning of St Valentine's Day, the rising sun peeped through a long rent in the clouds over the back hills, edging them with gilt. Its rays streamed out like long fingers, reaching to caress first the eaves of Charter Hall and the tops of the hedges lining the driveway. The rays wandered across the buttresses of St George's Church, making the stone glow like honey. Down the steeple of St Finbar's they bled, limning the black boughs of the ancient yews, lightly brushing the ancient, mossy roof over the village well. Then they pulled back the shadow of Whitethorn Hill to tinge with gold the thatched cottages of the village, upon whose roofs grew clumps of stonecrop, reputed to ward off thunder.

From one of the outermost houses arose a scream.

The scream went on and on, punctuated with almost unintelligible outbursts of 'Jesus, Mary and Joseph!' and 'Lord save us!'

John Delacey leapt from his bed. Rushing into the kitchen he found Lizzie running in circles, sobbing. Margaret, Katherine and Mary discovered her at the same time.

'Oh Jesus,' shrieked Lizzie, 'she's all a'blood. She's killed herself, by God. She's murdered.'

Still dressed in their nightshirts, everyone hastened into Rose's bedchamber. There on the bed the young girl lay, but the pillow and the linen all around her was soaked with crimson ichor. Bearded with a sticky, red viscosity, her face was almost unrecognisable.

'Mother of God!' exclaimed Margaret, clapping her hands to her mouth.

Her father looked stricken. 'Where's all the blood coming from?' he cried, kneeling beside her. 'Where are you hurt?'

'It's nothing,' murmured Rose, opening her eyes to prove she was still alive. ''Tis only a nosebleed.'

Her father flinched. At that moment he had caught a strange look in his daughter's eyes, and the phantom of a smile on her face, a smile almost of beatific joy.

'Pinch your nose,' ordered Mary, businesslike. 'Pinch it hard together, like this. Lizzie, quit your puling. Go and rinse a rag in cold water, then squeeze it out and bring it here at once. Maggie, you go and rouse up the fire under the hob. Kitty, pull the sheets off the bed this minute and throw them in the tub with cold salt water.'

'I'll not!' squawked Katherine indignantly. 'I'm not the servant!'

Mary said sharply, 'For goodness' sake, I only have two hands!'

Rose caught her sister's eye, nodded and made the secret sign with her hand. It was a signal they had used since childhood, to indicate that there was a private matter they promised to share when others were not listening.

'Oh, very well,' mumbled Katherine sourly.

Mary's prosaic method prevailed, and soon Rose's haemorrhage was staunched.

'I've never seen you with such a nosebleed,' fussed her father. 'I'd better have the doctor here to make certain you're all right.'

'I'm all right, Papa,' said Rose, 'truly. It looked worse than it was.'

'We'll have him here anyway.'

'Sure, if you go spending money on doctors, I'll have another nosebleed with the strain of it,' said Rose energetically.

Her father sighed. 'Well then,' he said, 'have your way. But you'd better be resting for a day or two, at least.'

His daughter noticed the haunted look in his eyes and by it she knew he remembered her mother's face lying amongst blood-stained sheets. Putting her arms about his neck she kissed him. 'I'm sorry, Papa.'

'Nonsense,' he said gruffly, stroking her hair.

Mary gave Rose a suspicious look.

'You're pale as a ghost,' she said. 'It wasn't anything Ilvenna McGinty told you to do, was it?'

'Oh no!' Rose said, cursing Mary's astuteness and praying inwardly that this wasn't a lie, since it had in fact been Ilvenna's mother who had advised her. 'No, truly, it was not.'

After breakfast Papa and Margaret went to work. Mary was out hanging freshly laundered sheets on the washing line, Lizzie was looking for eggs in the henhouse and Rose, wrapped in shawls, was sitting in the rocking chair by the kitchen window.

Katherine hissed in Rose's ear, 'What were all these leaves of yarrow doing in your bed? I found some tied up in a stocking, and another mixed up with the linen. And there was an awful soggy one floating in the washtub.' She grimaced. 'I threw them away. It was a love divination, was it not?'

Rose nodded and said happily, 'And it worked, Kitty.'

Katherine gasped.

Rose nodded. 'He is a living man.'

Months passed. For the Delacey family, life continued as usual.

On Midsummer's Eve a merry multitude of villagers bearing flaming torches wended its way up Madigan's Leap. Every year they celebrated the solstice this way. Those who had reached the clifftop stood outlined against a red and gold sunset slashed across the sky, its splendour reflected in the ocean far below.

By the time Rose and her sisters began the climb, the sun had drowned in the ocean and stars were shimmering. Against the darkness torches flared, dazzling.

As she strode up the hillside, Rose observed two falling stars streaking the skies over Madigan's Leap. She dropped back from the crowd and averted her eyes from the torch-glare. On retreating into the blind shadows, she felt someone fall into step beside her. She looked up to see who it was, and came to an abrupt halt. He halted, too.

The crowd parted around them, hurrying along without pause. For a full minute, Rose and the newcomer stood and stared at one another. They seemed to drink each other in with their eyes, like thirsty wanderers in a barren land who have found a well of clear water.

A youth of perhaps seventeen summers, this stranger was tall and strong, with hair as dark as a crow's wing. It fell down his back, tied in a horse tail, and he wore no cap. He was handsome, oh yes – strikingly handsome, with a beauty that commanded attention. Lean and taut was his countenance, as though carved out of stone, yet youthful and lively. His jaw was shaven and the line of it was well moulded and firm. Dark were his lashes and eyebrows. His eyes were as grey as the sea in a storm, but she who stood before him knew, as if by instinct, that they could flash hard and bright if his passion were aroused. There was a depth to those eyes that was fathomless. A white cravat encircled his neck. Over his linen shirt he wore a waistcoat, subtly patterned with the colours of heather and bracken. Beneath the shirt, his broad shoulders tapered to an elegant middle. He was girded with a belt to which a sheath was attached, with a scian tucked therein. The newcomer's long legs were clad in trousers of soft leather, over which were tied leather gaiters. He stood now as straight as a spear, but Rose was well aware he could move with the grace and power of a wild horse. To his enemies he might appear to be the devil himself, but as a lover, she had no doubt, he would be matchless.

The faces of these two as they gazed upon each other were the faces of people in pain. To look at them, anyone might have guessed they experienced the keenest agony or the most intense sorrow. Slowly the young man's hand moved towards Rose, and then, with a sudden movement, he had seized her by the wrist. In the same instant her other hand found its way up to his face. Her fingers slid into his hair and gripped tightly.

When at length they released each other, her wrist bore his fingerprints in the form of bruises, and her hand came away tangled with several livid filaments torn from his scalp. Despite the fact that they had inflicted violence on each other, and as if by these actions they had verified the other's existence, the expression of hurt in their eyes softened. It appeared that whatever anguish pierced them had now diminished to an ache. As though at some signal, they turned and began walking side by side, following the last of the crowd up the slope.

They had spoken not a word.

Kaspar

Justin D'Ath

'This is Kaspar,' Chase Jensen announces grandly.

'OMG!' gasps his visitor, peering dewy-eyed through the heavy gauge chain-link fence. 'He's magnificent!'

Lost in the wonder of the moment, she lightly touches the back of Chase's hand.

So far, so good, he thinks. But the next bit is what counts.

Taking a deep breath, Chase slo-o-o-owly turns his hand to meet hers, then one by one captures her warm fingers supergently in his. Her attention is so focused on what's in the pen that she doesn't notice.

It works almost every time.

Chase wishes his friends could see him now, holding hands with Lola Daylight, the hottest girl in Year Nine.

'Kaspar is the last of our original breeding stock,' he begins his well-practised spiel. But today his voice is quieter than usual, less assured, because the creature is

watching them with its head lowered, and a mean glint in its eyes.

Has it been given its medication today?

'Kaspar is a hundred and sixty years old,' Chase continues, almost whispering now. 'My great-great-great-grandparents imported him from Norway, just before a deadly new virus called *Enhjøning sykdom* wiped out the entire northern hemisphere population. So, ours are the only ones left.'

'Wow!' cries Lola.

Chase will never know whether Lola's wow comes in response to what happened 160 years ago, or to what's happening in the here and now. He will only know how fortunate it was that he was still holding her hand. He yanks her out of the way just in time.

CLANGGGGG!

Kaspar hits the fence at full gallop. His metre-long horn pokes out through the wire, wobbling like the pointy end of a javelin, exactly where Lola was standing. Had Chase's reaction time been even half a second slower, the hottest girl in Year Nine would have been kebabbed.

The echo of her startled scream still rings in his ears. Chase doesn't blame her for screaming; he almost screamed himself. But is glad he didn't. Leading her well out of horn-range, he wraps Lola Daylight protectively in his arms.

Thank you, Kaspar, he thinks.

Aloud, he says, 'Sorry about that, Lola. It was totally my fault. I shouldn't have let you go so close to the wire.'

'I thought unicorns were supposed to be nice,' she murmurs into his chest.

'Mostly they are,' he agrees. 'Kaspar wasn't always like this. I used to ride him when I was little.'

'I didn't think you were supposed to ride them.'

'It wasn't like riding a horse. I was only about four or five years old. Mum and Dad used to lead him around the lawn on a rope and I'd sit on his back.' Chase shakes his head at the memory. 'He was so lovely and gentle back then.'

Lola looks up at him with her big, brown eyes. 'So what's going on with him now?'

'The vet thinks he's getting some form of animal dementia. Basically, he's forgotten what humans are,' explains Chase. 'Now he seems to think we're his enemies.'

'That's so sad!' Lola says softly, turning her head in Kaspar's direction.

Chase follows her gaze. The unicorn is trotting up and down the fence, snorting at them and rattling the splintery tip of its horn – *tinktinktinktink* – along the wire. 'We've got some special medication to calm him down,' he tells Lola, 'but Mum must have forgotten to give it to him this morning.'

Then he remembers that his mother is away for the weekend. She and Aunty Jess have flown up to Melbourne to see some Russian dancing show. She left Chase a list of jobs to do while she's gone. Looking after Kaspar's medication is one of them. Oops!

'I suppose I'd better go and sort it out,' he says with a sigh, reluctant to end the hug.

———

All the unicorns' vitamins, food supplements and medicines are kept in a little supply room at the back of the stables. It's a long, low building with stalls along each side. Lola's head swivels back and forth as she and Chase walk between them. All the stalls are empty.

'Where are the others?' she asks, sounding disappointed.

'In the top paddocks,' Chase says. 'I'll take you up there as soon as we get Kaspar sorted.'

He opens the small fridge where most of the medications are stored. The vet left a ziplock bag of tiny vials when she visited last week. Each one contains 10 mls of milky liquid. Chase counts how many are left. Only four. That means they'll run out on Tuesday.

So, they're going to do it on Wednesday while he's at school.

There are half a dozen small red apples in the crisper tray in the bottom of the fridge. Chase puts one in his pocket and hands a second one to Lola. 'Don't eat it,' he says lightly, but there's a catch in his voice. 'It's . . . it's for Kaspar.'

A wide-gauge reusable syringe rests in a stainless-steel bowl on the workbench. Chase fills it from one of the four remaining vials, making sure he gets every last drop. Then he takes the apple from Lola and carefully injects the contents deep into the fruit.

'What is that stuff?' she asks as they make their way back outside.

'I don't know.' He tosses the apple over his head and catches it behind his back. Showing off. Because that's how you impress girls. Getting sentimental over a dying animal doesn't cut it. 'Some sort of tranquilliser. Whatever it is, it calms the old fella down.'

Kaspar watches them approach. He snorts threateningly and paws the ground. Dust swirls around him. His eyes are weepy and bloodshot. A trickle of fresh blood runs down from just below his horn. He must have hurt himself when he charged the fence. One of his ears is torn from a similar incident last week while the vet was here. It's horrible what's happening to him.

'Can I give him the apple?' Lola asks bravely.

Chase passes it to her and shows her the metal chute to put it through. There's a double layer of wire in this section of fence; it's horn-proof.

'But be careful he doesn't bite you,' he warns.

She slips the apple into the chute, then jumps back when Kaspar charges the fence. *CLANGGGGG!* The reinforced wire does its job, but Lola squeals anyway. Chase doesn't do the hugging thing this time, even though the opportunity is there.

He's more concerned about Kaspar than about bragging rights on Monday. The poor old unicorn has just opened another wide red gash above his left eye. The blood looks shocking on his silver-white fur.

'How long will it take to work?' Lola asks, watching Kaspar eat his medicated apple.

'About half an hour,' Chase tells her. 'Then he'll be okay for the rest of the day. Well, not really okay – it's like he's half asleep, but at least it calms him down.'

'Is he going to get better, Chase?'

'No. There's nothing we can do for him. You can't cure old age. He's had a hundred and sixty good years, I guess.' Chase blinks, then quickly wipes his eyes. Stupid! he thinks. 'The vet's coming on Wednesday, I think. She's going to . . . to . . . you know . . .'

Lola gently takes hold of his hand.

'Let's go and see the others,' he says, with his face turned away.

Girls are absolute suckers for unicorns. And if you happen to live on the only unicorn farm and breeding facility in the world, any girl you ask will come and visit you. Unfortunately, these visits never lead to anything ongoing. Chase has never had a girlfriend. But he has probably held hands with more girls than any other boy at school.

It's unusual, though, for a girl to hold hands with him for a second time.

But that's only because she feels sorry for me, Chase tells himself gloomily as he and Lola Daylight walk hand-in-hand up to the nursery paddock.

'This is where we keep the unimares with unifoals,' Chase says, resuming his well-practised visitors' commentary. 'All the other . . .'

He falls silent when he sees the quad bike parked outside the gate. His father stands at the edge of the paddock holding a rope.

'Can you give me a hand?' Mr Jensen calls when sees Chase and Lola. 'I'm trying to round up Ziggy.'

Ziggy is the seventh or eighth unifoal out of Marta 2, one of the stud's oldest and most reliable breeding females. He's nearly three years old. Strictly speaking, he should no longer be in the nursery paddock. But Ziggy is a lot like Kaspar used to be – he has such a lovely, gentle disposition that his presence there has a calming influence on the younger animals, some of which can be skittish and prone to accidentally injuring each other with their sharp little horns. All the unimares love him, too. As do

Chase and his parents. Ziggy is *everyone's* favourite! Chase can't wait to introduce him to Lola.

He opens the gate for her and together they enter the nursery paddock. They are no longer holding hands. The unicorns stand in a small group (called a blessing) over in the far corner, watching the three humans curiously.

'So, who's this one?' asks Mr Jensen, giving his son a sly smile that Lola probably isn't supposed to see. He often teases Chase about his many girlfriends, which just shows how out of touch he is.

'This is Lola.'

She and Mr Jensen say hi to each other.

'What's happening with Ziggy?' asks Chase.

'I need to get him down to the yards,' his father says. 'He's being picked up in about an hour.'

'What do you mean? Who's picking him up?'

'His new owners.'

'But, Dad, Ziggy doesn't turn three till June!'

Even though there's a five-year waiting list for unifoals, and prospective buyers pay $5000 deposit on the day theirs is born, the sale isn't completed until it's three years old, which is when unicorns reach maturity.

'They want him a couple of months early.' Mr Jensen shrugs. 'I don't see any harm in it.'

'Does Mum know?' Chase asks.

'Of course she does,' says his father, busy with the rope.

Chase hates how his parents keep secrets from him. 'You and Mum should have told me!' he says hotly. 'Just like you should have told me that Kaspar's being put down on Wednesday.'

Part of him wants his father to contradict him and say that Kaspar isn't being euthanised on Wednesday, but that doesn't happen. Instead, Mr Jensen meets his eyes and says, 'I'm sorry, Chase. We just didn't want to upset you.'

So it's true. Chase takes a deep breath to steady himself. He's aware of Lola standing next to him and doesn't want to make her feel awkward by having a big blow-up with his father in front of her. But a couple of things need to be said.

'I'm more upset that you *didn't* tell me,' he says. 'And I think it's time you and Mum stop treating me like a kid. Jensen Unicorns is a family business – that's you and Mum and *me* – and I'm old enough now to be included when important things are going to happen.'

His father rubs his chin thoughtfully and nods. 'I guess your mother and I have rather left you out of things,' he admits. 'It's hard to draw the line between being a parent and being a business partner.' He pauses and gazes out across the paddock, where the glossy white unifoals and their alert-looking mothers are staring back.

Then Mr Jensen does a surprising thing – he walks up to Chase and extends his hand. 'Let's do things differently from now on,' he says. 'Welcome to the firm, son.'

Chase has no option but to shake the proffered hand. It's embarrassing with Lola watching and he feels his face turn red. But he's more pleased than embarrassed.

For the first time in his life, he feels like a man.

'All right, guys,' Mr Jensen says energetically, bringing Lola back into the conversation. 'Let's get Ziggy rounded up, shall we? If you two go around behind the unis and herd them slowly along the far fence line to the top corner, I'll come from this side and see if I can throw the rope over his head.'

Chase doesn't move. 'There's an easier way, Dad,' he says.

He whistles loudly, calls 'Zig, Zig, Zig, Zig', and a tall, slender unicolt separates from the blessing and comes prancing across the paddock towards them.

'Impressive work, son,' Mr Jensen compliments him.

'He's totally GORGEOUS!' gasps Lola, referring to Ziggy, unfortunately, not Chase.

The animal stops about ten metres away. He nickers and shakes out his long, silky mane. And Chase has to admit that Lola's right – Ziggy *is* gorgeous. Sleek as a deer, glistening silver-white in the sunshine, he could be straight out of a fairy tale. Except, yeah, his horn still has a bit of growing to do – it's barely 15 centimetres long, which is perhaps slightly short for a unicolt his age.

Taking the rope from his father, Chase catches Lola's hand (she lets him) and leads her out into the paddock. They stop a couple of metres from the unicolt and Chase places the apple that wasn't injected with tranquilliser in Lola's free hand. 'Give him this while I slip the rope around his neck,' he says.

She seems a bit hesitant. Chase doesn't really blame her after her bad experience with Kaspar. 'Don't worry, he won't hurt you,' he says. 'Their mothers teach them to be careful how they use their horns. It's like puppies learning not to bite.'

'*He* won't bite, will he?' she asks, perhaps still thinking about poor old Kaspar.

'No. But keep your hand flat so he can take the apple cleanly. Yes, that's good.'

While Ziggy is busy with the apple, Chase passes the rope over his neck and clips the head loop closed. He offers the free end to Lola. 'Do you want to lead him down to the house?'

'Will he let me?' she asks nervously.

'Of course he will. Look, he loves you already.'

It's true – Ziggy is gently nuzzling her shoulder, with his head tilted carefully sideways to make allowance for the horn.

Lola takes the rope, leans forward and kisses the unicolt on its nose. 'Ziggy, aren't you just a lovely, lovely, lovely boy!' she coos.

Waiting to open the gate for them, Mr Jensen catches his son's eye and winks.

———

The buyers are late. They were supposed to arrive at midday, now it's nearly one o'clock. Mr Jensen has tried calling them, but their phone is either switched off or out of range. He keeps coming out of the house and peering down the long, tree-lined drive towards the road. He's supposed to be playing tennis at two and it's a half hour drive to town.

Chase and Lola are waiting in the holding yards with Ziggy.

'I wouldn't mind if they never come,' Lola says, busily weaving another braid into Ziggy's mane. She has made a long row of them. He's beginning to look like a Rainbow Pony.

'Me too,' says Chase, although he doesn't mean it. Breeding and selling unicorns is his family's livelihood – you have to learn to say goodbye to them.

But he's going to miss Ziggy.

His father comes walking down from the house. 'He just called,' he says, holding up his phone. 'It seems his phone number has changed. He's had some sort of car trouble and won't be here for another forty-five minutes.'

Lola smiles to herself and begins another braid.

'That's bad luck,' says Chase. He knows how much his father enjoys his Saturday afternoon tennis. He and his playing partner, Rolly Stephens, were last year's regional champions in the men's doubles. 'Will it matter if you're late?'

Mr Jensen rubs his chin thoughtfully. 'Actually, Chase, I've got a favour to ask of you. In light of what you were saying earlier – about becoming more involved in the business – do you think you could handle today's sale if I'm not here?'

'Of course I can,' Chase replies, pleased. 'Is there any paperwork or official stuff I have to take care of?'

'It's all up at the house. Come and I'll show you.' Mr Jensen turns to their visitor. 'Why don't you come too, Lola? You and Chase can get yourselves some lunch.'

She gives him a big, sunny smile. 'I might just stay here and keep Ziggy company, if that's okay?'

'Of course it's okay. I like what you're doing to his mane, by the way.'

'I'm going to start on his tail next.'

Chase's father laughs. 'Perhaps we can employ you as our regular unicorn hair stylist.'

'That'd be cool, Mr Jensen.'

'She seems like a nice girl,' he says approvingly, as father and son walk together up to the house.

Chase shrugs noncommittally. He knows it's only about unicorns.

The paperwork is all in a folder marked

Wolfsbane.

'What's Wolfsbane?' asks Chase. The word seems vaguely familiar.

'It's the client's name,' says his father.

'Unusual.'

'He's an unusual client.' Mr Jensen pulls a computer print-out from the folder and hands it over. 'Take a look at this.'

It's a form titled Client Details, but most of the spaces have been left blank. The surname has been supplied, *Wolfsbane*, but there's no first name or initial. And there's no tick in any of the boxes for Mr, Mrs or Ms. The spaces for the residential and postal addresses have been left empty, too. In the contacts box, there's an email address that begins '*wlfbn@*' and the phone number that his father said no longer works.

'Why is he being so secretive?' Chase asks.

'I have no idea,' says his father. 'But he always answers my emails and he seemed friendly enough on the phone.'

'Has he paid yet?'

'The final payment came through yesterday. Including an extra thousand dollars so he could take Ziggy this weekend.'

'That's a lot of money just to get him a few weeks early,' says Chase.

'Do you know what I think?' His father raises an eyebrow. 'I think someone is having their birthday soon – his wife or one of his kids – and Ziggy is going to be their surprise birthday present.'

Chase smiles at the thought of it. 'If it's for a girl,' he says, 'she'll think it's the best birthday present ever.'

He's looking forward to meeting the mysterious Wolfsbane.

There are two men in the black RAM ute that comes crunching slowly up the gravel driveway towing a dusty blue and white horse trailer. It's not long since Chase's father left, so it's possible the two vehicles passed each other somewhere down the road. But it's equally likely that Wolfsbane came from the other direction. He could be from just about anywhere, reflects Chase, remembering the empty address box on the client details form. Wherever Wolfsbane is from, Ziggy will be going back there.

Chase misses him already.

The two men climb out of the ute. The driver is a large, bearded man wearing a black T-shirt, black jeans and a faded red and white beanie. His passenger is short and thin, dressed much the same as his companion, only his hat is made of brown leather and has a funny pointed crown.

'Looks like Santa and one of his elves,' Lola says quietly, and Chase has to suppress a giggle.

He and Lola are waiting with Ziggy on the strip of lawn in front of the holding yards. Lola has just finished braiding the unicorn's long, silver tail and he's quietly grazing behind them while she and Chase sit side by side on the sweet-smelling grass. Chase passes Ziggy's rope to Lola, rises to his feet and walks down to greet the client.

The resemblance to Santa fades as Chase approaches. The big man's arms are covered in tattoos of knives and chains and grinning skulls, and his ears are heavily pierced. Chase holds out his hand. 'Mr Wolfsbane? I'm Chase Jensen.'

Santa ignores his hand. 'He's Wolfsbane,' he says, nodding in the direction of the 'elf'.

Chase turns to the smaller man, who has similar tattoos to Santa's. He doesn't offer his hand this time – one time left hanging was once too many. 'Hi, Mr Wolfsbane. You've come for Ziggy?'

'Ziggy?' asks the man called Wolfsbane.

'Your unicorn,' Chase explains. 'We call him Ziggy.'

Wolfsbane nods. 'Let's go and look at it.'

Chase was about to lead the way, but the two men are already walking ahead of him up towards the yards, where Lola stands waiting with Ziggy.

'Hi,' she says.

'Hiya, doll,' says Wolfsbane. He takes the rope from her without asking and roughly pulls Ziggy closer. 'What's this nonsense?' he asks, running his fingers through Ziggy's carefully braided mane.

'We wanted to make him pretty for you,' Lola answers in a small, hurt voice.

Wolfsbane just shakes his head. He hasn't noticed the tail yet. He and Santa are examining Ziggy's horn.

'Runty little thing,' sneers Santa.

Wolfsbane turns to Chase. 'Who are you, again?'

'Chase Jensen.'

'Where's your dad?'

'He's not here,' Chase says, but he's beginning to wish his father *was* here – these guys aren't exactly friendly. 'I'm looking after things today.'

'Your dad said its horn is fifteen inches.'

'He wouldn't have said that,' Chase tells him. His face feels hot. 'We only use metric measurements. He probably said fifteen centimetres.'

Wolfsbane swears under his breath, but not so quietly that Chase and Lola don't hear. What is his problem?

'He's not even three years old,' Chase says patiently. 'His horn will grow.'

'It won't grow much overnight,' growls Santa.

Well, obviously! Chase almost replies, but holds his tongue. These are clients and you can't be rude to them. He makes a decision.

Taking a deep breath, he says, 'I'm sorry you aren't satisfied, gentlemen. If this animal doesn't meet your expectations, Jensen Unicorns will refund your money in full, and . . . um . . . we'll add five hundred dollars as a goodwill gesture.'

Wolfsbane is silent. He must be considering Chase's rash offer. Part of Chase hopes he *won't* accept it. What will his father say when he finds out that Chase has not only cancelled the sale, he's added five hundred dollars to the refund?

It's Santa who comes to the rescue. Leaning close to Wolfsbane, he whispers into his ear: 'We *have* to go ahead, Wolf! Everything's set up for tomorrow. Members have flown in from all over the worl –'

'Shut it!' snaps the smaller man, eyes darting in Chase and Lola's direction.

If he's worried about them overhearing Santa's words, it's too late – Santa's lungs match his large size and even his whispers are loud.

'I'm just saying,' Santa persists, his voice lowered even further (but still not enough), 'it's too late to call it off.'

'But when they see the size of the horn, we'll be a laughing stock!'

'Doesn't matter. We can ham it up a bit – use daggers instead of swords, and wooden practice maces instead of iron ones so it goes on for longer.'

'Yeah, maybe,' Wolfsbane says doubtfully. 'I guess we don't really have any other choice, do we?'

What are they talking about? Chase wonders. His father was wrong, they certainly don't want Ziggy for a birthday present.

What *do* they want him for?

Suddenly it comes to him. Wolfsbane is the name of one of the most violent henchmen in the TV series, *Shame of Thrones*. And the tattoos on both these men's arms are replications of the design on the flags that the original Wolfsbane and his warrior clansmen carry into battle.

These guys are Thronies – cult followers

of the TV series who dress up and act out scenes from the show. Not much is known about them because members take an oath of secrecy when they join, but rumour has it they're a bunch of fanatics. They fight with real swords and steel-tipped tridents and heavy spiky clubs called maces, and sometimes even kill each other.

Chase and his parents used to watch *Shame of Thrones* until the episode in Series Two where Wolfsbane and his right-hand man, Giant, fought a unicorn in a gladiator stadium before a huge, cheering crowd. The unicorn put up a good fight, but it was no match for the two heavily-armed warriors. It wasn't a real unicorn, of course, just a clever piece of computer-generated animation; but its gruesome on-screen death was enough to put Chase and his parents off the show forever.

Chase has broken out in an all-over sweat. He feels sick. Because now he understands why Mr Wolfsbane (it's probably not his real name) and Santa-aka-Giant want a unicorn. What they are planning has probably never been done before. For the first time in the cult's history, a pair of Thronies are going to enact in real life what the makers of their beloved TV show could only achieve though the use of animation.

Ziggy isn't going to be someone's birthday present, he's going to be ritualistically killed!

The event will no doubt occur in some secret location, witnessed by a cheering audience of Thronies from all over the world. Each member has probably paid a huge fee to be there. And it's likely the entire event will be filmed and then sold on the Dark Web to other Thronies who aren't able to attend. Apparently, there are thousands of them worldwide. No wonder these two guys can afford to buy a unicorn – and they aren't cheap! – only to put it to death the following day.

It won't be much of a spectacle. No matter how much Mr Wolfsbane and Santa-aka-Giant provoke him with their daggers and wooden clubs, sweet little Ziggy won't fight back. It'll be a slaughter.

Chase can't let it happen.

'Gentlemen,' he says, 'come with me; there's something I'd like to show you.'

And using his newly granted authority to make decisions on behalf of his family's business, Chase sets in motion a series of events that will not only save Ziggy's life, but will teach a worldwide audience of not-easily-shocked Thronies that, when it comes to doing battle with them, CGI unicorns are absolute kittens compared to the real thing.

And lastly, four months and sixteen days after Chase Jensen becomes her boyfriend, Lola Daylight will receive the best birthday present ever.

Ancestral Trees

Pamela Freeman

I wish they'd allowed me to have a willow tree. I might be gone by now, in its quick-growing roots.

But no. When – at twenty-one – I said, 'I'd like to be buried under a willow,' the whole family said, 'No, no, willow's a soft wood. It'll never keep you contained.'

At fifty – at my second choosing – they said, 'Willows are quick to grow and quick to die. It'll let you loose on the children.' And the week before I died, my brother said, 'A willow isn't safe, Cara. It has to be planted near a stream, and your corpse will contaminate the water.' Which was a reasonable argument, so I gave in.

My daughter chose a jarrah for me. 'Such beautiful wood, Mum,' she said. 'Such a pretty tree.'

I was relatively young – eighty-three – when I died. We tend to live long lives in my family. One hundred isn't unusual. So, the body grove gets filled slowly.

The oldest tree here is my great-grandmother, under a red gum. She's gone completely, fully muffled. I pray that she – and some of the other old ones – have no awareness left. It takes a good long while for the roots to fully bind them but, once bound, that's it. Until the tree dies, maybe, but we haven't been in this country long enough to find out what happens then, here. In the old country, the trees were oak, and oak binds forever. But it doesn't grow well in this soil, so we've had to find alternatives. It will be a few hundred years, we hope, before we find out if eucalypt binds as strongly.

The oldest one still talking is my grandmother, Bridget. Not that she says much. It's a struggle, now, for her to make it out of the roots, to get herself up above and awake. Won't be long before she settles down. Right down.

The others aren't much company. Old relatives never are, are they?

At the hospital, Clancy ignored it all. There was red tape. 'All bodies . . .' began the nurse – 'I'm sorry to call him that, honey, but that's what the regulations say – all bodies have to go to a registered funeral home.'

So she decided to steal him.

'I just want a moment,' she said, and they all nodded, even Patrick, who was red-eyed and wild-haired and looked as if he'd explode at any minute. He didn't like not knowing what to do. It wasn't just grief with Patrick; he was in his 'I can't cope with all these people' state, but she had no energy left to help him.

She had to get her baby to the body grove before his spirit started to walk.

She could survive his death, but she knew she wouldn't survive his haunting.

So, 'I just want a moment,' she said, and once they were alone, she wrapped him – Benedict, after her father's father – tenderly in the shawl her mother had crocheted, and slid him, his tiny face decently covered, into the empty nappy bag she'd bought with such excitement only two weeks before.

And then she called her cousin Mandy, slid out the opposite door in the 'family room' where they'd brought her to grieve, got the lift down to the lobby, and simply walked out.

The cab to Mandy's used up the last of her cash, but that was okay. Mandy was ready, her car waiting in the driveway, a couple of overnight bags in the back.

Clancy got into the front passenger seat.

Mandy slid into the driver's seat, and they were off without a word.

Gently, soothingly, Clancy brought him out. His little body was stiffening. They had until it softened again before his spirit would walk, so that was all right. They'd make it in time.

God, she hurt. A hard labour, and too long because Benedict had given up, exhausted with trying to be born. No. She mustn't blame him.

These things happened. That's what the doctor said. And the nurse. And the midwife.

These things happened. Still.

She knew the numbness would wear off soon. But she didn't want to think about what would happen afterward, once she'd done what she had to do. There was a tsunami of grief waiting to crash down over her, but she didn't have to think about it, not yet.

'You'd better text Patrick,' Mandy said, 'or he'll get the police after you.'

Shit. Yes.

One-handed, she texted:

I'm fine. Taking Benedict to be buried in family plot. Come if you want.

Was that mean? Too bad. She couldn't worry about Patrick right now. He was an adult. He'd coped with being on the spectrum all his life. He could cope now.

He answered immediately.

How could you leave without me? He's my baby too. I'm coming.

She suspected that the tsunami would have a fair bit of guilt mixed in with the grief. But she had to get Benedict to his tree.

His tree.

'What kind of tree?' she wailed at Mandy. 'What kind did you choose?'

'A Sydney red gum. But they're so big, and he's so . . . little.'

She rocked him. His eyelids had tiny blue veins. His eyelashes, long and brown, lay in perfect semicircles on his cheeks. Only the top of his head was discoloured, from the suction cap.

'It won't start out big,' Mandy soothed her. 'Just a sapling.'

'No, no. It's not the right tree. He needs something softer.'

'Soft isn't safe.'

They'd all done it as kids – gone to the grove to meet the tethered spirits. They'd been taken by their parents, to meet their ancestors. And snuck out in the gloaming, to scare themselves with the dark eyes and the long hands and those grating, difficult voices in your head. Her bowels had turned to jelly and she'd desperately wanted to pee when her grandfather had loomed over her and called her 'sweetheart' in a voice which wasn't his.

But you could run, run, run, back to the house and be safe. Because the spirits, the dark crowd of ancestors, couldn't leave their trees.

Would he be all right in their company? Was she doing wrong, not letting him haunt her? He was only a baby, after all . . .

'What about a nice mulga?' Mandy asked. 'They're not too tall.'

'Rose gum,' Clancy said. 'The heartwood is pink. He'll like that.'

'And it's fast growing.' Mandy nodded with approval. 'Good choice.'

Mandy's brother Tom ran the town nursery, and she rang him as they approached. He met them out the front, a sapling of rose gum in hand, which he stuck in the boot. Neither of them got out of the car.

'I'm so sorry, Clancy,' he said. 'How's Patrick?'

'He wanted a funeral home,' she said.

'Well, we can't have that.' He shook his head. 'Not on your life.'

She was comforted by Tom's simple

conviction. No, they couldn't have that.

'I'll just close up here and follow you out,' Tom added. 'Jan's heading out there already with Aunty Chloe.'

'Thanks, kid,' Mandy said. 'We'd better get going.'

He thumped the roof lightly in goodbye and they kept on, taking the western road out of town, over the river, up into the foothills. Dry country, this, and the soil not rich, but perfect for eucalypts. Others grew wool here, or fattened steers, but their family were tree-growers. Furniture makers, harvesting no more than one hardwood tree a year, planting a dozen. (Apart from the family trees, of course. No one ever cut down a tree in the bone grove, or planted one there without a family corpse underneath.)

In her arms, Benedict's little body grew stiffer. His face, paler, as the blood settled. His tiny nose, a tad sharper.

They were taught the signs, as children. So they would know, when it came time to bury their elders, how long they had before the spirit was free and could no longer be bound.

'The soul goes first,' her mother had said. 'It goes into the light and returns to God, and all is well. The body goes next. And the spirit last, if it goes at all.'

'The spirit,' her father had said, 'is the accumulation of everything the soul has lived through, which it no longer needs. Identity, personality, memories – none of these are of any use to God, so the soul leaves them behind, to fade away. Mostly, this happens within minutes of death. Days at the most.' He had glanced fondly at her mother. 'But your mother's family – your family – has particularly strong spirits.'

Very strong.

As a teenager, she had gone to the grove to talk to, to learn from, the elders. She was interested in history, and what a treasure trove of information they were!

But most of them were mad. As the identity frayed, the personality disintegrated, madness grew. And every single one of them was a poltergeist.

Or whatever you called a spirit that could move physical objects.

'Is it hard, being stuck here?' she'd asked her grandfather, and all hell had broken loose.

She'd been hounded out of the grove, sticks pelting her, twigs ripped off trees smashing into her face, wind howling.

What if Benedict wasn't safe there?

But no. When the funerals happened,

everything was always quiet. Calm and peaceful and welcoming.

Her nanna would look after him.

―

The clan had gathered. Her parents, in tears, ushered her out of the car. Tom, pulling up behind them, got the sapling from the boot. The others, crowding around, patted her on the shoulder with wordless murmurs.

In the hospital, all that sympathy had made her crazy, made her want to run away and hide. Here, it lapped her in love. Her hands were starting to cramp from holding Benedict, but she shook her head when her mother offered to take him.

'Should we wait for Patrick?' Mandy asked.

For a moment, she considered it. But a baby's body went through the after-death changes faster than an adult's because it lost its heat so quickly. She wasn't sure how much time they had.

'No. Let's just get it done.'

Her father carried the spade. Her mother walked, tears on her face, with her hand on Clancy's back. Her brother, Jimmy, came running out of the forest. He'd been up on the heights when the news came, and it had taken him as long to come down as it had taken her and Mandy to drive here.

She was glad he was there. The tsunami was building, and soon it would crash down on top of her.

As they approached the grove, she breathed a little more easily. It was a refuge, not a prison. A place for Benedict to be with family. A place he'd be looked after, and returned to the land, as spirits should be.

It just took a bit more effort with her lot.

The trees reared up, heights ranging from enormous, for great-great-great-grandmother's ironbark, to middling, for Uncle Brian's messmate. The most recent one was Nanna's. A jarrah, planted by Aunty Chloe. That one was barely more than a sapling – only five years old and reaching just above her father's head.

'Put him by Nanna Cara,' Clancy said.

'Good idea. She'll look after him.' Her mother nodded, tears still streaming. Around the gathered family, the spirits started to appear.

Slowly, softly, at first just flickers of light, brief and confusing. And then, more solid, tall figures in old-fashioned suits, shorter ones in long dresses. No children. Children's spirits didn't last long, being not as full of memories, and their bodies small. They were bound quickly, in the first flush of root growth, and slept easily in the brown earth.

So it would be with Benedict.

Her grandmother came at last, floating next to her own tree, the jarrah. Nanna Cara smiled with pity at Clancy.

'Oh, lass,' she said, her voice echoing in Clancy's head, dark and harsh-sounding, but full of love. 'I'm sorry.'

For the first time, tears began to heat her eyes. 'Will you look after him for me, Nanna? His name is Benedict.'

'Of course I will.' Nanna reached out to gently touch the baby's face. Here it came. The tsunami. She could feel it gather, feel her whole body tighten to face it . . .

'Clancy! Clancy! What are you doing?' It was Pat's voice, loud and enraged. He pushed his way through the crowd angrily. 'Goddammit, Clancy!'

She faced him down, Benedict still in her arms. She couldn't blame him for being angry, and yet she did.

Two years ago, she'd tried to explain to him about the spirits, and he'd brushed it off as superstition.

When she'd read about maternal mortality statistics, she'd tried to get him to promise that he'd bring her back here to be buried quickly if anything happened, and he'd laughed and promised, but she hadn't trusted him.

'He needs to be buried before his spirit comes alive,' her father said, being gentle. He'd learnt to believe. Pat would too. Couldn't he see the spirits?

But no.

'Don't be ridiculous. This is illegal. The – the body has to go to a registered funeral home.'

'No,' her mother said calmly. 'It doesn't. The family is allowed to retain the body for up to five days. And this is a fully approved private cemetery. Do you think we're fools, Patrick?'

Dumbfounded, Patrick stared at her.

'Technically, the only wrong thing Clancy has done is not get the funeral director to put Benedict's body in a body bag.'

'We know the rules, Patrick,' Dad said.

He seemed dazed. The tsunami stayed poised, for a moment. She remembered all the days and nights of planning, of painting the nursery, of laughing as Patrick put his hand on her belly to feel Benedict kick. Of anticipation and joy and exuberance. Of care lavished upon her.

She had to remember this was his baby too. Carefully, she disentangled one hand from Benedict's shawl, and held it out to him.

'Come and stand next to me,' she said. He grabbed her hand as a lifeline and looked down at Benedict's pale little face.

'You'd better hurry,' Nanna Cara said, and he didn't even blink. No, he couldn't see or hear her. And yet Dad could. How did that work?

She couldn't think about it now. Her father started to dig the grave, but Patrick took the spade from him as if it were his right. Maybe it was.

'Six feet down?' he asked.

'No,' Jimmy said. 'Nine hundred mills is what the law says, but we put it a little more shallow. So the roots can grab hold.'

Patrick let out a snort, a combination of anger and disbelief, and Clancy knew that this was it. The end of their marriage. He'd never forgive her for this; never forgive her the 'superstition'.

Maybe that would be easier than trying to rebuild everything – everything. Trying to decide what to do with that nursery room. Packing up Benedict's clothes together. Putting away the mobiles and the quilts on the wall. Just walking away would be so much easier.

It was time.

Patrick got out of the hole, sweating, and she knelt by its side. After a moment, he knelt too, and their joined hands laid Benedict in the earth, the shawl gently over his face so his little eyes and mouth would be free of dirt.

Then, the tree. Tom freed it from its pot and handed it to her. Tenderly, she teased out the roots, and placed it over the tiny white form.

'You first, Patrick,' her father said, indicating the pile of earth.

As if in a trance, Patrick patted down a couple of handfuls of soil, and then the others came, one by one. The living members of the family first, but then the surviving spirits, taking handfuls and patting them

down, making the sapling secure around their baby.

And finally, Patrick saw. Not the spirits themselves, but the dirt. He pointed to it, a handful moving through space, and his face went stark white.

'That's my grandfather,' Clancy said, taking pity on him. 'The others are here too.'

He edged back but didn't leave her; she had to give him credit for that.

Gradually, with everyone helping, the hole filled in. Finally, she could let go of the sapling's trunk.

But she couldn't.

She couldn't.

She couldn't let him go.

The tsunami hit, full force.

It flung her into Patrick's arms.

Spirit babies are not quite as annoying as real babies. They don't cry quite as much. But they are just as cute.

I'm enjoying coddling this one. Benedict. A big name for a little tyke. He's a sweetie. His mother visits, but I told her last time that he was being drawn down by the roots, and he wouldn't be here much longer. He only had a few breaths of life, after all. He doesn't have many memories to be bound.

I think she regrets not letting him haunt her, but her instinct was sound. She has a life ahead of her, even if the knot of grief under her breastbone never goes away.

It doesn't, you know.

My second girl was dead after three days. That's her tree, over there. The blue gum. She bound easily, too, which was a comfort.

That's what Patrick doesn't understand. To know their spirit isn't wandering, that it's settled here, in the bosom of the family, safe and calm . . . that's a comfort.

But until then . . . just as well they didn't put me under a willow, or I wouldn't be here to take care of Benedict.

Uncertainty

Ian Irvine

We've been hunting the so-called 'Gifted' for decades. Maybe centuries. Maybe for all time, because magic is an abomination. A lie that undermines the sacred Laws of Physics and our Bible. Magic, and the magickers who perpetuate it, must be expunged from the world.

We're the grunts who do the dirty work. Orders come down to one squad or another, or sometimes a whole company if the target is sufficiently dangerous. 'We've found another magicker. Exterminate the mongrel.' And we do.

When they say *exterminate*, they mean *utterly expunge*. We can't just shoot them, check the body and identify unmistakeable signs of death. More than once, magickers have come back from death. Heck, some have returned after their bodies were shredded and burned. A few years ago I was there when one – admittedly a hoary old sorcerer – re-formed from a smoking

pile of ash and erased a platoon of hunters. Not something I ever want to see again.

We've been tracking this magicker for days, herding her, and now we have her trapped in a vast concrete labyrinth. I lean against a shaded wall and wipe sweat out of my eyes. It's sweltering down here, with not a wisp of wind, and the white concrete radiates heat.

I get a glimpse of her, not enough to aim, then she's gone again. Not a visual sighting; magickers can disappear even in the brightest light. But my helmet headset also shows radar, magnetics, IR and UV and multispectral images, and not even a master can hide from all of those.

We've driven her deep into the labyrinth and she must know there's no way out. The readouts say she's no more than eighteen, small and fine-boned. Under fifty kilos. The calibrated aura checker indicates she has limited magical power, and the head-scanner shows only normal activity in the brain areas you would expect after such a long and desperate hunt.

So, not an adept. A girl of no great experience and little magical learning – if we can rely on our instruments. But they've been fooled before, and our orders are to treat every target as if they're an adept.

'Can you get a shot?' says Kropps, from behind me.

He's hoping I'll say no. He wants the kill, desperately. A certified kill means status, prize money, promotion to a safe desk job. Out of this shithole for good. And this is his chance.

Our target is believed to be the last magicker left alive on Earth. Proof that you killed the last one – exterminating magic for all time – might take an ambitious man or woman all the way to the top. Even to the presidency.

I'm not giving him the chance. This is my hunt. I've been doing this filthy job for eleven years. I've been on teams that have taken thirty-seven magickers down, some of them mighty adepts. One had to be killed three times – after she took out two-thirds of the squad. She'd erased a whole company of hunters before that.

Eleven years, and I've done the donkey work all that time. Carrying the captain's pack as well as my own – often, sharing his sleeping bag after eighteen-hour days on the hunt. Scraping up the magickers' remains and doing the thrice-burn, then dissolving the ash in fluoroantimonic acid. Not for the faint-hearted . . . or the clumsy.

Eleven years, and I've never been at the

front during a kill. Never had a magicker in my sights.

But the last kill erased the captain and most of my team, and finally I got the chance to lead. No one's taking this kill away from me.

'Chill down your weapons,' I say, over my shoulder. 'Do *not* shoot until I say your name, and, "Fire!"'

Kropps rolls his eyes. They all know the rules. I guess, after so long as a grunt, power has gone to my head.

Using gloves, I eject the chiller from the magazine well of my automatic rifle, take a magazine from the cryothermos and slide it into the slot. It's a waste of time shooting magickers with normal bullets. Cold iron doesn't work either, despite the myth. Nor silver, nor even enriched uranium – which shows how desperate we were, back then.

Only bullets made of quicksilver can take down a magicker. Mercury metal, chilled to well below 40°C so it's still solid when it hits its target. No one knows quite how it brings them down, but that doesn't matter. Once they're writhing on the ground we have a whole range of options – none pleasant to watch – but magickers aren't human, are they?

'Chilled down!' says Kropps.

The other six members of my squad echo him. I check my augmented reality readout. The chamber is at -44°C, the magazine at -47°, but they won't stay at that temperature for long in this heat. If the temperature drops to -41°, the magazine will auto-eject so the bullets don't liquify, and we'll have to chill down all over again.

A day in the life.

'Visual!' whispers Nat-Lee. 'Three hundred and eleven degrees. Distance, sixty-two metres.'

Ahead and to the left. I scan and pick the magicker up, crawling along a stormwater drain. I track her in the sights.

'Are you going to shoot, or not?'

Kropps again. I wish I had *him* in my sights.

My arm shakes, then she's gone. I curse inwardly, wave everyone forwards. 'We've got to get closer.'

We move ahead. An alert sounds, *ding*. I keep going. I really want this kill.

'Squad, stop!' says Nat-Lee. 'We're at fifty metres.'

'I give the orders,' I grate.

'I'm safety officer,' says Nat-Lee. 'And unless she's hit, and down, we're not allowed to go closer than fifty metres without a permit.'

'All right! Anyone got a visual?'

No one has. We don't know where she is. I shiver. She might be coming our way. Magickers are unpredictable; they don't obey the sacred laws. I lift my visor, wipe my brow again, and see her *with my eyes*. But she vanishes again.

'There she is!' cries Kropps. He has his visor up as well.

'Where?' I say, and the others ask as well. No one else can see her.

'There!' Kropps runs past, aims and fires a burst.

'Got her with five bullets!' he exults. 'Mid-chest. I got the last, stinking magicker!'

Now I see her, on her back on the ground. 'You insubordinate bastard!' I grind out. 'That was my shot!'

'You haven't made a kill in eleven years, magicker-lover!'

A mortal insult, but I maintain self-control. 'My record stands. I've done the hard yards, the dirty jobs. That – was – my – kill!'

'But when you didn't take it, it became anyone's!'

'You must give me the first shot. I'll have you cashiered for this.'

'Do your worst. *I* killed the last magicker. Nothing can touch me now.'

'Enough!' says Nat-Lee. 'We've got to

make sure she's done – and this time we follow the Standard Operating Procedures to the letter.'

My chamber is at -42°C, the magazine at -43°. They'll stay cold long enough to finish her. I lead my squad forwards. Closer. Closer.

The young magicker hasn't moved. With five mercury bullets in her chest she's got to be dead, but we have to be sure.

Thirty yards.

Twenty.

Ten. She's tiny.

It's stifling inside the headset. I take it off and put it on the ground. My face is running with sweat; it's running down my neck and back. I wipe my face on my sleeve.

'There's no blood,' says Nat-Lee. 'Magickers bleed, don't they?'

'I've seen plenty of dead magickers,' I say. 'They bleed!' My nightmares are drenched with their blood.

'Why isn't there any blood, then?' says Kropps.

Horror shivers up my backbone at the realisation. 'You had your visor up! I saw you aim and fire – *and you didn't close your eyes.*'

He stares at me, uncomprehending.

'The observer effect!'

'What?'

'The Law applies to our work. *Observing* the shot can change the outcome.'

'You mean she's not dead?' Kropps whirls, aims and, eyes closed, sprays the rest of his magazine into the body.

The girl's body doesn't jerk, and no blood appears. Of course it doesn't – we're all looking at her and it changes the outcome again.

'You cretin!' I say. 'I'll make sure you're scrubbing toilets for the rest of your miserable life.'

'Like hell! Turn away!'

We obey instantly, by reflex.

Kropps snatches Nat-Lee's rifle, turns away from the body and, firing backwards, unloads the full magazine. Most of the brittle mercury bullets shatter on concrete, but when I turn there are two small bloody wounds on the girl's chest.

'She was the last!' exults Nat-Lee. 'Magic is dead!'

A heavy splash alerts me and I look down. The magazine of my rifle is at -37°C and liquid mercury is running out of it. The rest of the squad's weapons are in the same condition. But it doesn't matter. The magicker is down.

'We have a procedure to follow,' I say.

'We burn the body to ash. Kropps, dissolve the ash in fluoroantimonic acid. Nat-Lee, neutralise the sludge and dry it. Then we'll go up in the chopper and scatter it along fifty nautical miles of ocean.' That's so it can never come together again. Only then will the last magicker be dead, their abominable law-flouting magic erased from the world, and the Laws of Physics safe from blasphemy.

I dry my face, pick up the heavy helmet and settle it over my head. It's still recording, and without thinking I touch Rewind and play it back, keeping an eye on the body.

The bullet wounds disappear. The magicker rises and, almost casually, extends a hand to Kropps. A flash. He falls. More flashes bring down Nat-Lee and the others.

'Your observer effect also works with recordings you make,' the magicker says. 'If you watch them.'

I knew that. Fool! I still have my rifle, and I consider running at her and using it as a club, but she could kill me before I went a metre. She's powerful. How did she fool our scanners? And how long before she kills me?

'Why do you hate us?' I say.

'Does a scientist hate a bug she's studying

under the microscope?'

I don't like the sound of that. 'Well, why do you undermine our sacred laws with your foul magic?'

'Your so-called Laws of Physics aren't sacred. Humanity worships them because it needs something to fill the void inside it. Neither are they *Laws*. They're just rules that work in one place, and not another.'

'How would you know?'

'This universe was one of our experiments,' she says, off-handedly. 'We made it, and others, to see what would happen if we imprinted each universe with a different set of rules – including applying the observer effect to certain macro-activities. There's a certain grim amusement to that, though –'

'Magickers *made* the universe? Preposterous!'

She shrugs. 'The first one was hard. After that, they were just variations on a theme.'

I'm struggling to understand. This has to be some kind of joke, or illusion. Or madness.

'You made it for your *amusement*?' I say.

'Call it *interest*, if you prefer. Or *study*. Life is infinite in its variety and potential – we could study it for a billion years. But the human race was one of our great failures.

Humanity could never coexist with any human or intelligent being who fell outside its petty, artificial rules. It set out to destroy us, and did us great harm – but also sowed the seeds of its own destruction.'

This is bad. 'I don't understand. Is . . . is any of this even real?'

'Depends what you call reality.'

'How do you know, anyway? You're just a kid – aren't you?'

'Humans are so quick to make assumptions.'

'Wait! Have I just found a loophole? You're watching me. What about the observer effect?'

She laughs. 'Magic is outside your sad little Laws of Physics. That's the whole point.'

'But humanity is unique. Irreplaceable.'

'Every *species* is unique. But humanity is too limited. Not worthy of further study.'

The magicker snaps her fingers. 'Gone!'

The Immortality Backup

Paul Collins

18 August 2034

'Report on the Dangers of Downloading Animal Minds and Life Experiences'

From the diary of Michael Schmidt, Dean of Faculty – Neuroscience, Gippsland University of Technology.

When the technology for vascular brain monitors was developed in the late 2020s, nobody could have known that non-mental telepathy was just around the corner. The device was simplicity itself. Probes a lot thinner than a human hair were inserted into the blood vessels of a brain by means of a needle and mesh catheter. Each probe contained hundreds of sensitive electrodes, and because blood vessels carry blood to the brain's electrical neurons, they were close enough to monitor thoughts.

At first, the scientists experimented with humans, and subjects were able to use their thoughts to drive cars, control bomb disposal robots, write social media posts and put themselves inside computer games. There were even projects to download the entire life experiences of people and put them into databases. However, people have a vast number of life experiences, so this turned out to be a very slow and expensive process. Data storage doesn't grow on trees, after all.

It was at this point that a small research group with limited funding decided that they should try to download a dog's life experiences. Dogs have lived with humans for tens of thousands of years, and although they can't talk, they are familiar with a lot of human words. A thought like: 'Tell me your earliest memories and there will be a dog biscuit in it for you' could easily be sent to a dog's brain through the electrodes of a vascular brain monitor attached to a computer, and hopefully the dog would *think*: 'What a good idea' and remember the time when it was a puppy.

What we humans didn't know, what we have never known, is that dogs have complex emotional lives, rich and complex histories, and myths so powerful and exciting that the exploits of King Arthur and his Knights of the Round Table would barely raise a yawn in canine circles.

The greatest myth of all is about the Bone.

No human has ever seen this Bone, nor ever will, yet apparently every dog in all the world knows about it. Every dog worth its weight in choice table scraps knows the tale; mothers tell it to their pups, and fathers re-enact the glory of it.

'Have you heard about the Bone?' they ask their pups. 'The dog that pulls it from the Tree, why, that dog's the King of Canines!'

Many have tried to do just that, of course, and each of them failed. None but the true King can pull the Bone from the stump where it was lodged long ago in the Making Time, when wolves were made into dogs.

What we humans knew nothing about is yapped and whined about in places like peaceful backyards, garbage skips, moonlit alleys, barns, graveyards and dugouts, in barns and backwaters. It is never barked loudly or howled, because it is not for the ears of urban foxes, cats or humans.

It is said that the Bone is like a map of unbearable dreams, notched with the tooth-marks of ten thousand dogs over thousands of years. Despite this, it never breaks or splinters. It is made of something else, not of this world, perhaps.

And how did it get there, in that Place that only dogs can enter and which no cat nor human can see? We scientists can't answer that.

Nameless himself appears to know about the Place. He told us through the vascular brain monitor that the Bone and Stump are seamlessly welded together. The Two That are One and the One That is Two . . .

As for the identity of Nameless, that is not easy to explain. When we were planning our experiment, we just needed a dog with no council registration number or ID chip, a dog with no official past. For the first time a dog would tell its story, and we were sure that it would be a simple tale of sniffing trees, chasing balls and trying to hide when any human said 'bath'. How very wrong we were, but I should let Nameless himself explain why.

Start of translated narrative:

They call me Nameless. Mainly because no one ever bothered to give me a name. Unless you count 'Lucky', which I don't.

My story begins on a farm as a three-day-old pup. Someone tried to drown me along with my siblings. They shovelled us into an old hessian sack, the mouth tied shut with string and the bundle flung into a dam.

I should have died (some say I did, but that was many years later). My brothers and sisters didn't survive. Not one. Their piteous cries echoed in my poor head for many years after that, and still when I was an old dog – the kind you can't teach new tricks to – I could be seen at times shaking my head, as if trying to dislodge something from it. A tick, humans guessed, but it was something far more sinister.

I survived. The bag somehow stayed half afloat, even though my lifeless siblings dragged it down. Someone saw that sack bobbing in the murky water and hauled it out.

Trembling and bewildered, I was pulled from that murderous sack and lodged by a warm fire with a bowl of dry food. And a boy with a heart as warm as the fire took care of me.

But it didn't last. If ever Fate played a part in any dog's life, it was mine.

Soon after my rescue, the boy's family had to sell up and shift. They paused in a local town on the Cudgegong River to stock up on supplies. While they were shopping, a vagrant stole their van. Within the day, he had decided he'd had enough of my whining and dumped me on the outskirts of another town.

This part of my life was indeed a mystery to me. Shrouded in guesses and cloaked in shadows, I managed to make it to another town.

For a week or more, I hid under verandas and in sheds, or kept to vacant blocks. I was forever desperately hungry. And as hunger will, it drove out all sense of pride and made me three times the dog I was. I scavenged and ate scraps whenever I could find them, through cat and dog flaps at night, or stealing from others even less fortunate than me.

I learnt to give a wide berth to other dogs, not just the big bruisers (the mastiffs and the rottweilers) but the little ones, too, like bull terriers, whose smallness seemed in inverse proportion to their terrifying ferocity.

It was during this period that I first heard about the Bone.

One night as I lurked in an old alley, I saw three scavenging dogs. I couldn't help but overhear them talking.

A little spaniel whined, 'What are we waitin' for?' He looked at the big German shepherd, missing one ear and with a scar across his snout. 'Jack and his pack are headin' east next week.'

'So? So?' growled the German shepherd. He looked as if he found it hard to sit still.

'Jack's gonna try for the Bone.'

The third dog, a mongrel mix with a white slash on his flank, said, 'Really?'

There was something in the way he said this that made my ears prick up. It was like he was talking about a god. Even though I knew little of Him, it seemed the mongrel was all hushed, and dipping his head ever so slightly, like he was giving the tiniest of bows. Respectful, and a bit scared, as I remembered it in later years.

The three dogs didn't say much more, but they seemed a bit bothered by this mention of the Bone, whatever that was.

Anyway, I grew up in that town, but I never called it home. I kept to myself, and tried to fit in with everyone. I wasn't a big dog, nor a little one. There was nothing visibly special about me, and few took any notice, dog or human . . .

Then one day one of them did. Or two, if you're counting.

The first was a lady who worked in a gambling hotel. She spotted me in the alley out back and coaxed me inside for some water and a meaty marrow bone. She took pity on me, I suppose. Perhaps she'd had a dog like me and her memories came back when she laid eyes on my thin, flea-infested body.

Either way, she took me inside and fed

me. And I felt an old ache, of some other time, like an echo of warmth and kindness. I couldn't properly recall it, but it filled me with sadness in spite of that juicy bone.

Well, to cut a long story short (or at least, shorter), I lived in that kitchen for a few weeks, and to my great surprise – and even discomfort, for I wasn't used to it – I was liked by all.

In the process, I met Sam, a regular. He was the type who said little and saw much. I think one thing he saw puzzled him.

He picked that I had a peculiar talent. More than once, when Sam had what he thought was a great hand of cards, he'd hear a soft growl from me. I'd often lurk around and under the table whilst a card game played out. So, it came to Sam's attention that, without fail, whenever I growled and Sam didn't fold, he lost that hand. But when I gave an equally soft bark, Sam always won.

Sam's fortunes changed overnight. From being a luckless kind of gambler, he shot to local fame as the man who could never lose. Indeed, his reputation got so lofty, he was forced to flee town one night when the locals he'd fleeced set out to teach him a lesson.

And of course, he took me with him, and

even named me – though it wasn't his right to do so – calling me Lucky, which wasn't what you'd call imaginative. Nor did it stick.

For the next three years, Sam and I toured the bigger towns and the cities, leaving the outback due to its poor pickings. The cities were where the money was.

One might think that having a dog like me, helping to make you rich, would ensure that dog was treated like a prince, or a friend at least. But it wasn't so. Sam became a mean-spirited human with a nasty streak, and more than once he didn't bother to feed me.

Then one evening my luck turned, if you could call it that. I wasn't on form as I was very malnourished, and Sam lost a lot of money. He dragged me outside and into the laneway.

A strapping guy dressed in army fatigues passed by the mouth of the laneway and, hearing loud curses and whimpers, hurried over to see what was happening.

He saw Sam in all his whisky glory kicking me out of his way. The soldier leapt forward and knocked Sam out – along with several of his teeth – with one hit. Then he picked me up and carried me from the darkness.

I won't relate the next part of this

tale, except to say that Tyson was a dog handler in the Defence Force. It didn't take him long to figure out that I wasn't your average dog. After all, I knew how to please humans. He adopted me and trained me to ferry messages and sniff out explosives. After a year or so, World War III – the Asia-Pacific War – broke out. I went with him on a tour of duty to Myanmar, Cambodia and Bangladesh.

Don't ask me how, but I just know things. Sam was right about that. And Tyson's luck became legendary. He came to appreciate that when I gave one of my signs, he'd best do as I said, if he wanted to keep breathing.

It's a fact that whenever I gave a special kind of bark, Tyson ducked, and every time he ducked or dived, he narrowly missed being wounded or killed. If Tyson came to a building and I gave a special growl, Tyson refused to enter or to let anyone else enter, and every time it was later found the house had been booby-trapped or else contained enemy soldiers lying in wait.

I saved Tyson's life several times, or more, and many other lives as well. And if you want to know the irony, his mates renamed Tyson and called him Lucky – lucky to have such a marvellous dog.

The only time Tyson was wounded in

that tour of duty was the one time he didn't have me with him. And that's something to think about.

After the war, Tyson went home, as did a horde of others. And somewhere in all of this, with tens of thousands disembarking ships and boarding trains and getting orders and discharges, we became separated.

If you ask me, it was Fate. I reckon I had a mission to fulfil, one that only I could manage.

Note:

At this point I should bring to the reader's attention that translating the thoughts of Nameless has been difficult, because dogs experience the world very differently to humans. They have a much more limited range of colours, while their sense of smell opens up a world of experiences and communications that we humans cannot even dream about. We have had to translate and edit the story of Nameless for our minds, which cannot begin to grasp a dog's hopes, fears, values and sense of wonder. To us their myths may be hard to grasp, but that is only because our language is not designed for a dog's thoughts.

One day in the autumn of some year, a great band of dogs made their way separately, and in small groups, to a place in the east. I can't tell you where this is; words fail me when I try. Or maybe it's an unspoken rule that dogs can't name the place.

I went along. I was thin and weak and had the look of a scrounger. After I lost touch with Tyson, life reverted to its meanest level.

I had recently been recruited into a dog pack whose leader – an arrogant bull mastiff – was called Butch. My job was to fetch and carry and do the menial kinds of things that dogs like Butch felt were beneath them.

So, we journeyed eastward, and over the course of a few days, more than 500 dogs gathered at the Place where the Bone protruded from what appeared at a distance to be an old blackened stump. It was deep in a forest somewhere, and part way into a gorge. The air was full of bird sound and water noise and early evening mist. The 500 dogs sat on their haunches, and made no sound. It was an eerie sight. It made me think of countless mangy cats I've seen waiting to pounce on unsuspecting rodents.

I was almost shaking; the Place had

such an effect on me. No human had ever stepped here, nor any dingo or possum or kangaroo. And certainly, no cat!

The moon rose, and still all the dogs waited. When it stood straight up in the sky, a movement occurred. A very old dog, ancient as the Earth, I reckon, limped forward and spoke.

'Every few years we gather here,' said the Old One, his voice gravelly. 'You all know the story. The dog that pulls the Bone from the tree will be the King of Canines, and a new day for dog-kind will begin.' He paused to compose himself. 'Let all those who dare, come forward.'

I was less than ten metres from the stump and could clearly see the Bone protruding from it. I watched Butch march forward, his head held high.

'I am Butch,' he proclaimed loudly. 'I am the King of Canines, and I will prove it to you now.'

Butch seized the Bone in his jaw and tugged. Nothing happened. I saw him adjust the grip of his jaw on the Bone and try again. A kind of growling groan issued from his throat. Every muscle in his body shivered with the strain. The tendons in his neck stood out. Suddenly, he leapt back, livid and snarling, and barked furiously at the Bone.

'I will try again,' said Butch, but the Old One shook his head.

'No,' he said. 'You have tried, and failed. Give up your place.'

With a low growl, Butch turned and strode away. Another dog came up then. He was powerfully built and sleek, as if he lived on the best kind of food.

He too clamped his jaw around the Bone and pulled. He twisted and hauled, but all to no avail. Another dog followed him, and another followed her, and so on throughout the night. Over a hundred dogs tried. And all failed.

The mood, which had been so charged and joyful earlier, had now slumped. Some dogs were whining or slobbering, others were wrapped in silence. It appeared there would not be a True King from this pack.

The Old One spoke. 'Is there no other who would test themself?' Heads shook, throats growled softly; all those nearest backed slowly away.

I had been gazing at the Bone as if hypnotised, and barely heard any of this. Nor did I move.

In a few moments, the entire pack

had fallen back. Only the Old One and I remained near the Bone.

'What about you?' asked the Old One, eyeing me.

My ears flattened. 'Um, sorry, I was just –' I stammered.

'What is your name?' asked the Old One, his voice kind.

'Uh, I don't have a real one,' I said. 'They call me Nameless.'

The Old One blinked, then peered more closely at me. 'Don't you wish to try?' he asked.

'Me?'

'Of course. Every dog has the right to try.'

'But I am nobody,' I said. In my heart I felt that you had to be big and strong and maybe a little bit famous before you could try to pull out the Bone.

'What have you to lose then, Nobody and Nameless?'

There was a murmur from the crowd.

'Go on, try it!' said a red heeler.

'Give it a go,' yelped a kelpie.

Then Butch's voice. 'Don't be ridiculous!' he barked. 'He's just a useless mongrel. He doesn't even know who his parents are. Let me try again!'

But those nearest to Butch growled and shoved him back. He snarled at them but said no more.

The Old One spoke again, his voice low and gentle. 'Will you not try?'

I swallowed. And wished they weren't all looking at me. I knew I was about to make a fool of myself. But I felt cornered, so I slowly stepped forward and approached the stump from which the Bone protruded.

'Just take it in your jaw and pull,' advised the Old One.

If I could have rolled my eyes like a human, I would have. Butch was right. This was stupid. I was just a worthless cur. So worthless they'd even tried to drown me as soon as I was born!

I looked at the Bone for a moment. It was mere inches from my face. I could see all the notches made by dog teeth. And it occurred to me that if I could leave my mark upon this Bone, then in a thousand years – long after I was forgotten – my tooth marks would still be here, still be seen by future dogs.

That gave me an odd kind of strength. I stretched out my neck and very gently closed my jaw around the Bone. For a moment I did nothing. The Bone felt rock-hard in my mouth. Immoveable. Unbreakable.

Then very gently I pulled. And the Bone slid out of the stump as easily as a stick comes out of water.

There was a moment of stunned silence, then a great baying rippled through the assembled dogs. Next, they were growling and yapping and yipping and prancing about in the madness of joy and amazement.

I blinked and, still with the Bone clamped in my mouth, looked over at the Old One.

'You are the One,' he said. 'You are the King of Canines. And the nameless is now named!'

End of translated narrative

By now it must be clear why the project to download the whole existence of a dog into a database was halted. Nameless has shown us that dogs have a society that we had never dreamed possible. Yes, we can put the very being of a dog into a computer, but is this a good idea? We may be tampering with forces that could come back to bite us.

Remember, of all the dogs to choose for our experiment, we somehow chose Nameless, the King of Canines. How did that happen? Nameless did not tell us that. Do dogs have powers that Nameless did not even hint at? Most importantly of all, why did he present himself to us and tell us his story? Was it to warn us to stop doing computer experiments with animals? After all, what might happen if a downloaded dog got loose on the internet? Chaos and a lot of messed-up files? Perhaps, but it could be a lot worse. Dogs are our friends, yet some of us mistreat them. Let us not forget that they are descended from wolves . . .

Postscript

Nameless escaped our facility shortly after we aborted this experiment.
 He is still out there.
 Somewhere . . .

The Way up to Heaven

John Larkin

The weather-beaten old farmer stared at the contraption, but he couldn't make head or tail of it. It had been lying in his south field since landing there a few hours before. The thing had started as a distant speck of light in the cold night sky earlier that evening, and now, here it was, sitting on top of his wheat crop, hissing like a cornered snake. Something wasn't right about any of this. Not right at all. In the distance, back at his farmhouse, he could hear the porch wind chimes tinkling away like crazy, and yet there wasn't so much as a hint of a breeze.

He put down his walking stick and clutched his chest. He'd been having searing pains there since he'd first spotted the light just above the horizon, and now, with the thing sitting there in his field, it felt as if his chest was on fire.

The thing hissed again and so he backed away from it. He'd seen the movies. This was exactly the sort of contraption that aliens liked to use to take over the Earth. Take over the Earth and suck out your brain through your ear with a straw. Or else make off with your wife or your prized cow. He wasn't taking any chances, not with his cow at least, so he kept his eye on it as he backed away.

The contraption was about the size of a small car. If there were any aliens in there, they'd be pretty cramped, or else really small.

Suddenly, the thing gave a more violent hiss and then seemed for a moment to split in two.

'C'mon then. Show yourselves if you've got the guts.'

He clenched his fists and glared at the contraption. If any aliens wanted to suck his brain out with a straw, or else make off with his wife or cow, then they'd have a fight on their hands. Though of course he didn't actually have a wife anymore.

When the smoke had cleared he realised that there was no one, or no thing, in there. The craft was empty. He stepped closer and peered inside. There was a control panel of sorts and a single seat. For some reason, he felt a strange urge to sit down in it. The pain in his chest had subsided the moment the contraption had opened, but he could sure use a rest. He clambered on board, plonked himself down in the seat and looked at the control panel. Like the rest of the vehicle, it was sparse. There was a small screen with a heading marked 'Destination', but the screen itself was blank.

With yet another hiss, the contraption closed itself around him, but for some reason that he couldn't explain, this felt right. He didn't know why or how but what he did know was that shortly he would be journeying to another world.

The small screen in front of him flickered to life. Well, this was all right. He was going to get some in-flight entertainment on the way to the stars. But rather disappointingly there wasn't much on. The only channel showed this frankly horrible little kid being cruel to a succession of animals and school friends. The boy was a terrible bully. The worst kind in fact, as he seemed to derive pleasure from his victims' pain.

He looked closer at the boy and realised that the kid was him. What sort of entertainment did these aliens have? Did they really fly down from the heavens just to show you what a terrible brat you were? Hardly a cordial way to conduct interstellar relations.

He looked back at the screen and

realised that his younger self had morphed into his older one. And his younger version was positively angelic compared to what he eventually became. His wife was there on the screen with him. She'd always been a big woman, but after their boy had disappeared up the heavenly staircase, she'd swollen up like a life raft. Had he really called her all those horrid, hurtful, disgusting names? Compared her to a cow. Compared her to a hot air balloon. Told her if she got any fatter, she'd have to get her own postcode. And then when she'd refused to leave the bed or stop her wailing, he'd thrown her out into the snow with nothing but the clothes on her back.

Well, he had to teach her a lesson. She might have managed to walk all the way to town if it hadn't been so cold. At least that's what the police had said. Like the police, he often wondered what happened to her. Still, he'd taught her a lesson and that was the main thing.

She wasn't always so useless, so lifeless, so grey. Although he never told her so, never encouraged her, he supposed she was a pretty good artist. Well, she always won first prize at the town fair for her watercolours. She only had one of her works on display in the house. She called it 'The Way up to

Heaven'. She'd painted it while their little boy was in hospital. It was a staircase to that world beyond the clouds that she'd made nice and pretty, with a kind of floral handrail. Reckoned it was something for their boy to hang on to if he ever needed it.

Six months later, he did.

She returned home from hospital, put away her paintbrushes, retired to bed, and piled on the kilos. He hung the painting at the top of the stairs, trying to encourage her. It didn't matter. But farmers didn't have the time to be moping about for lost infants, not when there was work to be done, fields to harvest, cows to milk, and butter to churn. And so, when there was no room left in the bed for him, he encouraged, cajoled and finally insisted that she go back to her family, as the child that bound them was no more. *He'd* taken the floral staircase and had left his pain behind.

With his wife carried off by the snow, the farmer embarked on a series of business ventures. He selected his partners carefully. They were usually old and vulnerable. He would convince them to trust him with their life savings on the promise of making them very rich. In this he was half right. *He* became rich while they ended up with nothing but the clothes on their backs.

And if they threatened to go to the police, well then, he would drop in for a little chat to convince them that that was not such a good idea. Not conducive to their long-term health. He also made them rewrite their wills, often with shaky hands. They never usually had much when they took the staircase, but what they did have quickly became his.

The screen flickered for a moment and the craft began to hum. Finally, he would be heading off into the darkness of space. Okay, he hadn't been the nicest person on the planet but now, thanks to these aliens, he would be going to another world. He could feel the little craft lifting gently off into the night.

The Destination screen began to flicker to life as the spaceship circled his farmhouse. He wondered where he might be going. Jupiter? Mars? Venus? Neptune? Maybe even to another galaxy.

With the pain in his chest now totally gone, he looked out the small window that was built into the craft and saw a body lying on the ground clutching his chest.

Then the words appeared on the Destination screen and he had to adjust his eyes.

It took a moment for him to realise what

was happening.

'NO!' he screamed at the top of his lungs. But nobody could hear him because he didn't have any lungs. Not anymore. His rapidly cooling body was lying on the ground in his south field, while the little craft hurtled through the abyss of space with his soul.

Destination: HELL.

A Dog of His Own

Bill Condon

It had rained a few days before and now the grass looked soft and inviting. The dog was straining so hard on the lead that she was choking.

'Go on, then – run!' As he spoke, the boy unclipped her lead and she bounded free. He knelt in the grass and watched her. She was flat out galloping.

'Please, Gemma, don't go getting hurt.'

He was talking softly to himself, but hoping somehow the dog would hear and understand. But she'd been locked up all day and she was just a pup without sense. Now that she was free, she was doing stupid, dangerous things. He thought that at any second, he would see her fall.

He'd often been to the dog races with his father – seen them fall plenty of times. Usually, they just went down and rolled. It always looked bad. But most times they'd get straight back up and trail the field; hopelessly beaten, but still trying with all their might.

Sometimes though, he'd seen them go down hard and there'd be a huge gasp from the crowd – just for a second – and then they'd go back to cheering on their dog as if the fall hadn't happened. If the fallen dog lay on the track motionless, it could mean it was knocked out, in which case it would probably recover.

But of course, it might have snapped its neck and be dead. As terrible as that was, it was far better than seeing a badly injured dog struggling to stand, with a broken leg. No one could forget seeing something like that.

'That's why you never let yourself get attached to them,' his father would say. 'They're not pets, mate. Always remember that.'

Now she spun herself in tight circles around him and he felt her paws dig into his back. Then she was down and away again, up high in the air and then tumbling end over end in the long grass, puffing loudly but still full of power.

For a moment, he turned away. His heart was pounding hard against his chest and he felt sick. He wished he'd never let her go. Then she would have been all right. She wouldn't have been hurt.

He thought back to a few months ago

when he first brought her home.

'I'm going to call her Gemma,' he said.

That had been his mother's name. She'd died a year ago.

'You're not thinking this through.' His father shook his head. 'You should give her a name that doesn't mean anything to you. Then, if she's no good and we have to get rid of her, or if something happens to her, it won't matter so much.'

'Nothing's going to happen to her, Dad.'

In that moment, he truly believed that . . . and he still did, for when he dared to look again, he saw that she was fine; only just able to stand, her feet wide apart, mouth agape and dripping saliva, gasping for air and exhausted, but so obviously happy and proud of herself.

He gave her the grin he kept only for his dogs; the one they saw when they tore up their rugs or cried to be taken for a walk at two in the morning. And all it meant was that he loved his dogs, far, far too much.

Now he lay full length on the grass and looked up at the sky. He wanted to see only the sky, but slowly, as he knew he would, he began to see all the dogs he'd had before. They were like friends, and they'd trusted him completely – that was the thing that made abandoning them so difficult.

Most of them were sent away on trains up to the country when they got too old or too slow. He could never forget any of them; standing alone, tied up on the railway station and looking at him, wondering what was happening as he hurried down the stairs. They were supposed to be going to good homes, but he hated to see them go.

He kept worrying about them being mistreated – shut out in the rain or being belted – or maybe half-starved and crawling with fleas. Sometimes he wouldn't think about them for a long time – a year or two – and then he'd see a dog that looked like his and he'd automatically work out how old his dog would be and wonder if it could still be alive.

It was like dragging out old photographs of people he'd loved and could no longer touch.

But he couldn't help but think of Molly. She was absolutely black; not one speck of any other colour. His father used to say she was the one he'd been waiting for: – 'She's a champion, she is!'

The boy smiled as he thought of her first win; the windscreen smashing on the way to the track, everyone in the car almost freezing, his father cursing all the way, and vowing 'to give up this crazy dog game forever'. And then, when she won, the windscreen wasn't mentioned once going home. No one complained about the cold. Everyone just kept retelling the race, saying over and over how good she was going to be.

Molly had courage. Some of the dogs were afraid of their own shadow, but not her. She'd run until she dropped if you let her. And the other dogs could jostle her and savage her and all but put her over the fence, but she'd just keep on coming. His father never sent her away. She was the exception. And he swore he'd never have another one after she died.

Having her put down had cut deeply into

him and he vowed he would never allow himself to feel that kind of hurt again. But the boy had pleaded for just one more. A dog of his own. And this was her: this mad, beautiful thing crouched in the grass just ahead of him.

Now overhead there was a massive cloud of the deepest shade of grey. It was steamrolling the light from the sky as it came.

'You've got two more minutes, Gemma,' he said, 'and then if we're lucky we'll get home before it comes down.'

She took off again, tossing away her tiredness and flat out sprinting after a piece of paper, pouncing on it and ripping it to shreds and then charging gleefully across the park to make the most of every second.

In front of her was a willow tree. She was gathering speed and hurtling directly at it as though she hadn't seen it. She was only a breath away when she wheeled, missing it easily and then darted off in search of more adventure.

Yes, you can run, the boy thought. And he wasn't concerned about her safety anymore. But now, with the rain so close, it was time to go home.

'Come on, girl,' he yelled. 'I'll bring you back tomorrow. Come on.' He whistled and called her, but she wouldn't come. She was over at the other end of the park. As he got closer, he saw that she was burrowing underneath the fence. Her head was already through.

He'd never run so hard. But before he was even near her, she was out into the world, loping down the street, looking everywhere around her, breaking into a trot along the footpath and shying away as the cars whizzed past – and not for an instant noticing his frantic calls.

Then the storm hit. She must have thought the thunder and lightning were being aimed at her. She was terrified and cringing, and she didn't know where to go.

He could see it all but there was nothing he could do. He couldn't catch her. He screamed out for someone to help but the rain had driven everyone from the street and the people speeding by in cars just stared. She kept going further away from him until she was out of sight. He walked on in the rain, calling her name again and again, until it was dark. By then he was drenched to the bone, but he hardly noticed.

Late that night the phone rang. His father reached it first. The boy was outside the room, listening. But most of all, hoping.

'Really?' his father said. And then, 'Thanks,

mate. Thanks a lot. I'll see you soon.'

'Dad?'

'A bloke a few streets away found her.'

'Was she . . . is she okay?'

'Yeah.' His father nodded. 'She was in his front yard. Playing with his dog. Not a scratch on her.'

'I didn't think I'd ever see her again,' the boy said, his voice breaking.

'Come on.' His father put his arm around the boy's shoulder. 'Let's bring her home.'

Shifting Edges
Dianne Wolfer

Aiko steps off the plane into intense heat. She walks across the tarmac, squinting in the glare. How can the horizon be so wide? And where are all the buildings? After life in a tiny apartment, Aiko feels strangely exposed.

She scratches her skin and frowns at the blood on her finger.

In the terminal, Aiko checks her phone. Tokyo is one hour ahead. With the Perth connection, she's been travelling for an entire day.

Her aunt is easy to spot. Cho is dressed in shorts and a colourful shirt, like the butterfly she was named for. Her easy smile and wide hat make her look like a local.

'Aiko!' Cho hugs her niece. So casual after two years in Australia! 'How's your mum?'

'The same.' Aiko holds back for a moment, used to bowing. 'Still tired.'

'And you?'

Aiko shrugs then relaxes into the warmth of her favourite aunt.

'I hope you can rest here.' Cho doesn't mention Aiko's rash. 'Caring for someone is hard.'

Aiko nods.

'Long Covid must be terrible, especially for someone like your mum.'

She nods again, remembering her mother's parting words, asking Aiko to decide what she wants to do with her life. Aiko's skin prickles. The question feels too big.

They heave the suitcase into the tray of a dusty ute and head south.

'It's a hundred and forty kilometres to Coral Bay.' Cho overtakes a dawdling caravan. 'Just over an hour.'

Sweat trickles down Aiko's back as they drive into a barren landscape. The earth is the deep red of *maguro*, dotted with tall misshapen mounds.

'What are they?'

'Ant hills.'

Aiko wonders whether Cho is joking, until they stop in a layby. There are no signs of life on the baked mud.

'Where are all the ants?'

'Inside. Termites seal the edges of their home against extremities.'

'So weird . . .'

Cho asks about the flight. 'Was it okay? You were brave coming so far on your own. I couldn't have done that at fourteen.'

'I was glad your friend helped me change terminals.' Aiko remembers the vivid blue sky around Perth airport and the bizarre screeching birds. The sky was impossibly wide. Too wide. There was nowhere to hide.

Cho smiles at her niece then nods at Aiko's phone. 'Want to plug that in and play me the latest hits from home?'

'I have a few covers of classic oldies . . .' Aiko chooses a playlist and Cho sings enthusiastically. A comfortable steering-wheel-tapping settles between them.

As they pass road signs with images of cattle, kangaroo and emu, Aiko asks, 'Will we see wild kangaroos?'

'Hopefully not while we're driving, but there are mobs of them in the dunes behind our caravan.'

'*Hontō!*'

The road stretches ahead. Endless, overwhelming openness. Aiko grips her phone, fighting the urge to scratch. They pass roadkill after roadkill on the edges of the highway and Aiko understands her aunt's meaning.

'So many dead kangaroos . . .'

'It's horrible, isn't it?' Cho beeps the horn at scavenging wedgetail eagles. They hover, pecking until the last possible moment before lifting their enormous wings.

At last, they turn off the main road. In the distance Aiko glimpses a vast, deeper blue – the Indian Ocean. They drive twelve kilometres to a small beachside community.

'Home,' Cho announces, parking next to a caravan at the end of a sandy track.

Aiko looks around, feeling like she's inhabiting a parallel universe. Three weeks here stretches into an unimaginable eternity. But the van is cosy with *kabuki* character posters on the walls and a maniacally waving Welcome Cat.

'The *maneki neko* is solar.' Cho laughs. 'It never stops!' She indicates a curtained-off area. 'Your bed's in there. Sorry it's so small.'

Aiko looks around. 'Is there a bathroom?'

'There's a loo for night-time wees.' Cho repeats the strange information in Japanese. 'During the day I use the bathroom at the caravan park.' She points down the track. 'It's that long building by the tennis court.'

Aiko takes a deep breath.

'Are you hungry?' Cho serves delicate

snacks from the fridge. 'Your visit is a good excuse for me to cook Japanese.'

They carry pickled vegetables, sashimi and rice balls outside, watching the sky shift into layers of pastel, orange, pink, mauve. As they eat, the first stars appear, then an almost full moon.

'Pretty amazing, hey?'

Aiko nods, trying to remember if she's ever actually seen stars in Tokyo.

After showering in weird-smelling mineral water, Aiko settles down in the curtained cubby space and falls into a deep sleep.

'Morning, sleepyhead.' Cho opens the blinds. Aiko blinks. How can sunlight be so stark? 'I'm heading off to work. Today is the half-day turtle tour, so I'll be back just after midday. Help yourself to toast and cereal.'

'Thank you.'

Cho points to a mask and snorkel on the table. 'Those should fit. The bay is safe if you want to explore the reef.'

'Okay.' Aiko pulls the pillow over her head and drifts back into an odd half-sleep until her phone wakes her. It's Mum.

They chat, then Aiko sleeps again until Cho returns with treats from the bakery.

'Do you like spinach and ricotta pasties?'

'I've never tried them.' Aiko bites and nods. 'Yes!'

'And there's this for after.'

The blueberry scroll is as big as Aiko's face.

'How was your cruise?'

'Great, we saw turtles and manta rays before the wind picked up, so the tourists came back happy. Want to go for a snorkel after lunch?'

Aiko hesitates, embarrassed by her angry raw skin.

'Here,' Cho offers, 'you can borrow this rashie.'

'Rashie?'

'A swim-shirt. It keeps off the sun. Most people wear one during the day, otherwise you'll burn.'

Aiko smiles and pulls the rashie over her head, relieved to be safely covered.

Cho gives her a wide hat and they cross the road to a stunningly beautiful beach.

'So much sand!'

'The tide's out,' Cho replies.

They walk past families digging moats, sunbaking and paddling boards in the shallow water.

'I know you're a strong swimmer, Aiko, but have you ever used a snorkel?'

'Only once.'

Cho explains how it works and adjusts Aiko's mask for a tight seal.

'Okay, let's practise by the drop-off.'

They wade through ankle-deep water towards the edge of the reef. Aiko sits on the sand as Cho checks her mask.

'Okay, it's only two metres deep here so you can easily step back. Ready?'

'Yes.'

'Look below.'

'Fish!' Aiko squeals lifting her head. 'Huge ones.'

'Our resident Emperors are curious.' Cho laughs. 'They like swimming beside people.'

As Aiko tries again, two more Emperors join the first. Being so close to such big fish is freaky. It's hard to steady herself.

Okay? Cho signs.

Aiko takes deeper slow breaths and looks into the non-judging black eyes of an Emperor. She soon gets the hang of snorkel-breathing and they fin-kick further out. There are so many fish. Schools of small blue ones, multi-coloured beaked ones, long striped ones. Cho points to a roundish fish with black criss-cross stripes and a yellow patch. She takes out her mouthpiece. 'Butterfly fish, my namesake!'

They drift over a garden of cabbage-shaped coral. Aiko watches electric-blue and purple fish peck at its edges.

'Parrotfish,' Cho tells her, then points to a ray nestling in the sand.

Aiko splashes backwards, trying not to flounder about with her fins.

'It's okay, it won't bother you. Just try not to step on it.'

They explore a lavender-coloured reef bed, then at last Cho signals for them to return.

'That was amazing!' Aiko takes off her fins and shivers despite the heat. After they warm up, she asks, 'Can we go in again?'

Cho grins and leads her to another area further up the beach.

'I'll show you where I sometimes see a turtle, though only early morning or late afternoon when it's quiet.'

The bay's colour of hydrangea blue, the flower of abundance, seems fitting. Each day Aiko snorkels. She examines the tide charts and swims at both high and low, learning which times are best for different fish. She begins to recognise unusual individuals and a massive, blue-lipped clam. Sharing discoveries with her aunt and checking images in Cho's snorkelling guidebook is a daily joy. The turtle remains elusive but Aiko keeps searching. One day she thinks she glimpses it in the distance.

By the second week, the salt water is drying her eczema. It's less angry and red. Or perhaps she is. Aiko's mother calls, sounding stronger, and Tokyo feels like forever away. As she scans the horizon for the tourist boat's return, Aiko wonders where her edges end. If she folds herself again, and again, like a new origami shape, using the same worn piece of paper, could she fit into this strange land, like Cho?

One afternoon Cho tells her that two of the casual boat staff have left.

'It's the way of it here. Backpackers don't stay long. Our skipper, Bob, asked if you'd like a part-time job while he tries to find someone for the rest of the season.'

'What would I do?'

'Cut fruit, make tea and sandwiches, general things.'

Aiko looks out to the boats on the horizon.

'Just here in the bay to start with . . .'

'Okay.'

Aiko's surprised by how much she enjoys greeting the tourists and preparing their snacks in the little galley. They cruise around the sheltered fringing reef, looking for turtles and viewing coral. Her confidence grows, and the next day Aiko helps on the manta ray tour.

'Manta are filter feeders, completely harmless to humans,' Cho explains as the divers lift their tanks. 'They're smart, with the largest brain-to-body weight ratio of any fish. If you look at their undersides, you'll see their different markings, kind of like our unique fingerprints.'

The divers step into the ocean, check their regulators and descend. Aiko watches Cho lead them down amongst the gentle but terrifying-looking rays. Front fins surround their wide mouths, and some wingspans stretch seven metres.

Aiko prepares plenty of food. Cho said the divers will be hungry. They ascend in a burst of bubbles. She helps them balance their tanks as they wobble back on deck, talking over the top of each other in an adrenalin rush as they share details.

That evening, Cho points to the Southern Cross and tells Seven Sisters star stories as they sip tea.

'Bob says you're great with the tourists, especially the kids. He wants you to come with us on a whale shark dive tomorrow.' Cho hesitates. 'I'm sure you'd enjoy it.'

'I've never been in deep water.' Aiko instinctively scratches her skin. 'What if I panic?'

Cho holds her hand, 'You've travelled from Japan, flown 1000 kilometres north of the most isolated capital city in the world . . .' She kisses Aiko's forehead. 'You have an adventuring spirit. You'll be fine.'

Aiko chews her lip.

'Trust me, you are brave enough.'

Aiko looks away, but the next morning when Cho asks again, she agrees.

After the practice snorkel, Cho sorts the tourists into two groups of eight. Then the catamaran picks up speed and they sail beyond the bay into deeper water. Bob cruises along the outer edge of Ningaloo Reef, in constant radio contact with the spotter plane. Suddenly he yells, 'Hold on everyone, we've found one . . .'

'Group One, kit up.' Cho repeats the rules. 'Remember, only eight people in the water at any time, that's why we have you in two groups. Keep out of the shark's way and definitely no touching. Once the pectorals pass, if you're strong enough, you can swim alongside the whale shark. Any questions?'

Aiko knows Cho is a marine biologist but seeing her take charge with such assurance is impressive. She gives her aunt a thumbs-up and as she zips her wetsuit she asks, 'How can you be so confident?'

'Practice.' Cho grins. 'Okay, Group One, let's go!'

One by one they step off the back of the boat.

'Bonzer work,' Bob says as Aiko helps a nervous teenager adjust his mask. 'How about you stand on the side now and help Rosa count heads. I don't want to lose anyone.'

Aiko grips the boat rail, keeping watch over the swimmers.

'Keep in line,' Cho shouts, floating in front like a mermaid with her gold rashie, elongated fins and streaming dark hair. When the snorkellers are corralled, she calls, 'Now look underwater.'

An enormous shadow appears, its grey-blue skin camouflaged by spots. The whale shark drifts closer. It's enormous, almost the size of a subway train carriage.

Some swimmers drift back as the whale shark passes. Others swim with all their might, trying to keep up. Despite its bulk the biggest fish in the world is fast.

Cho herds the swimmers back on deck,

then tells Group Two to get ready. Bob speeds ahead of the whale shark and they repeat the process.

Aiko has snacks and warm drinks ready for Group One, then she keeps watch over Group Two. The energy onboard is exhilarating as swimmers buzz with excitement.

'Did you see the size?'

'Three times me, I reckon.'

'How cute were the cleaner fish?'

'I know . . .'

'It's a good day,' Bob calls as the spotter finds another whale shark and they repeat the process.

By the time they reach a third whale shark, the shivering swimmers have warmed and are sunbaking on the bow.

'How many want to go back in?' Bob asks.

Only five stand.

Bob taps Aiko's shoulder. 'Looks like it's your turn, mate.'

Aiko stares across the deck into endless ocean.

'*Senri no michi mo ippo kara,*' Cho mutters.

Aiko nods. A journey of a thousand miles begins with a single step. The cheesy proverb feels apt as she pulls on a mask

and scissor-steps off the back of the boat, like she's seen the others do.

The small group floats into line. Cho stays close as Aiko peers down, trying not to remember how deep it is. Then the whale shark drifts up. Graceful, enormous, majestic. She holds her breath. Aiko sees the perfection of the shark's design, the light shafts camouflaging with the mottled rows of spots. Her breath releases in a stream of bubbles.

Time slows. Her breathing settles. Her sensitive edges are salt-crisped, sealed tight as a termite hill. Being here on the deep edge of a magnificent reef, something shifts. She is such a small cog. What is the worst that can happen, Aiko wonders, laughing at her previous self-importance. She swims beside the whale shark, feeling at peace.

―――

Sailing back into the bay as the sun sets, Aiko sees the caravan park clinging to the edge of the continent, a limpet on an ancient rock.

'I'll miss you when you go,' Cho whispers. 'Perhaps you can come back next year, for longer?'

Beside the boat a turtle pops up to breathe and Aiko knows there are so many things she can do with her life. She hugs her aunt. 'I'd love that.'

Author's Note:

Cho:	*butterfly*
Hontō!:	*really!*
Maguro:	*lean raw tuna*
Kabuki:	*type of Japanese theatre*
Maneki neko:	*welcome cat*
Sashimi:	*raw fish thinly sliced*

Message Me

Michael Earp

I think it's just the street that is empty. Dusk has passed. The tea-stain shadows that grow out of every corner now cover each house. Night is thick like molasses.

To try and fight the feeling of being utterly alone – seriously, not even one person and their dog, no lights at any of the windows – I text Hamish.

Walking home. Kinda creeped. Where you at?

I hold my phone, as if it's more company in my hand than my pocket. Usually, Hamish isn't too bad in getting back to me before too long. Hopefully he can sense my need tonight.

It's only nine-thirty. I can't work out why everything is so dead tonight. I'd lost track of time studying in the library plenty of times before, but never had this feeling on my way home. It may as well be the small hours for how deserted my slice of suburbia is.

There aren't even many cars lining the

curb. The Dimitrious' navy Falcon is still there, thank goodness. Otherwise, I might start thinking I am in the wrong town. It hasn't been moved since I was a kid. But so many others are gone. The thought that maybe I'm on the set of some post-apocalyptic film makes me smile, but only for a moment. Then that thought joins the others that are making my anxiety spike rapidly.

I look at my phone again – still no response from Hamish – and the brightness is disorientating in the dark. So I lock the screen.

My exhalation when I see my house is a mixture of relief and disappointment. I want to be inside more than anything right now, but there are no lights on, which means my parents are out. Not unusual. They often go to friends' places on Saturday nights and get home late. But I want to be around people more with each passing minute. Even if they are in another room.

I let myself in and lock the door behind me. Still nothing from Hamish, but the familiar surroundings do a small amount of soothing.

'Mum? Dad?' I know they're not here, but I need to hear a voice bounce off the walls, even if it's mine. There's no point in going upstairs to check. I trudge down the stairs to the basement which I converted into my bedroom a year ago. Mum and Dad resisted, because the only window is a tiny one that's not even a foot high, right at the top of the wall. I convinced them with promises of studying.

The first thing I do is turn on all three of my lamps. I hated the fluorescent, overhead light, so I went to a bunch of op shops and got some daggy lamps. All mismatched. One's a floral touch-lamp, the other two were probably ten dollars when they were brand new. I got them for a dollar each.

I fall onto my couch. Hamish's silence is getting louder. And not seeing a single person since leaving the library? Just plain eerie. It's nine fifty-eight and I want to text him again. I know he hates it when I blow up his phone, but two texts in half an hour when I'm feeling super unsettled isn't that bad, right?

Home now. Could chat, if you're free.

I open Instagram and scroll through the images, letting them smooth the ruffled edges of my mind. I haven't got far when I hear a noise coming from the wall. At first, I ignore it, sure it's just pipe noises. But when it doesn't stop, I turn my head to face the wall.

There's definitely something there. But it's too quiet to discern. A hiss, perhaps, but nothing that I can place.

I experiment by moving closer to the wall. It sounds like I could almost work it out, but not quite, so I put my ear against the painted concrete.

So faint I can barely hear it, there's a whisper. It's repetitive and it takes me a few times before I catch the words mixed in the muffled breathy noise.

'He's not free.'

When I hear it, I pull back from the wall with a start. What the hell? I get up from the couch and stare at the wall. But I can't hear anything now. Is it too late? Should I go to bed? I just want to hear from Hamish. Then I'll be at ease. It's been a long day. I close my eyes for a moment and then look again at my phone. Ten-o-seven. Surely, it's been longer than that.

I sit back on my couch, make sure I can't hear anything, then stare at my phone for a full three minutes watching the clock. It's a technique I developed to both stop the feeling that if I'm not typing or receiving a message then I'm not really wanted, and to alleviate the load on Hamish's inbox. When I'm like this, I wait until there's a zero on the end of the time before I send another message. I'm lucky it's only three minutes because I'm pretty damn tense right now.

Sorry to unload on you, but I feel a freak out coming on. Xo

I don't know what that noise is about. Overactive imagination, Mum would say. Not that I'd tell her. I'm never super open about what's going on with me. She and Dad had to piece together that Hamish and I were even boyfriends. But he is the first person I've ever voiced my insecurities to. The first I told how extreme my anxiety could be. It is a miracle that he is also able to hold all of it, and support me whenever he can.

I just wish he would reply. There's a part of my brain that tells me that he's just busy. I know he had a family thing tonight. The rest of my brain thinks that part's worthless, and clearly, he's avoiding having to deal with me.

The room seems darker, like I haven't tapped my touch lamp enough times and the bulb is still on its dim setting. I reach over to tap it again. It takes three taps to be completely bright. But as soon as my fingers hit the cold metal it turns off, which means it was on full. In the weaker light of only two cheap lamps, I hear a whisper from right next to my ear.

'Not another freaking episode.'

I spin around and shout, 'Who's there?'

There's no answer, of course, because there is no one there. My heart is trying to be heard, banging loudly. I tap the lamp three times then walk to the door and flick the light switch too. The harsh white light flickers on. It should be a relief, but it's a spotlight on my loneliness.

Voices are new. I've never heard voices before.

I'm not even sure I did hear them, except that my heart is objecting wildly to whatever the hell just happened.

I turn on my speaker and wait for it to connect to my phone. Then I search through to the playlist Hamish made me to help calm me down. Pressing play firmer than I need to, the first song starts and the bright beats distract me enough to steady my breathing.

I don't think about how long it'll be till ten-twenty. I don't think about how I'm alone until then, or until Hamish messages back and maybe even after that. I don't think about how he probably doesn't want to message me because all my emotional and mental baggage is too much for him. I don't think about that. I just think about the recognisable rise and fall of the melody that's coming through the little speaker in my hand.

I turn it up.

My eyes are darting around the room, but I'm not hearing anything other than the song, so I'm starting to feel less freaked. The rising tide of anxiety that nobody will ever understand me or be able to handle me is still there, of course. It seems to echo louder in this empty night. But it's a hand on my shoulder I've almost gotten used to.

The second song on the playlist comes on. It's a cute one about going to the beach with friends. It's not deep, but that's the point. I know it's on here because he's trying to remind me of the times we go to the beach with people. *See*, he's saying, *remember you have friends?*

I do, but I don't tell them all this head stuff. I'm scared I'll freak them out and they won't want to hang with me anymore and then Hamish will resent me for driving all our friends away. So, are they really friends if they don't know me well?

The song's not deep. But my mind has a will of its own. I look at my phone, thinking I'll skip it, even though it does usually help me, but I see that it's ten-twenty already so I quickly text.

Hamish?

I wait to see that it's sent properly, then skip the track.

In the silence before the next song starts: 'He doesn't care.'

The whisper is right in front of my face this time, although no one is there.

The bright sounds of a marimba start but I crumple to the floor. I feel broken like I am not meant to fit into this world. A jigsaw piece with no companions. As if there are instructions on how to be around people, and around yourself, but I missed out on them.

I'm crying. The tears feel like they're spilling from the gash that splits my heart and my mind. The gap that won't let reason in.

The music stops mid bar, and I'm filled with panic that the voice will say something. But it's because my phone is ringing.

I look at the screen. Hamish is calling.

I'm worried this is some other trick of my mind. I thought he'd just message me.

But I'm too desperate to care. I answer and put the phone to my ear.

I wait for the voice to start taunting me again.

'Babe, you there?'

'Hamish?'

'Sorry! Family dinner went super late, I

got caught up getting my ear gnawed off by my uncle who wanted to recap his entire life and couldn't stop to check my phone.'

'You're actually there? Calling me?' His voice is bringing me back to where I can construct a rational thought.

'Yeah, of course I am. Always here for you, even if I can't text. You know that.'

'I know that?'

'Yeah, of course. Should I come round?'

I nod, but realise I haven't made a sound. 'Please.'

'Okay. I'm going to keep talking to you all the way there. You'll never believe the stories he told me . . .'

At that moment, the small window near the ceiling lights up with a flash. I flinch at another hallucination. No, it's headlights. Hamish already? No, he's still talking to me through his car's Bluetooth. Mum and Dad are back.

I breathe out in one long, slow breath.

Guess there wasn't an apocalypse after all.

Faith and the Elephant God

Susanne Gervay

As Faith pounds her arms through the surf, her surfboard dips and rises. With her back arched, she looks for the gleaming line behind the swell of waves – out to sea into the beyond. She makes a final charge ahead, riding against the curling rolls before they arch and crash into white fury. When her board reaches smooth waters, she surveys the horizon, dividing the Earth and heavens. She checks her leg leash to make sure the board is tied to her. Then she flips her board around and calls out to Caleb.

'What kept you?'

'Someone had a head start.' Laughing, Caleb skims his hand over the glassy water before the wind sweeps it into waves. It crashes onto the sand. With a quick flick, he splashes her.

Faith splashes him back. The water

catches the lights in the rainbow of colours and sun. Faith smiles as the warm glow of the universe surrounds her.

Faith and Caleb float beside each other, watching the swells, the gaps between sets, the currents, the wind direction and other surfers riding waves. Caleb points down the beach to a pod of dolphins, flying and bounding like champion aerialists. Two dolphins spin in the air.

'I'd love to surf like that.'

Faith watches the dolphins dive away. She looks up at the sun, gleaming between the white clouds. Her blue eyes soften. When Faith was younger, her mother's heart just stopped. She always remembers that day. Her mother was resting on the lounge chair with her hand extended. Faith squeezed her hand, but her mother didn't move or speak again. Her father held back his tears and told her that she was born with a fault inside her heart. Faith didn't want to believe him. So she held onto her mother's hand and waited for her mother to wake up. She never did.

'Come on, Caleb. Let's ride a wave.'

Caleb and Faith have been beach buddies since they were five. Caleb arrived from India with his parents. His mother wore saris and she gave them a small Ganesh, the elephant God. It brought them wisdom, understanding and regeneration. They settled next door. Caleb knew all about cricket, but didn't know anything about surfing. Soon, he did. Faith's dad was a surfer and he was keen to teach Faith. He wanted to teach Caleb, too. Nothing could be better than Faith having a buddy. They lived near the beach and could carry their surfboards down there. There was a headland there too. It gave them the vantage point; they could see the rips and wind directions.

Faith's mother loved the incense at Caleb's front door and the welcoming scent from the altar inside their house. She put Ganesh on the windowsill. It brought light into their home. Caleb's mother gave Faith a sarong made from a sari with the sparkling universe and the colours of the sea. She tied it over her shoulder after every surf.

Caleb and Faith became best friends.

'He just has to learn to swim better.' Faith laughed. He learnt quickly, like a fish darting between waves and underwater tunnels.

They were nine years old when Faith's mother passed away. They scattered her ashes and their broken hearts into the ocean. The creamy frangipanis with their

sweet scent were laid on the water, drifting to infinity. The white and grey of seagulls shimmered above them, flying in a V formation as a salute. Caleb whispered to Faith that her mother's spirit was still alive.

'I'm a Hindu and I know these mysteries. When someone dies, the soul is reborn as a different form. Their soul remains and continues until it reaches its true nature.' He took the Ganesh from her windowsill and put it into Faith's hand. 'You need it now.'

Faith always wore it around her neck. Faith's mother had become part of the sea.

Surfing became fundamental to their days. Every morning they'd check the Coastal Watch and know where the swell was coming from, the number of seconds between sets and from which compass point the wind was blowing. They would head down to the beach in the mornings, most afternoons and on weekends.

They are now thirteen and as always, the sea calls them. They dive into the water.

'Hey, Caleb. I'm taking that wave.' Faith paddles fast, catching the swell. Standing on her board, she drops into a wall of water. She skims at incredible speed, flying with the wind in her face, salt on her lips, sun on her back. Raising her arms, she is like a seagull soaring.

Caleb laughs. He raises his arms too, then paddles for the next wave.

A familiar voice calls from the shore. Faith turns. Her father has followed them down to the beach. 'Faith! Faith! Faith!' He's waving.

Faith smiles and waves back. Paddling to the line where the swell begins, she waits and watches. That is what surfers do, wait and watch. She studies the swell, wind, sun, currents, sea, sky. She watches Caleb. He is on a rip-roaring ride. Faith admires him as he spins into the air, flipping his surfboard 360 degrees.

Faith rests on her surfboard, beckoning the warmth of summer to trickle through her. She looks towards the horizon. From the corner of her deep blue eyes, grey lights ripple under the glassy swell. She loves dolphins as they play in the sea in the days of sun and the flickering cosmos.

Caleb calls to Faith. He points to a wave coming. 'A perfect A-frame. Do you want to do it?'

Her father forgotten, she nods. 'Yeah. It's amazing.' Only a surfer knows the feeling of the ocean. It can be so magnificent, breathtaking but peaceful. The rest of the world disappears. The wave is all that matters.

They both paddle as hard as they can. Faith is up and riding the wave. Caleb is beside her. They reach the peak, then down the face as they ride the tunnel. As the wave peters out, they are breathless.

'Let's do it again?' they both say together.

The conditions are always changing: offshore, onshore, low tide, high tide, mid tide, close outs, barrels, point break, reef break, beach break, shores. It's endlessly challenging. Endlessly encompassing. Endlessly eternal. Faith paddles out past the waves.

Caleb stays on the shore to repair his leg bank.

Faith loves the freedom of being so deep in the sea. She can't see the dolphins playing anymore and rests her head on the surfboard. She glances into the water, and runs her fingers over the surface. Suddenly, a chill zigzags through her. A large oval shadow ripples under her board. Too big for a dolphin. The fin doesn't swerve into a dolphin curve. It is knife-straight. She gasps and her heart pounds. She starts paddling, hoping to lose the predator. But the huge shadow tails her, worrying the water. Worrying.

Slowly, a dark blue eye without eyelids

emerges beside her. Then it disappears. Faith paddles faster than she has ever done before. Breathless, she splashes the glassy surface into shards of light. Maybe she has escaped. Then everything erupts. Water spits and swirls, all-consuming like a tornado. As she spins downwards, she holds onto her surfboard for her life. But she is not strong enough. Her surfboard trembles and she's sucked into the sea.

The great white attacks. Instinctively, she punches its white belly. Her arms are swinging. Her legs are pounding. She kicks and kicks and kicks. Startled, the shark retreats. Faith scrambles back onto her surfboard and frantically paddles towards the beach. But she knows she can't out-surf the shark. Is it coming back? Fear grips her like when her mother died. Like her nightmares that her father will abandon her. Like Caleb who could leave her. Is she alone forever?

Beneath the water, the dark shadow glides towards her, gaining speed, slicing the sea, moving like a whirlwind. Faster and faster. She has to escape. She's splashing so hard now, when it surges. The water parts into monumental foam and spray. Breaching high into the air like a super-god, the great white arcs, its mouth open wide. Double rows of jagged teeth glare from its enormous jaw.

Screaming, Faith hurtles off her board. In the face of whirls of thrashing fins, she clasps her board like a warrior shield. The great white charges again, hitting the board hard, again and again. Dragging the board and Faith into a deathly spin. Suddenly, the shark falters, dizzy and momentarily confused. Unable to get its bearings.

Panting, Faith struggles back onto her board.

The water is calm again. Faith is spent. She glides along the outer line, where the swell begins. The great white shark re-emerges. It glides beside her, with one eye staring at her. Slowly Faith turns her head. She stares with her deep blue eyes into the shark's one dark blue eye. A calm spreads through Faith, as the great white silently watches her. Her panic scatters, like confetti playing in the sea breeze. She looks up. Is it her mother standing watch over her? The sun warms her back. The sparkling blue of the water surrounds her. She feels the peace of the sea.

Disturbing murmurs make her glance back to shore. She doesn't want to hear them. See them. Caleb is paddling frantically towards her. Her father has leapt onto his board. He is coming for her. She looks up. Her mother's arms are around her.

The shark glides beside Faith. Their deep blue eyes connect again. Faith stares at its enormous jaw and smooth skin. The shark watches her intently. She doesn't paddle or panic anymore. She just lets go, trusting the sea to take her home.

With a smooth swish, the shark swerves away, disappearing beyond the swell, into the infinite sea.

Her father's arms are around her. Caleb is beside her. Her mother's heart is hers and she feels her hand. The sea surrounds them. Ganesh presses against her chest. Or does she press Ganesh against her?

She is not afraid anymore.

Author's Note: This story was inspired by an interview with a surfer who survived a great white shark attack at Cellito Beach, NSW. He fought off the shark, but at the end of the attack, when he felt calm and at peace, the shark stared at him, turned away and let him live. He felt it was a spiritual experience about acceptance of life.

The Knight

Tony Thompson

Tom thought the townhouses where he lived with his mum looked like a medieval castle. He imagined that he was the knight who lived there. Maybe it didn't look exactly like the pictures in the book he'd taken out of the library, but there were big walls and a gate at the front.

It was Sunday and Tom was sitting on a small patch of grass beside the gate, watching the cars come down Bayview Avenue. He tried counting all of them at first, then just the dark blue ones, hoping that one would turn into the street and stop in front of the gate. It would be his dad and he would say, 'Hi, Chief! Hop in.' They'd go to the model train shop on Mount Pleasant Road. It was closed on Sundays, but Tom loved seeing the small N gauge trains journeying through mountains and colourful villages in the large store windows.

He'd lost count of the dark blue cars, and something about the afternoon light told him that it was getting late. He had come out after lunch so that he would be ready at one o'clock. That's what his dad had said on the phone. 'Be out there at one o'clock, Chief! Don't be late.' He wasn't late. In fact, he'd gone out as soon as he'd finished lunch, even when his mum told him his dad wouldn't be there for another thirty-five minutes at least. It didn't matter. Maybe he'd be early. Was his dad ever early? Tom tried to remember. Actually, his dad was late sometimes so maybe he was just late today. How long had he been waiting? He looked at the sun. You were supposed to be able to tell the time by the sun. He'd seen a sun dial on a school excursion but he didn't have one. If the sun was right overhead, that was noon. He looked for it, but it was behind the clouds. He shivered in his thin jacket.

Tom started to wish he was doing something else. He wanted to see his dad but he imagined a different kind of Sunday afternoon, one where he was building a model airplane or setting up his castles and taking out his toy knights for a big battle in his bedroom. Tomorrow, he would have to get up and go to school. He didn't hate school, but it was boring and the other kids didn't seem to like him. Some

of them did, he thought. But a lot of them thought he was weird because he liked to read. It wasn't that he was the smartest kid in the class. Actually, he was probably the dumbest kid in maths in all of Year 7. He loved history and anything to do with stories, but he had terrible handwriting. Still, he could name every English monarch. He looked up quickly, hoping that his dad's car would suddenly be there before quietly starting the list. Alfred The Great, Edward, Athelstan . . . the Saxon ones were complicated and different, depending on the book. Then there were the Danish ones. He'd start with Edward the Confessor.

His mind wandered after Henry VIII. Two Year 8 kids who lived in the townhouses came through the gate. One of them was Jack who had moved in a few months earlier. Tom had befriended him but had then dropped him when Jack realised that Tom wasn't a particularly cool kid. He was with a boy named Kelly who had once knocked Tom off his bike for no reason at all. Jack waved and Tom waved back.

'What are you doing, Tommy?'

Tom did not like being called Tommy.

'Waiting for my dad.'

The other boys looked at each other and laughed.

'He's probably not coming,' said Jack.

'He probably hates you,' said Kelly.

Tom had no idea what to say but knew laughing usually worked with kids like them. Jack and Kelly kept walking, probably heading to the mall to get someone to buy them cigarettes. Tom watched them cross the street. Jack turned back to him briefly but looked away before Tom could read his expression.

His jeans felt damp from sitting on the grass. He climbed onto a wall near the gate. There was a better view of Bayview Avenue from there. He imagined that he was a knight guarding the gate against . . . who? The Vikings? No. The Normans? No. Knights came later, Tom thought. The French maybe. Saladin's assassins. Yes, he was a knight in Richard the Lionheart's army. He was in the Holy Land on a Crusade. His armour was shiny and he was wearing a tunic with a big red cross on the front. His eyes moved slowly across the desert landscape. The assassins wore black and carried large curved swords. He had to be very careful. But he was one of Richard's favourite knights because he was brave and very good at sword fighting. Tom shifted on the wall. He was on a horse, a large black one that he'd brought from his castle in England.

'Tom, have you been out here the whole time?'

The armour and horse dissolved, and his mother was standing by the gate. She looked annoyed but Tom couldn't figure out what he'd done wrong.

'I'm waiting for Dad. He said he'd pick me up at one o'clock.'

His mother looked at her watch and shook her head.

'It's after three, Tom. Come inside and I'll phone him.'

'But what if he comes?'

'Don't worry, he'll come to the door.'

Tom looked up at Bayview Avenue, hoping that his dad's car would be among the cluster coming down the hill. He followed his mum through the gate and past the other townhouses back to his own, 110D.

'Take off your jacket, Tom,' said his mum.

Tom saw, for the first time, that there was another way this afternoon could end other than his dad picking him up. He would be in his room, reading maybe, or listening to The Beatles in the study. It was too late to start anything like a game with the castles and he didn't have any airplane models that he hadn't built. There was a yellow chair in the living room. He sat in it while his mum phoned his dad. Her facial expression remained the same, a slight look of irritation as she waited before hanging up.

'No answer,' she said.

Tom jumped up and grabbed his jacket.

'He must be on his way. He's probably waiting out there!'

'Tom,' said his mum. 'Your dad might . . .'

'He's coming, Mum. He said he was coming.'

She nodded and Tom burst out of the screen door and ran back to the gate, certain that his dad would be there. 'Where were you, Chief? Hop in, we can still get to the model train shop. Maybe it will even be open, and we can get you that train engine you wanted.'

He wasn't there. Tom walked through the gate and climbed back up on the wall to watch the cars.

Hopefully, it would just be his dad. Martha, his dad's girlfriend, was okay but if she came, she would sit in the front seat and talk about the restaurant where she worked. Dad would talk about it too and it would be 'grownup talk' about who didn't know what they were doing and who should just leave if they weren't happy. Martha was a waitress and she always complained about the service when the three of them went out for dinner. One time, after she mentioned that the waiter had forgotten to bring garlic bread, Tom had said, 'You must be the greatest waitress on earth.' He had meant it to be a compliment but as soon as it had left his mouth, he knew that it sounded sarcastic. 'That's enough, Tom,' said his dad and Martha didn't speak to him again that day.

But Martha had been nice to him too. Once, when he was a bit younger, his mum had dropped him at his dad's house because she had to go to a funeral. Martha was standing outside and came over to the car. She spoke very quietly to Tom's mum and then stepped back. His mum turned to him.

'Tom, your dad isn't feeling well, so Martha is going to take you to see a movie and for lunch at McDonalds.'

Tom knew that his dad wasn't really sick, as in a cold or something. There was a problem. They weren't lying to him but he wasn't getting the whole story. It turned out to be a fun day. Martha was a lot younger than his dad and sang along to the music on the radio. They'd had Big Macs and seen an excellent movie that he normally wouldn't have been allowed into except that the guy behind the counter obviously liked Martha and let him in. It was a horror movie and Tom loved it. Afterwards, they went to a used bookstore where Martha bought him two Thor comics and a paperback called *Norse Myths*.

Tom suddenly felt furious with his dad. He clenched his fists and decided that if Jack and Kelly came back, he was going to fight with both of them. Tom wasn't very good at fighting but he thought that he was angry enough that he could make at least one of them cry. Then kids would be scared of him. Watch out for Tom. He beat up Jack and Kelly one day. And all the stupid kids at school who flicked his book when he was reading or tripped him in the halls. He'd take on all of them. That's what the knight in the Holy Land would do. Hand-to-hand combat. Tom needed to start doing push-ups or lifting weights. Maybe he'd go to karate class. There was a kid at the Catholic school who knew judo.

His dad always did this stuff. He promised things and then didn't do them. Tom pictured his dad and felt bad for being so angry at him.

His dad was funny and told great stories. They sometimes went for long drives where

Dad talked about his time at university or his travels overseas. He told Tom about old girlfriends and his favourite jazz musicians. He listened to Tom talk about the Middle Ages and added interesting things about the kings and queens. Once, on a drive to visit Tom's grandparents, his dad told him that Richard III probably hadn't murdered his nephews. Tom couldn't believe it. Sometimes, he would sleep over at his dad's apartment and was allowed to stay up late, really late if Martha was cooking. It was fun sometimes although it could be boring if they got talking about someone he didn't know and how that person just needed to be realistic.

The cars had their headlights on now as they came over the hill. It was probably getting close to dinner time. Maybe his dad would come soon and they would go out for a meal. Tom liked the pizza at a restaurant near his dad's place. Or maybe they would go back to his apartment and Martha would make French fries. She'd done that once and they were really good. Tom felt hungry and wondered if he should have a snack while he waited.

The sun was almost gone when his mum came out to the gate. Tom had been thinking about his knight in the Holy Land

and what adventures he'd had on the journey out there.

'Tom, you better come in. Your dad isn't coming.'

He knew, he thought. He'd known for hours. His mum didn't look happy. Tom was pretty sure now that she was mad at his dad and not at him. He followed her back through the gate and to their townhouse.

'He's going to explain why he didn't pick you up. I'll just phone him.'

Tom had a feeling that he didn't want to talk to his dad but couldn't think of any reason why he shouldn't. His father would make an excuse and tell him about the fun thing they would do next time. This had all happened before.

His mum handed him the phone and he heard his father's voice.

'Hi, Chief. I'm really sorry.'

Tom knew this voice. It was the one where his dad talked about sad things. Tom didn't like it at all.

'You know, you're a great kid, Tom.'

'Thanks, Dad. You're a great dad,' he said, not really knowing what else to say.

His dad started to sob.

'No, I'm not, Tom. I should have come today.'

Tom's mum gently took the phone and

walked into the kitchen. He heard her speaking softly and saying goodbye. She came out and smiled at Tom.

'Would you like me to order pizza tonight?'

'Yes!'

'Okay.'

'I'm just going to go out and play for a while,' he said.

'Sure, Tom. Come back in soon and I'll phone the pizza place.'

It was dark outside as Tom walked back towards the gate. But he wasn't Tom anymore. He was in the Holy Land and Saladin's assassins were making their way up the driveway. He reached for his sword and drew it slowly. There were a lot of them, but he wasn't scared. The cars continued to pour down Bayview Avenue as the knight prepared for battle.

Rabbit Life

David Metzenthen

Apprentice gardener, Simon Best, liked digging holes. He was good at it and surprisingly quick, considering how small he was. His arms were thin, his hands soft, but he was tireless. This annoyed his boss, Jarrod Foxman – or Foxy, as he liked to be called. Now Foxy, the head gardener, liked apprentices who knew footy scores, cricket scores, called Foxy 'Foxy' and laughed at his jokes. Simon was not one of them.

'You, Simon *Pest*.' Foxy signalled to Simon at the start of work on a cool Monday morning.

'Get over here. I gotta job for ya.' Foxy smiled as he always did when he had something unpleasant planned. 'C'mon. Hop to it.'

Simon crossed the courtyard to where Foxy stood in front of the wooden shed that was his office. The head gardener, wearing sunglasses and holding a clipboard, smiled nastily.

'So, *Pesty* –' Foxy waited, as if he hoped Simon might say something about this nickname, but the small gardener simply stood blinking in the sunshine. 'Go to the north-west corner of the gardens. Take a wheelbarrow and tools. Weed the whole area. Dig it over then rake it. Take your lunch, Pesty. You'll be there all day. Possibly all week.'

Simon nodded, leaving Foxy to wonder if he'd actually seen the kid's ears twitch, or had just imagined it. Really, the head gardener thought, that dopey kid was like some kind of feral animal. He gave Simon his favorite pest-scaring stare.

'Get a move on, Mr Pest.' Foxy curled his upper lip to scare Simon but Simon had already gone.

———

Simon pushed the old metal wheelbarrow – the other gardeners always took the new plastic ones – towards the far corner of the Royal Botanic Gardens. Not too far away, he could see city buildings and apartment blocks but here he was quite alone, which made him happy.

Overhead, lovely old gum and pine trees spread their branches across the sky. Trimmed shrubs and neat flower beds bordered the path. It was too early for visitors to enter the gardens. There were no noises or smells that Simon found disturbing. So, Simon Best was quite content. Ahead, he saw the wild and weedy north-west corner.

It was an untidy and little-known area that met the tall diamond-wire boundary fence. For years, broken branches and dead plants had been dumped here. Weeds had flourished as the rubbish piled up. Foxy called the place the Bermuda Triangle and complained he didn't have the time to fix it. At the sight of this lonely and uncared-for corner, Simon's chest swelled with pleasure. He liked it here.

Simon worked hard pulling weeds, digging, and raking over the dark soil. By four o'clock he had made some progress. But the area was large, and Simon Best was small. When Foxy arrived to see what had been done he was not impressed.

'Not the best, Pest.' Foxy surveyed the piles of dead branches and uprooted stumps. On purpose, it seemed, he overlooked what the small, brown-haired gardener had achieved. 'You'll be here for a few days yet.'

Simon nodded but said nothing. Secretly he was relieved. He did like the beautiful flower beds and perfectly planted trees of the Royal Botanic Gardens, but this wild

place suited him better.

'I expected more, Pest,' Foxy said. 'Because I like everything in good *order.*' He smiled, showing sharp, uneven teeth. 'Tomorrow, you have to push all the piles into one big one. Because this place is doin' my head in.'

Simon knew that was unfair. There was no way he could move the heaviest stumps and thickest branches. He also knew he would have to try because Foxy fired anyone who disobeyed his orders.

'Yes, sir,' Simon said. 'I'll try.'

'No, no, no, Pesty,' said Jarrod Foxman cheerfully. 'You *will.*'

The next morning Foxy sent Simon straight to the wild corner.

'On yer way, Pesty.' Foxy waved him off. 'Be like a rabbit and start runnin'.'

Simon collected his barrow and tools and headed down the path. He didn't like being called a pest, but he didn't mind being called a rabbit as he loved rabbits. At home with his mum, in their tiny dark cottage, Simon had a large black pet rabbit called Mister Buttons. No one except Simon's mother, Bethany, knew about Mister Buttons. And Simon would never tell the other gardeners because they hated rabbits, although not one had been seen in the gardens for a century.

Arriving at the wild corner, Simon studied the place. Slowly a smile lifted the corners of his mouth. There were thistles, patches of bracken, and a few clumps of blackberries. The cut branches, even if he piled them together, would stay because Foxy didn't have the machinery to move them. This, Simon thought, would be the perfect place to live if you were a rabbit.

Simon worked hard at piling branches and stumps. He moved them downhill towards the fence, as far away from the path as he could. And when Foxy turned up late in the afternoon, the wild corner looked quite tidy. But in fact, Simon had only succeeded in pushing some of the heavy things into a place where it would be nearly impossible to get them out.

'This joint will be your worst nightmare, Pesty,' Foxy said happily. 'You'll be here for days.'

Simon smiled secretly. He was quite happy with his work in the wild corner. But he knew, like Foxy knew, there was more to be done. The difference was Simon's ideas of what would be done were a lot different to Jarrod Foxman's.

In the cool of the evening, Simon sat cross-legged in his tiny backyard feeding celery leaves and slices of carrot to Mister Buttons. The black rabbit, silky and strong, nibbled his way through the vegetables with amazing speed. Yet he was also totally alert, as any smart rabbit should be.

'What I need from you,' Simon whispered to Mister Buttons, looking into the rabbit's coal-dark eyes, 'is some sort of a rabbit-type miracle. Maybe a miracle where something good happens to me. And something bad happens to Foxy.'

Simon then scooped up Mister Buttons, took him to his hutch, and put him gently on his bed of clean hay.

'Go to sleep now,' he said, although he knew Mister Buttons didn't sleep much at night; he was always busy doing rabbit things. 'Tomorrow is a new day. And maybe something wonderful will happen.'

———

The next morning, Foxy sent Simon off to the wild corner to continue weeding and tidying, so Simon did exactly that. By the wire fence, Simon dug out a dead plum tree and threw it on the ever-growing pile. Then, seized by a feeling he couldn't explain, he dug a hole under the fence. Simon knew if Foxy found out what he'd done, he'd be fired. But Simon also knew his boss would never bother to visit the weediest corner of entire botanical gardens.

'Very good,' Simon murmured, admiring the hole that was like a burrow. 'Let's see what happens now.'

As the sun was about to set, Simon sat on a log to have afternoon tea. Blackbirds called, signalling that dusk was on its way. The end of the working day was close.

'Nearly home time,' Simon whispered, sitting still, his brown hair and green shirt blending into the background of piled branches and stumps. 'But not quite.'

He watched little birds flutter over the ground looking for worms and insects. He listened to the sounds of a city that came from a long way off. He smelled grass, flowers, dirt and wood. Then, with a start to his heart, Simon saw someone moving silently outside of the fence.

Knowing often the best way not to be seen was to not move, Simon sat still. He watched as a girl carrying a brown sack appeared. She was about his age, he guessed, and had short, black hair. Whatever was in the sack wriggled. At the fence, she knelt, and looked around.

Normally Simon would not talk to a

stranger. But he thought this girl might be doing something rather unwise or rather interesting. He called out gently.

'Hello.'

The girl looked around, startled. Simon held up a hand.

'Don't worry, you're not in trouble.'

The girl crouched, ready to run.

'Don't go. Please.' Simon walked over, looking at the sack she held in small round fists. 'Maybe I can help you.'

The girl shook her head. Like Simon, she also had brown eyes, and large teeth.

'Don't think so,' she said. 'What I have, you don't want.' She lifted the sack. 'I got rabbits. We got too many at home. So, I'm lettin' some go. Two boys and two girls.'

Simon smiled. He felt a strange and growing joy. This girl and her rabbits must be the miracle Mister Buttons made happen.

'Oh, I love rabbits.' Simon glanced around. 'They're exactly what I want. Come here. I'll show you something.' He led the girl to the burrow under the fence. 'Put them in. They'll be safe on this side. There are no cats, dogs, foxes or poison in here. They can breed as much as they like.'

The girl looked uncertain. 'But if they breed, they'll eat all the good plants.'

Simon shrugged. He'd decided that this person, so small and so perfect, was the most beautiful girl he'd ever seen.

'Oh, they might eat some.' He shrugged. 'That's what rabbits do.'

On a cold misty Friday morning, Foxy dispatched his teams to all corners of the botanical gardens. Soon enough, Simon was the only apprentice left standing in the courtyard.

'Oh dear,' Foxy said. 'The last one left is my best pest. I think that's gunna be the story of your life, Pesty. Now and forever, Amen.'

Simon didn't agree or disagree. It was as if he and Foxy spoke different languages. Simon also knew to be quiet or Foxy would only get meaner. So, he nodded obediently when he was told to go back to the wild corner.

'Yes, Mr Pest?' Foxy stood with his hands on his hips. 'Yes?'

'Yes,' Simon said. 'Yes, sir.' He quickly collected his tools and wheelbarrow, headed off down the path into the fog, and disappeared.

As Simon pulled bracken and weeds, the mist gradually lifted. He thought about the rabbits that had been released into the gardens. They would be somewhere close, he knew. They would be establishing a new colony under the stumps and branches. They would soon be having families. These were blissful thoughts to Simon. The rabbits would breed, spread far and wide, and hop around at dawn and dusk.

Soon, Simon knew, more rabbits would dig more burrows in the rich dirt and in the mind of Jarrod *Foxy* Foxman. Things had worked out perfectly. So, cheerfully, he worked through the day, even though the wind rose, the temperature dropped, and the sun shone with hardly more than a golden glow.

A feeling of loneliness entered the gardens. The visitors had gone, the gates were locked. It was time for Simon to return his tools to the toolshed and go home. He packed away his spade, trowel and clippers, then set off in search of his rake.

'Well, it can't be too far away,' he told himself as he walked along the fence. 'It has to be here somewhere.'

In a patch of sunshine, he found the rake. He also found, sitting as still as a hare in a golden nest of grass and old branches, the beautiful black-haired girl who had brought the rabbits.

'Come in,' she whispered, smiling, pushing aside a tall curtain of weeds. 'There's just enough room for the pair of us.'

Simon hid the rake and crawled into the grassy squat, thinking this was the warmest, safest, nicest place he'd ever been. He and the girl smiled and held hands. They were totally hidden. And Simon knew they could stay here, for as long as they liked, for ever and ever, and no one would ever know.

Into the Wild

Deborah Abela

'There he is!'

Kalash swung his schoolbag onto his shoulder and ran. He bolted away from the swarm of kids and parents and headed for the bush that butted up against the oval.

He'd planned to sneak there after school. It would take longer to get home and he'd have to explain to his mum why he was late, but it would be worth it if he could make it without being caught.

That was the plan, until Niko, the biggest of the three boys, saw him as he tried to escape.

'Get him!'

Kalash wished his legs would run faster, but Niko was captain of the AFL team and outran everyone, even some of the adults.

He scrambled over the fence but the strap from his bag caught on the wire and jerked him back. His fingers fumbled as he tried to untangle it.

'Come on!' Niko's cry cut the air like a chainsaw.

Kalash ripped his pack from the fence and ran.

If he stayed on the track, they'd catch him, but if he turned into the bush, he might have a chance.

He also might get lost.

But Kalash had no choice. He sprinted into the scrub, ducking and weaving between the branches, hoping to lose them.

'He went that way!'

The boys' feet crushed leaves and snapped twigs. Their yells were like battle cries.

'We're coming for you, Kal!'

He was never going to get away. Not when Niko was this mad. Niko had made it his life's ambition to pick on him, but when Kalash stood up to him at lunchtime, in front of everyone, he knew he was going to pay.

But those few seconds, telling Niko what he thought of him, were worth it.

Kalash pushed through the branches. They tore at his arms and legs. He didn't feel the pain, just the blind panic of needing to get away, when he stepped too close to the edge and slid down a bank. He lay sprawled on the ground. A stream gurgled beside him. He lifted his pounding head. The place felt familiar.

That's when he remembered. The cave Roberto showed him when they were kids, before he moved away leaving a giant hole where his best friend used to be. His only friend. They'd read comics by torchlight and make plans to escape. He hadn't been there for years, but he knew it was nearby.

Voices cackled above.

Kalash sprang to his feet and thrashed at the branches. Sweeping and tearing. It was here somewhere. He knew it.

Then he saw it. The entrance to the cave. It was narrow and hidden by bushes, making it the perfect hideout.

Kalash fell to his hands and knees and crawled inside.

He sat on the damp earth and tried to catch his breath. The cave was quiet and thick with darkness. He blinked a few times, hoping his eyes would get used to the dark.

He peeked through the cave mouth and saw the tangle of scrub in the sunlight. He stayed as still as he could, listening.

Footsteps crashed through the silence. Three pairs of shoes lurked in the undergrowth.

'Can you see him?' Niko snarled.

'No,' a voice answered.

'He has to be here somewhere. Keep looking!'

Their steps pounded away.

Kalash breathed out in a rush. He slumped forward over his knees. All he had to do was wait until they got bored, then he could go home.

But that's when he heard it. A low, deep growl.

And it was coming from inside the cave!

He squinted, trying to make out what it was, when two piercing eyes emerged from the darkness.

He'd heard rumours of panthers from the kids at school. Some said they'd seen them in their backyard, scaring the chooks. One kid said he was woken by growling and never saw his pet rabbit again.

He had to get out, but Niko and his friends were still there. If he went now, they would tear him apart.

But so could the beast.

He squeezed against the cold cave wall, breathing as quietly as he could.

Kalash's eyes adjusted a little more to the darkness. He saw the outline of the creature, limping towards him.

'It's okay, fella. I'm . . . I'm not going to hurt you.'

There was another low growl as the animal stepped into a trickle of light.

It was a dog. A Dobermann.

'Buddy?' The dog was thinner than when he'd last seen him. 'It's me, Kalash. We wondered where you went.'

He held out the back of his hand, like his mum taught him, hoping Buddy would recognise his smell. The dog licked him.

'You and Mrs Novak went everywhere

together. I bet you miss her, don't you?'

Buddy whined and sank to the ground.

Kalash noticed a thorn lodged in his paw. 'That's gotta hurt. I can help you.'

His held his thumb and pointer finger like a pincer. He'd have to be careful. Injured animals could be unpredictable.

His skin prickled with sweat. The cave was small, so if the dog pounced, he'd have nowhere to run.

'That's it. Not long now.'

In one quick movement, he pulled the thorn out. He sprang back, in case Buddy attacked, but instead he yelped and licked his face.

Kalash slumped in relief. 'You're welcome.'

He slipped off his backpack and poured water from his drink bottle onto the wound.

'I bet you're hungry, too.' Kalash took out his lunchbox. 'It's lucky we met today. I've got Dad's meatloaf. He always gives me too much. He hopes it'll make me big and strong, but I think I'm always going to be short and puny, like Niko says.'

The dog ate the meatloaf and barked.

'I know.' Kalash smiled. 'Dad's a good cook.' He put on his backpack. 'If you come home with me, I'll get Mum to look at your paw. Make sure it's not infected. And we're having roast chicken for dinner. Dad's meatloaf is good but you'll love his roast.'

Kalash crawled through the mouth of the cave and listened for voices. Nothing.

He crouched low. 'It's okay, they've gone.'

Slowly, the dog got to his feet. He put his weight on his good legs and followed him outside.

The sun was falling behind the trees but there was enough light to make it back to the path if they hurried. And if he didn't get lost. Kalash tried to retrace his steps, hoping he'd remember the way.

The dog whined.

'Sorry, fella. I'll find it, don't worry. I think it might be . . .'

He stopped. His skin went cold.

Blocking his way were Niko and his two friends.

'Told you I heard barking.' Niko was smug.

Buddy growled.

'It's the kid who ran away from school. Did something scare you?'

'I just wanted to get home.'

'Home to his mummy,' one of the boys teased.

'Mummy's boy,' the other sneered.

The dog inched forward.

'It's okay, boy,' Kalash whispered.

'If you wanted to get home so badly,' Niko

said, 'why are you hiding like a chicken?'

Niko dropped his bag to the ground. He flapped his arms and began to cluck. The other boys laughed.

'Chicken! Chicken!'

He danced and clucked.

Buddy bared his teeth; his muscles tensed.

'No, boy!'

But Kalash was too late. The dog lunged at Niko and knocked him to the ground. He stood over him, snarling.

'Get him off me!'

The two boys went to help but Buddy barked. They backed off.

Kalash slapped his thigh. 'Come on, boy.'

But the dog kept barking only centimetres from Niko's face. He tried to slide out from beneath him, but the Dobermann jammed his good paw onto his wrist.

'Help!' Niko cried. 'He's going to kill me.'

Kalash tried again. 'Come on, fella!'

Buddy gave one last snarl before he hobbled to Kalash and sat by his side.

'Are you okay?'

Niko scrambled to his feet. He was breathing fast and his face was white. 'Yeah. Of course I am. That dog should be locked up.'

'He was being protective,' Kalash said.

'Protective? He attacked me! I could've been hurt.'

'If he'd wanted to hurt you, he would've done it.'

Niko brushed the dirt from his hands and uniform. 'You tell anyone about this and you're dead.'

Kalash nodded.

Niko slung his bag onto his back and turned away. 'You just stood there,' he hissed at the boys.

'He was going to kill us.'

Their voices faded.

The dog licked Kalash's fingers.

'Hey, fella.' He tickled him under the chin. 'You just made my day a whole lot better.' He thought for a moment before realising. 'Maybe even tomorrow as well.'

Kalash stood a little taller. 'And for that, you deserve *two* servings of roast.'

Buddy barked and together they walked all the way home.

Three Days and Three Nights

Sean McMullen

Lara noticed there was something strange about Claws while she was doing her homework. The tabby was called Claws because she ate with her claws, pulling chunks of fish out of her bowl and holding them up to her mouth. She was twenty years old, almost twice as old as Lara.

Most of the time she slept on the desk as Lara did her homework, but on this night she just sat on the floor, staring at the doorway. Lara checked the door. There was nothing to be seen, but there was a strange, faint smell of burning that seemed to be coming from nowhere in particular. Claws continued to stare at the doorway, unblinking.

Once she had finished her homework Lara reached down, gathered up Claws in her arms and put her on her lap. The cat jumped down at once, sat beside the desk and continued to stare at the door. Claws was supposed to eat in the kitchen, but Lara fetched a bowl of dry cat food and put it in front of her. Claws ignored it, and just glared at the door, eyes wide.

Gran was in the kitchen when Lara found her. She had grown up on a farm in Scotland and knew a lot of strange folklore about animals.

'Gran, I think there's something wrong with Claws,' Lara said. 'She just sits by my desk and stares at the door.'

'Be there in a minute, child, mustn't let dinner burn.'

Lara was back at her desk when Gran came in. She took one look at Claws and shook her head.

'The cat's dying, poor thing,' she said.

'That can't be right,' said Lara. 'She looks fine, she's just stopped eating.'

'Ah, but she's doing what only cats can do when Death comes calling.'

'What's that?'

'Staring at Death, warning him not to come any closer.'

'Death? You mean the skeleton in a black robe? He's not real.'

'Believe what you like, child, but remember this. When Death comes calling, a cat can stay alive for an extra three days and three nights by staring at him.'

'So, cats can see Death?'

'Oh yes, and if Death reaches out a bony hand too early, it's claws are out and slash! How long has puss been like that?'

'Maybe two hours.'

'Then in three days she will be dead, so give her lots of love while you can.'

'And all I can do is let her know I care about her?' asked Lara, kneeling beside the desk and stroking the cat.

Gran just shrugged. 'Afraid so.'

Gran never dressed up the truth in pretty words, or tried to make a joke about bad news. That was the sort of thing that Mum did. As far as Mum was concerned, children should not talk about upsetting things like death, and Lara found that very annoying. That was why she pretended that nothing was wrong when her mother got home from the Neighbourhood Watch meeting.

Dad was sure to be useless as well. He would just smile and say, 'There's sure to be an engineering solution'. That's what he always said, because he was an engineer. The trouble was that this was Death, and you can't stop Death with a screwdriver and a circuit tracer. Lara was actually relieved that he was away at a conference.

At school Lara found it hard to concentrate. Whatever class she was in, the faint smell of burning was always present. She wanted to talk about it with her friends, but what could she say? 'Death's hanging out near my desk at home, and Gran reckons he wants to kill my cat'. No, she would just get a lot of strange looks.

Claws was still beside the desk when Lara got home. Before starting her homework, she set out bowls of dry cat food and canned fish, and even put the kitty litter tray beside her desk. Claws was not interested.

'What about some water?' Lara asked the cat as she put down yet another bowl. 'You can't go for three days without drinking.'

The cat ignored her. Lara opened her laptop and started her homework. The smell of burning was stronger. Did that mean Death was closer? Claws continued to stare at the doorway.

The next morning Lara changed the cat food and fetched fresh water for Claws. She even changed the cat litter, although Claws had not used it. It was Friday. Lara always looked forward to Fridays because the weekend was next, but on this Friday, it meant that Claws had only two days and two nights left.

What would Dad do? Lara wondered. Be

scientific, of course. Study the problem, work out a solution. Lara picked up Claws and carried her across the room. The cat's head turned as Lara walked. No matter where Lara carried her, Claws always stared at the same spot. Something's really there! Lara realised. Claws can see something that I can't, and now it's inside my room.

On Saturday morning Gran stood watching as Lara tried the experiment with Claws again. She worked out that the old cat was watching something that had moved a little closer to the desk during the night.

'Death's walking to the place where Claws will die,' said Gran. 'He doesn't have to follow her around.'

'Well, I'm going to stay with her until the very end,' Lara said as she set her down by the desk.

All day the smell of burning got stronger, but Lara did not even leave her room to have lunch. Claws was more than just a cat, she was Lara's friend. You don't dump your friends when they are sick, or worse. For the first time that she could remember, Lara had her homework finished on Saturday. She then surfed the Internet about what to do about sick cats, but none of the websites were any help. Claws was not sick; she was just very old for a cat. Lara stayed up for the whole of Saturday night, staring where Claws was staring, even though she could see nothing.

On Sunday morning Claws was still alive. Lara ate her breakfast at her desk, helping the cat to stare at whatever was slowly moving across the floor. Lara played an audiobook on her laptop, to keep herself awake while she helped Claws stare. She knew she would never forgive herself if Claws died while she was asleep.

In the evening her mum said she was going to the airport because Dad had texted that he was coming back a day early. There had been some sort of accident and the conference had been cancelled. Lara said she was staying in her room, even when Mum asked her to come along and give her father a big welcome.

'But Dad was nearly in a terrible accident,' said Mum. 'He might have been hurt.'

'Well, Gran says Claws is very sick, and I'm not going to let her die alone,' said Lara, quietly but firmly.

'I can't believe you love a cat more than your own father.'

'I love them both, but Dad's not dying. Claws is.'

'This is something to do with Gran's fairy stories, isn't it? I'm going to speak to her about that. You're twelve, that's too old to be listening to that sort of rubbish.'

'So should I listen to the rubbish on some pop star's podcast, like other kids my age?'

Mum had no answer to that, and she gave in. An hour later her parents were home. Lara was fairly sure that she was in trouble, and that Dad would not understand about Claws. Suddenly he was standing at her door. Lara scooped up Claws and held her tightly.

'I'm sorry about the accident, Dad, but Claws is very sick and I just can't let her die alone.'

To Lara's relief, Dad didn't seem to mind.

'Hey, that's all right,' he replied.

'Phew,' she said, now feeling guilty. 'What happened? Mum didn't tell me anything about the accident.'

'It was pretty dramatic but nobody was hurt. One of our demonstration laptops was powered by the new type of covalent lattice battery, the type that lasts a week without recharging. The problem is that the battery stores more energy than a hand grenade, and if something inside breaks . . .'

'Boom?'

'Really big boom. Luckily nobody was nearby when it exploded.'

'Scary.'

'Yeah, it was quite a surprise, but all good. Now tell me all about Claws. How is she?'

'Gran said dying cats can have an extra three days and three nights, if they glare at Death and don't sleep.'

'Yeah, I know. She told me all those old Scottish stories too.'

'I suppose you don't believe her, do you?'

'I keep an open mind. Yesterday's folklore may be tomorrow's science. Give me some details.'

'Claws started staring at something I couldn't see, about this time, three days and three nights ago. Gran said that means she's about to, well, you know.'

'Die?'

'Yeah.'

'Well then, you had better stay with her.'

'You mean it?' exclaimed Lara.

'Of course, I'll bring your dinner in. Hey, and I'll eat in here too.'

The relief Lara felt was like a huge weight being lifted from her shoulders.

'Oh, Dad, thanks so much! I just know Claws only has a few more minutes. I can't see Death, I don't have cat eyes, but I can smell him getting really close.'

'Smell him?'

'Yeah. He smells sort of like, well, weird fireworks.'

'Really? Do you think I could smell him, too?'

'I suppose so. Gran never said humans can smell Death, but I suppose she doesn't know everything. Maybe we can.'

Dad stepped into the room, then sniffed the air.

'Funny, I know that smell,' he said, scratching his head and frowning.

Suddenly Dad's eyes bulged with terror. He dashed forward, scooped up Lara and Claws in his arms and ran out into the passageway. They collided with Mum, who was coming to tell them that dinner was getting cold. Just as they went sprawling on the floor, the laptop exploded.

The blast started a fire, and a few minutes later the family was standing in the street outside, watching the fire brigade pouring water through Lara's bedroom window. She was holding Claws, who was licking her hand and purring, in spite of all the noise and excitement.

'Thanks, Claws, you're the greatest,'

Lara kept saying, over and over.

'What do you mean?' asked Mum, who had lost count of how many times Lara had thanked the cat.

'Gran thought Death was coming for Claws, but all the time Claws was keeping him away from me,' Lara explained. 'Claws stared him down for three days and three nights, just long enough for Dad to get home and smell the fumes coming off my laptop's battery. She saved my life.'

'Lara, dear, you shouldn't think Gran's old stories are true,' said Mum. 'You might get nightmares.'

'Claws saved me, why should that give me nightmares?' asked Lara angrily.

'Because there was no invisible thing in your room. Claws didn't really keep Death away from you.'

'Yes, she did!' said Dad, Gran and Lara together.

Trick or Treat or Death

Kirsty Murray

'You don't have to wear a mask in the car, Olivia.'

'It's okay, Dad,' replied Olivia. 'I like it.'

'I hate masks,' said Atticus.

'You don't have to wear one anyway. It's not compulsory until you're twelve, though they'll have to change that rule sooner or later,' said Olivia. 'This pandemic is going to make the last one seem like a picnic.'

'I'm never going to mask up.' He scowled. 'I'm a sovereign citizen.'

Olivia rolled her eyes and stared out at the quiet, suburban streets. Time had no shape anymore. Journeys that should have been quick took forever. Yet the drive to her stepmother's house seemed so swift that Olivia couldn't catch her breath.

'Do we have to stay at Marin's place all weekend?' asked Atticus.

'It's not just Marin's place. It's my place, too. It's our house,' said Dad.

'It doesn't feel like "our" house,' said Atticus.

Olivia looked at her little brother and smiled with her eyes.

Marin had left a black plastic garbage bag by the front door as usual. When Atticus rang the bell, Marin opened the door but stepped back into the hall, keeping her distance.

'Tell them to put all their clothes in the bag. I have fresh ones for them inside.'

'Hi, Marin,' called Atticus. But Marin had already retreated into the house.

'Dad, I'm not stripping down to my underwear on the front porch,' said Olivia. 'I'm fifteen.'

'Just do it,' said her father.

Atticus was already undressing.

'Can I at least change in the garage?' pleaded Olivia.

Dad sighed. 'Leave your old clothes on the Ferrari, I'll put them in the garbage bag.'

It was cool and dark in the garage. The clothes Marin had bought were still in their Amazon packaging. It was always the same. The pandemic was just an excuse. Even before the latest viral outbreak, Marin had insisted Olivia and Atticus change their clothes before coming into the house. It was as if Marin wanted to strip away the vestiges of that 'other' woman, the children's mother. Marin had even suggested Olivia consider plastic surgery for her 'too big' nose.

'I like my nose,' Olivia had said. 'My mum has a big nose, too. We like noses that can breathe.' Marin had snorted through her tiny, snub, turned-up nose.

The problem with Marin, Olivia decided, was everything about her was too neat and tidy. All her furnishings were white or cream. White leather lounge suite, white walls decorated with insipid washed-out water colour paintings. The kitchen gleamed. Even Marin was a study in blandness with her perfect blonde hair, her white business suits, her shiny white shoes. And Atticus and Olivia were dark and grubby and left fingerprints on every pristine surface. Only occasionally did they do it on purpose.

'It's Halloween,' shouted Atticus, as he strode into the kitchen. He opened the pantry door and peered inside. 'Have you got any treats?'

'We don't live in America,' said Marin. 'Australians don't celebrate Halloween.'

'Some Australians do. Mum said we could. She even made me a costume. I'm a vampire.' Atticus fished out a pair of plastic vampire teeth that he'd transferred from the pocket of his old clothes into the pale blue jeans that Marin had bought him.

'Will you take us trick or treating?' asked Atticus, turning to his father.

'Atticus, no one will open their door to you,' said Marin. 'It's not hygienic.'

Atticus ignored her and spoke directly to his father. 'Do you want to see my vampire costume?'

'Atticus!' Marin interrupted, 'I don't want you bringing your bags into this house. You don't need them here. You have your Alphington wardrobe waiting for you.'

'But I don't have a vampire costume here. You didn't make me one, did you?'

Why didn't Dad intervene, thought Olivia. All he did was avert his gaze from his children and set the table for dinner – laying out white plates on the shiny clean glass tabletop.

Olivia stared down at her plate. At least the food wasn't white. Rocket salad, tiny tomatoes, a thin strip of grilled salmon. When Olivia had finished, she could hear her stomach rumbling for carbs.

'How can you eat fish without chips!'

shouted Atticus. Dad kept acting as if he were deaf, but his expression was thunderous.

'Dave,' said Marin, pointedly ignoring Atticus. 'Why don't you take the children for a walk in the park after dinner?'

'We don't need to be "taken for a walk". We're not dogs.'

'It will be nice in the park, Liv,' said her father. Of course, he meant it would be nicer for them all to be away from Marin. Or nicer for Marin. She wasn't sure which.

Olivia looked from her stepmother to her father and the weekend stretched ahead – a long, torturous dance of avoidance; avoiding complaining, avoiding a fight, avoiding the urge to punch Marin. Olivia took her plate to the sink and then put her mask back on.

'Okay, let's go,' said Olivia. 'Atticus, you can put on your vampire costume and scare the possums in the park. There are bats down there, too, you know.'

'He can't bring the costume into the house,' said Marin, her voice sharp and clipped.

'He can change on the porch,' said Olivia.

—

The light in the parklands was soft. Deep blue shadows fell beneath the olive trees.

Fruit bats wheeled overhead. In the shadowy dells, the bush was thick and wild and overgrown. Down by the creek, in the gloaming, someone had a flashlight and the beam shimmered on the surface of the water.

Atticus ran ahead, his cape flapping behind him.

Olivia walked in silence beside her father. When his phone rang, he stepped away from her to take the call. She could hear the irritation in his voice. It was Marin. Her voice was metallic, piercing the night air like needles. Dad's face grew red. Even from a metre away, Olivia could hear Marin's voice growing louder and more hysterical. Olivia wished her father would just admit that marrying Marin had been a mistake.

Without hanging up on the call, he turned back to Olivia. 'Olivia, honey, would you mind taking Atticus for a lap around the park. He needs to get his yah-yahs out and I have to sort something with Marin.'

'But how do we find our way back?'

'Just take the main gate out, turn left, then take the second street on the right,' said her father. 'You know where we live. Don't you have your phone?'

'It's in my bag, which is in your car because Marin wouldn't let us bring our

bags inside,' said Olivia.

'You know the house, it's only two blocks from here, for Pete's sake.'

'Okay, okay,' said Olivia. 'Just go.'

She watched her father hurrying out of the park, still arguing as he clutched his phone to his ear. Even at a distance, Olivia could hear the shrill rage of her stepmother's disembodied voice.

Olivia turned to look for Atticus. He was way ahead, turning onto a path that led across a small bridge. She had to jog to catch up with him. Atticus stayed six metres ahead as he careered down the hill, shouting with pleasure to be out in the open. She caught up with him at the stepping stones that crossed the Darebin Creek. An owl swooped overhead.

'It's getting late,' said Olivia. 'We should head back.'

'We can cross over here and then go back up the stairs over the bridge,' said Atticus. 'I remember the way.'

So Olivia followed her little brother through the wetlands and up the bluestone steps. The olive trees were so thick they blocked out the twilight. A dog skittered past them. Olivia jumped. At the top of the steps she asked, 'Which way now?' and Atticus pointed to the right. They followed a path through the darkening parklands that led them back to bright streetlights.

'This isn't the main gate,' said Olivia.

'But we're back in Alphington,' said Atticus. 'It's not far, is it?'

They walked down the quiet street. The houses were asleep behind their fences. The sky turned a deeper purple. Olivia knew they were lost. She grabbed Atticus' hand and made him stop at the next cross street.

'We've taken a wrong turn,' she said.

Atticus began to cry. 'I want to go home to Mum.'

'Hold my hand,' said Olivia, and she strode on.

The street turned into a cul-de-sac. The house at the end of the street had a carved pumpkin on its front porch. Fake spiderwebs and plastic skeletons were draped along its picket fence. An orange light glowed in a casement window.

'I wanna see that house,' said Atticus, drying his tears and dragging his sister to the end of the cul-de-sac. A wild rose garden, vibrant with scent, lay between the front gate and a squat Federation-style weatherboard house. Jasmine spilled over the picket fence and tangled with the spider webs. In the light of the glowing pumpkin, an old woman stood hand-watering the garden with a hose.

'Trick or treaters?' she asked, peering over the gate at Atticus.

'We're lost,' said Olivia. 'We took a wrong turn out of the parklands.'

'Where do you live?' asked the old woman.

'We're visiting our dad and stepmother. I think their house is in Fulham Grove. Or maybe Bennett Street. I can't remember,' she said, suddenly appalled that the address escaped her. Her head began to ache and her thoughts were foggy. 'Do you have a mobile I could borrow?'

'I have a landline,' said the old woman.

'What's a landline?' asked Atticus.

The old lady smiled at Atticus. 'I like your costume. I have candy,' she said.

'Thanks, but no thanks,' said Olivia.

'Olivia!' moaned Atticus.

'We're in the middle of a pandemic,' said Olivia. 'Don't you remember anything from when Covid happened? You can't take food from strangers. You might catch something.'

'It's only candy,' said the old woman. 'I put it in a jar with a special dispenser so children wouldn't put their hands in. It's very hygienic. Come and see.'

Olivia realised the old woman was American, her r's rolling off her tongue, warm and friendly.

Atticus let go of Olivia's hand and followed the old woman to the front porch.

'Come see,' called Atticus. 'It's cool.'

Olivia watched as Atticus cupped his hands under a glass dispenser. The old woman pulled back a small window that fed into a twisting plastic chute. Wrapped sweets in black and gold foil tumbled into Atticus' waiting hands.

'You're the only trick or treaters out tonight.'

'I'm not trick or treating,' said Olivia.

'I am!' said Atticus.

'Could you bring the phone into the garden?' asked Olivia.

'I don't have a portable handset. The phone is fixed to the wall. You'll have to come inside to call your parents.'

When Olivia hesitated, the old woman said, 'It's okay, honey. I haven't seen anyone in months. You're perfectly safe. You can take your mask off. You won't catch the virus from me.'

'You could catch it from us,' said Olivia, adjusting her mask.

'Oh, I don't believe little children as nice

as you two could be vectors,' she said, smiling at Atticus. 'You're not a vector, are you, honey pie?'

The old lady's hand hovered above Atticus's head as she resisted the urge to pat his dark, curly hair.

Atticus was thrilled to get inside. He stood in the kitchen, picking caramel from his teeth, while Olivia used the phone to call her father. She got his voicemail and left a message.

'Would you like a spider?' asked the old woman.

'A real spider?' asked Atticus.

'My lord, no. A spider is a special drink. An Australian drink! We call them ice-cream floats back home. I thought y'all knew about spiders.'

Atticus climbed up on a stool while the old woman stood on the other side of the kitchen bench. He watched, hypnotised, as the woman put a scoop of mint green ice-cream in a long glass and then tipped lime green soda on top. The ice-cream fizzed and floated to the surface and a foam of green ebbed against the lip of the glass.

'Would you like one, too?' she asked Olivia. 'Raspberry flavoured?'

'No, thank you,' answered Olivia, standing awkwardly near the front door.

While Atticus sipped the spider through a straw, the old woman laid out bowls of popcorn, gingerbread and orange marshmallows. More and more food poured out of her cupboards until the bench was littered with treats in small bowls – liquorice, tiny chocolate bars, gummy bears, Freddo Frogs and sour rainbow straps. Atticus crowed with pleasure. Tentatively, Olivia edged closer, picked up a piece of liquorice, lifted her mask and popped the sweet into her mouth. It made her want to cry.

'Did you call your parents?' asked the old woman.

'I left a message, but Dad doesn't listen to his messages. I need to text.'

'You just make yourself at home until he calls back. It's nice to have visitors.'

'I think it's against the law to have visitors during lockdowns,' said Olivia.

'Never you mind,' said the old lady, and something in her tone made Olivia shiver.

'I don't want to go back to Marin's,' said Atticus. 'I want to stay here with this nice granny lady until Mum comes to get us.'

'I haven't called Mum,' says Olivia.

'Your parents are divorced?' asked the old lady, as she sliced a piece of chocolate cake and offered it to Atticus.

'Yes, and we hate our stepmother,' said

Atticus, cramming cake into his mouth.

Olivia looked away. They should never have come into this house. No one knew where they were and the old lady was starting to unnerve her. Atticus sneezed, sending an explosion of snot and half-chewed popcorn and chocolate cake flying across the kitchen bench. The old lady wiped a blob of Atticus' gunk from her cheek.

'I'm so sorry,' said Olivia. She grabbed Atticus by his wrist and wrenched him from the stool.

'It's okay, honey,' cried the old lady, as they headed for the door.

'Thank you,' said Olivia through gritted teeth. 'We have to go.'

They ran blindly into the dark cul-de-sac and around the corner.

'I feel sick,' wailed Atticus.

'Serves you right,' said Olivia.

'Where are we going?'

'Anywhere but there. It was too weird. Like something from Hansel and Gretel.'

Finally, they reached a street corner that Olivia recognised.

'C'mon,' said Olivia, yanking Atticus along behind her. 'We're nearly there.'

The front door was open and all the lights were on. Dad was sitting in the living room on the white leather couch with his head in his hands. Marin stood above him, her hands on her hips.

'Tell them, Dave,' said Marin. 'Tell them! In my house, it's my rules!'

Atticus whimpered. He was a pale shade of green with blue patches under his eyes.

'I think I'm gonna be sick,' he said, and then promptly projectile-vomited onto the white leather lounge.

Their father shut his eyes. For a minute, three different thoughts collided in Olivia's head. Marin was screaming. Atticus was sick. Olivia couldn't smell anything. Not even the vomit. Nothing. How strange, she thought, patting the front of her mask.

Two weeks later, as Olivia sat propped up in bed, reading the news on her iPad, she saw a picture of the old lady from the cul-de-sac in Alphington. She clicked the link and it took her through to the *New York Times*. The headline read 'Those We've Lost'. The old lady had been a famous children's writer that Olivia had never heard of called Molly Sugar. She had died last week. As Olivia read through the obituary, she felt a sinking sense of shame. Olivia and Atticus had infected everyone in their family with the virus and probably the old lady, too.

Even though Molly Sugar had offered them so many treats, they had given her the worst 'trick' of all. When she was better, Olivia determined she would find Molly Sugar's grave and place flowers on it.

Olivia closed the article and checked the case load on the Health Department's website. Then she sat for a long time looking out the window, remembering the old lady and the strange evening in her kitchen with the fizzing 'spiders' and the mountain of sweets.

Since Halloween, the children were no longer welcome in Marin's house. The stains on the white leather couch would never come out. It was going be a long, long time before Olivia and Atticus would see their stepmother again.

'Thank you, Molly Sugar,' whispered Olivia.

The Trail of Gold

Sue Bursztynski

'Will, hurry up, the customers are waiting!' hissed my sister Kate. She was right, I needed to get on with delivering the tray of beer, but I couldn't help listening.

Old George Burgess wandered into our pub about once a month, when he was in town, and got talking with any new customers who hadn't heard his tale; they always bought him drinks to tell it.

George really did have a story to tell. He witnessed Frank Gardiner's gang's gold robbery at Eugowra Rocks back in 1862, when he was a boy. The bushrangers who had done it had been caught, and most of the gold retrieved, but there were still people looking for some gold which hadn't been found afterwards.

This time, his audience was a group of railway workers on their way through town. There were also two Americans, who sat at another table but were clearly listening and grinning.

'So, I was about the same age as young Will here when my dad sent me to the goldfields to sell food to the diggers. We had a dray filled with it; Dad was expecting a big profit –'

'Your dad never thought of digging himself?' one of his listeners asked, puzzled.

George laughed. 'Why would he? Ask anyone who remembers that time, plenty around in this gold mining town. Digging for gold might make you a fortune, yes, or maybe not. And I remember old Harry the German who *did* make a fortune, spent it all and went right back to poverty. But diggers are always going to need to eat, just like everyone else, aren't they?'

The entire table laughed.

'Getting back to my story, I was on my way here with Dick Bloomfield, who was working for my dad, when we got bogged down in the creek and had to find help to get out. If it wasn't for that, we might have made it here before the robbery. But we didn't. Frank Gardiner the bushranger caught up with us and made us come with him to the Eugowra Rocks. They needed carts and animals to block the road for them, and ours was one of three.'

'Did they kill anybody?' someone else asked.

'No. Look, it could have been worse. They just pulled our hats over our eyes and tied them down so we couldn't see . . . except I did. I was wearing a ratty old hat my mum would have thrown out if she'd seen me with it. There was a hole in it right here . . .' He touched his forehead. 'Anyway, after the bushrangers had robbed the gold coach . . .' He looked down at his empty glass. Someone waved me over to refill it. 'Thanks, Will. After the robbery, they let us go, and gave us each a pound to compensate us for our inconvenience. I spent mine on sweets. It lasted me two weeks! After the robbery, Dick and I continued on to this lovely town and sold nearly everything.'

'Speaking of money,' said one of the Americans, 'what happened to the loot?'

'Oh, they got back most of it,' said the old man. 'But before he was caught, Frank Gardiner managed to hide some of it, it's said. Frank was caught in Queensland and eventually went to live in the United States. He never came back. Nobody knows where it is, to this day. I don't live in Forbes, but I hear there are always people looking for the gold. Isn't that right, Will?'

'It is,' I agreed. Kate was calling me to come and fetch an order, so I returned to the bar. I was back, carrying a tray of food, before the

discussion
was over, and saw old
George turn to look at the Americans more closely. 'Funny,' he said, 'you two look familiar.'

'We haven't been here before,' said one of the men, who had mentioned his name was Monte. 'But our dad was from these parts before he moved to California, so you never know.' He winked. 'We heard this was a good place to go prospecting.'

'Good luck with that,' chuckled George. 'The gold dried up in this area about a year after that robbery.' He climbed to his feet and tipped his hat to his audience, saying

'Good evening!' as he left.

The story was over and George's audience went their separate ways, including the Americans, who said they were headed for Wheogo Station.

'How many times have we heard *that* story now?' complained my older brother, Phillip.

'Who cares?' Dad laughed. 'Every time he tells it, we sell food and drinks. And you know what? That story brings visitors to this town. It was the biggest gold robbery in our history – there was over seventeen thousand pounds worth of gold and cash stolen. Visitors need to eat and drink, don't they? I'll be sorry if that gold is ever found!'

'What if it was true, though?' I asked.

'It's nonsense!' said Kate. 'I've read about it in the *Forbes Times*, interviews with old people who remembered. Frank Gardiner had to dump some of his share of the gold just to get away. *That* was found!'

But I kept thinking about it. If there *was* gold around here, I would be able to buy a lot more than a few sweets. The hotel could do with some repairs. I went out to the stables to look after the guests' horses. There I met Joe, our stablehand, who went to school with me.

'Guess who was in today?' I said, rubbing down a bay mare which belonged to the local policeman.

'George Burgess? I know. I looked after his horse and helped him buckle her up to the trap. Was he telling that story again?'

'Well . . . yes. We always have people wanting to hear it.'

'That's because of the treasure, which doesn't exist.'

'What if it does?' I argued.

He stopped brushing for a moment and looked at me. 'You mean this, don't you?'

'We could use that gold. And I have some ideas about where it might be hidden.'

Joe burst out laughing. 'Fifty years nobody's found it and Will Hayes of Forbes knows where to look.'

'I just said I had some ideas. Look, I've heard that story over and over. There was a member of Gardiner's gang who lived around here – and who was released for "lack of evidence" – but got killed only a couple of years after the Eugowra robbery. Ben Hall.'

'And?'

'His wife Bridget was the sister of Gardiner's girl, Kitty, who went to Queensland with him. If Gardiner was in a hurry and didn't want to get caught with the loot on him, where would be a good place to hide it?'

'Somewhere on Hall's property at Sandy Creek? *Nobody*, of course, has looked there.'

'Very funny! But there's something else. The Americans. There were two of them in the pub today. They said they were going prospecting.'

'So is everyone else!'

'Yes, but they said their father was "from around these parts" before he went to America. And George said they looked familiar.'

He thought about it. 'You're saying they might be Gardiner's sons?'

'Why not? And if they are, maybe he told them where it is? Maybe even drew a map?'

'Maps! Buried treasure! It sounds like a

scene from *Treasure Island*!' But he was looking thoughtful. 'All right. What did you have in mind?'

'I go that way for supplies for the hotel. I was going tomorrow, in fact. Phillip usually comes with me, but he's always complaining about how busy he is. You can drive and my dad thinks you're reliable . . .'

'Well, I am! Oh . . . you want me to come with you? Oh, no, Will, no! I don't go on adventures. Besides, Mum will be furious if I lose my job getting drawn into your mad plans!'

'Look, we are just going on my usual route. We'll even bring back the supplies. I only want a little bit of time to see if I'm right. If I am, you'll have more than enough gold to satisfy your mum.'

'Where were you planning to look? You don't have a map, do you?'

I smiled, knowing he was caught. 'Leave it to me.'

———

'I can't believe you talked me into this!' grumbled Joe as he drove us, but it was only a mild grumble. 'You do know that even if we find that gold, we'll be expected to hand it over, don't you? It was a robbery!'

'My granddad was a miner at the time. He says most of it was found and there was compensation for the rest. Besides, tell that to all the treasure hunters who have come to Forbes over the years!'

We were nearly at Sandy Creek. It was time to put the cart somewhere safe and give the horses a chance to graze and drink while we walked on.

'Where now?' asked Joe.

I hushed him with my raised hand. Ahead, I could see a cart I recognised as the one belonging to the American brothers we had seen at the hotel. I pointed. It held equipment for digging. The owners were not there, though their horses were grazing nearby.

We walked quietly, slipping through the trees and brush till we came close enough to see beyond the horses and cart, to where two men were talking. One of them was Monte, the brother who had spoken to old George. The other was Mr Butler, who owned the Wheogo Station property; Dad bought from him sometimes.

'Are you sure?' Mr Butler was asking. 'Monte, lad, so many people have been here over the years.'

'But they didn't have maps.'

'Having a map is all very well, but it has been a very long time. The homestead isn't even here anymore. How will you know where it is in connection with what's on the map?'

'Were you boys looking for something?' said a voice behind Joe and me. Turning, startled, I found myself looking at one of the Americans. The man was Monte's twin brother, whose name, I recalled hearing, was Abe.

'Er . . . just looking around,' I babbled. 'We were on our way to fetch supplies and I thought we could take a look at Ben Hall's home . . .'

'And I'm the Emperor of China. Pull the other one, boy. I remember you from the hotel in Forbes. You served us beer. Come this way, both of you.'

There wasn't much we could do, judging by the look on his face. He hadn't actually threatened us, but his face was grim. We went with him to where his brother and Mr Butler stood, Joe muttering, 'Oh, thanks, Will, thanks very much!'

'Well, I was right about the map, anyway,' I whispered.

'Lookie what I found, fellas!' called Abe. The other two turned.

'Drat,' Monte said, 'does the whole of Forbes know our business here?'

'Not everybody, sir,' I said. 'You aren't the first to come here to look for buried treasure – and probably won't be the last.'

Monte smiled. 'I wouldn't be sure about that, Will boy. Who is this with you?'

'I'm Joe Simmons,' Joe said. 'I work in the stables for the Hayes family, so I got the job of driving for the supplies run.'

'I know Will,' said Mr Butler. 'Though I wasn't expecting him today.'

'And I bet his family had somewhere else in mind for his buying today,' said Abe. 'He's just nosy, isn't that right, Will?'

'I wasn't planning to spy on you, sir. We wanted –'

'We wanted to check out the buried treasure, like everyone else,' Joe interrupted. 'Not everyone comes here, though. Will had a good idea. Was he right?'

'We think so, yes,' Monte agreed. 'At least, that's what our dad said. And he should know. He was not a nice man, but he did want to take care of us after his saloon was knocked down in the San Francisco earthquake. It's been fifty years, nobody cares anymore about what happened then, except for the gold.'

'Mr Christie, you aren't going to do something violent, are you?' protested Mr Butler. 'I didn't see any harm in doing what dozens of people do every year, but –'

'And you won't see any harm now, Mr B,' Monte told him. He turned to us. 'Tell you what, boys, get on with your job and head for home and I promise you won't hear from us again.'

'What if they talk?' protested Abe.

'Who cares? We will be gone. But I don't think they will, will you, boys?'

I shook my head. Joe stared at me. 'That story about the missing gold has brought my family a lot of visitors over the years. I still would love to have found it, though.'

Monte burst out laughing. 'I bet you would! All right, off you go. We will not bother you.'

We hurried back to our cart, hoping they wouldn't change their minds and follow.

'Well, that was a waste of time, wasn't it?' Joe sighed.

'Never mind. We still have a job to do. Let's get on with it.'

It was two days later when Mr Butler turned up at our pub. He ordered some beer and asked for Joe to come in, telling Kate that Joe had done something for him and he wanted to reward him.

Kate agreed, but called out, 'Keep it short, please, Mr Butler, Joe has work to do. So does Will.'

'I promise I won't take long, Miss Hayes, and then I will collect your father's list for his next order.' She nodded reluctantly, then turned back to her own work.

The pub was quiet, so we weren't interrupted.

'Boys, I have a message for you – and something else, but first you might want to know what happened after you left.' We listened. We did want to know.

He gulped at his beer, nervously. 'They were who we thought they were, Frank Gardiner's two sons from his American marriage. And they did have a map. They told me they were going to start digging next day, and they stayed the night with me. But . . . it seems they had already dug up the gold their father had stolen. By the time I woke in the morning they were gone, leaving a note and a gift – something for me and a gift for the two of you.' He reached into his pocket. 'What they left for me was nowhere near the share they had promised, but it was fairly generous given that they didn't have to give me anything. For you . . .' He put a pouch on the table. 'Two pounds for each of you. And here is the note.' He placed that on the table between us.

We looked down at the note, written on decent stationery, probably from Mr Butler's homestead.

'Dear Mr B,' it read, 'we are sorry we

need to be gone without saying goodbye, but we have what we came to your lovely country for, and we are looking forward to arriving home. Here is a small share of the proceeds as promised, if not as much as you expected, and also two pounds each to the boys for their inconvenience. Please hand it to them for us. I believe our father gave the people his gang inconvenienced a pound each, but it has been many years since then, so we are giving them twice that, in hopes it will be enough to give them good spending money in 1912.

Your Obedient Servants,

Monte and Abe Christie (also known as Gardiner).'

We stared at the note and then at each other. I burst out laughing.

'What do you say, Joe? Shall we spend our ill-gotten gains on sweets?'

He understood my reference and chuckled. 'I never liked lollies, anyway. I'll think about it.'

'Thanks, Mr Butler,' I said. 'Very kind of you to come and drop this off. You won't tell anyone, will you?'

'Certainly not! It will make me look a fool. Well, I'd better be gone, I have to speak with Mr Hayes. Good day, boys.'

After he rose and went behind the bar,

we sat there for another few minutes.

'What gall!' Joe said. 'Still, we have something to show for your mad plan. Thank you. Are you going to show this to your family?'

'As Mr Butler said, certainly not! It would cause more trouble than it's worth. I'll think about how I can use it for the family a bit at a time without them noticing. Although . . .'

'Although what?'

'It's such a shame I can't tell the customers about it when George Burgess next arrives.'

Author's note: George Burgess was a real person, who witnessed the Eugowra gold robbery when he was thirteen. I'd like to think of him sharing that story over and over. The story of Gardiner's sons arriving in Australia to do some digging may or may not be true, but it's such fun, I'd like to think it is. Joe, Will and his family are fictional.

The Barefoot Thieftaker

Lucy Sussex

On a sultry summer's morning, at the country house of the Lord Chief Justice, the painter from London began his working day with some practice sketches from the window. The household's young black page was kicking a ball. Later, this page would sit still and be painted, when Her Ladyship's likeness was done. A maid in the kitchen garden cut cabbages. A ragged stranger come begging at the gate. Lastly, he sketched a servant like nobody else he'd met in the fine homes of his employers, a woman called the Thieftakeress. He did not see how a maidservant could catch criminals, but this was a legal household. The Chief Justice must have good reason.

He did not finish the image. Her Ladyship summoned him to her first sitting, wearing her best gown and jewels. Anne the Thieftakeress, from her seat under a plum tree, saw the window shutting, with

relief. A watcher herself, she disliked being watched. She had her own work to do, reading through a pouch of His Lordship's correspondence, the anonymous letters of denunciation. The next step, active investigation, intercept letters. 'I need the female touch,' the Chief Justice, her master, had said. 'We men cannot make sense of it.'

At the least, she will sift through letters of petty spite, at the worst, treason against King Charles II. Not many countrywomen read, but the household was used to her now. The garden had emptied, everyone about their own work. She read a letter intercepted en route to Europe. The writer was a lady of high rank, the red-waxed seal bearing heraldic arms of a pelicaness. Though it was broken, it could be faked and sealed again. She re-read the letter, then returned it to the pouch. Bees buzzed, her chin met her collar, and she dozed.

She woke to find the sun clouded over. Something had happened, for around the kitchen door servants clustered, excited and horrified. Clasping the pouch tightly, she burrowed between them. At the centre was Wat, the page, muddy to his breeches.

'My new shoes! Gone!'

She glanced down at his bare feet.

'Have you lost them?'

Wat stood on one foot, wiped the other on the boot scraper, revealing to Anne for the first time his sole, as pale pink as any other in the household.

'M'Lady ordered me to cut some lilies, to be in her painting. So, I took off my shoes to wade into the lilypond. I left them on the bank, and now they're gone!'

'Who would rob a Chief Justice's servant?' asked Anne.

A gardener shrugged. 'Someone who did not know who owns this country estate.'

'A stranger,' said Anne.

'They were the first pair I wore that fit!' cried Wat, wiping his other foot.

'A stranger with big feet,' said Anne. Wat had some growing yet but was already tall.

The cook suddenly exclaimed, 'That ungrateful vagrant! When I gave him bread!'

'Stale,' muttered someone.

'Was he shod?' asked Anne.

The cook thought. 'Only just. The soles flapped like tongues, and his toes stuck out.'

'Then he had reason and opportunity, if unobserved,' said Anne.

'I had them made for me, not some vagabond!' said Wat.

'Then you must hurry to get them back,' replied Anne.

'She's the Thieftakeress,' said the cook. 'She knows what to do.'

With the Chief Justice absent in London, permission for leave meant asking her young Ladyship. She, being occupied with the painting, granted it. The artist obliged too, with a precious sketch: the beggar captured, not in chains, but in ink and paper. Now Anne and Wat freely took the road to the village, following the thief's reported direction. Anne, mindful of the clouds, brought her cloak, but Wat strode barefoot, not wanting to lose time. As they left, the cook handed them a bag, new bread and cheese, to eat on the road.

'We should have requested His Lordship's foxhounds,' said Anne. 'For the scent.'

Wat paused, eyeing a tussock of grass by the road, trodden flat. He crouched, then lunged into the roadside hedge. When he emerged, he clutched two large, near-destroyed shoes.

'We do not need hounds!'

Sharp eyes, she thought. Wat could make a good thieftaker.

The find cheered them, but though they sped, they saw no other sign of their quarry.

'Wat, if we do not catch up with this beggar today, what then?'

'I will follow him to the end of the known world!'

'For shoes?'

'Cook said you walked from London to Essex during the Plague!'

'I sought my husband's murderer!'

'And I the first shoes I could buy with my wages as a servant, not slave.'

At the village they found Abel the parish constable, at his forge.

'Have you seen a well-shod vagabond? Like this?' – unrolling the sketch.

'Aye, passing through, good riddance!'

'Then,' said Anne, 'we must report a felony.'

That, and Wat's livery, with the arms of the Chief Justice, could not be denied. Abel lay down his tongs and picked up his official staff. The three continued under the heavy sky – until, at a boundary stone, the constable stopped abruptly.

'I can go no further. My authority stops here. You go on and find the next parish's constable, Praise-God Pratt at Crowntree.'

Wat eyed Anne.

'That is lawful,' she said reluctantly. 'The letter of it.'

They crossed the boundary into Crowntree parish, Wat shaking his head.

'You have parishes where Africa has tribes.'

'And how would you catch a thief there?'

'Warriors would chase him without stopping. Barefoot, too!'

'And when they found him?'

'If Mohammedan, they would chop off his hand,' said Wat.

'Wat, you wouldn't . . . '

'You cut off heads in this England.'

'That's for treason, against the King.' She thought again of the Lady's letters. There was something odd about them: a code?

'Then hanging will do,' said Wat.

They kept walking, encountering farmworkers heading homewards for the day. When asked, they too had seen the beggar sketched, wearing fancy new shoes. That kept them going, as the day dimmed, with a storm imminent. Only at the top of a hill did they pause, at the clear view of the darkening road before them, quite deserted.

'Only one way the villain could have gone: Crowntree Village,' said Anne.

'He must rest sometime,' replied Wat. 'And then we catch up!'

As if to disagree, thunder cracked overhead, followed by rain. Diverting from the road, they ducked into woodland, to see in the distance a tumbledown cow byre. What remained of the roof gave them shelter.

'My shoes are getting muddy, on another's feet,' grumbled Wat.

'If well-made, they will survive,' said Anne.

They waited for the rain to cease but it settled in for the night. Not wanting a wet and dark return, they shared the food. Then they settled too, at opposite sides of the byre.

'I sleep anywhere,' said Wat, and did just that.

Anne, in her cloak, lay restless. When she finally did sleep, she dreamt alarmingly. An apparition came, a noble lady in rose damask, her hair grey. Blood welled from shallow wounds in her chest, and her face was agonised. 'Beware, my daughter!' the visitant cried. 'Beware!'

Anne woke with a start, to find pre-dawn, and clear skies.

'What do Africans believe about dreams?' she asked Wat.

'They have meaning.'

'Us too. In plaguey London I dreamt of my dead husband, Thomas.'

'And that meant?'

'I should pursue his murderers.'

'And you did?'

'The dead's demands have precedence. Even above kings and masters.'

He nodded, and only then did she retell the night's dream.

He replied, 'A ghost-lady, but not seeking vengeance.'

'Not like my Tom.'

'A portent then. The meaning'll come.'

They made a breakfast from their remaining food, and rainwater, licked from leaves. Then they took to the road again: a hard passage, slogging through mud.

At Crowntree they passed empty stocks.

'Try the lock-up,' said Anne.

Inside a foul-smelling hut, they found Praise-God, the parish constable. With him was the man in the sketch, now chained to the wall. He wore shoes of good leather, with fancy red stitching.

Anne had to grab Wat to prevent bodily attack.

'Those are my shoes!'

Praise-God eyed his bare, muddy feet. 'The villain's arrested for vagrancy.'

'This is a separate charge, of theft,' said Anne.

'Charge away, but you need proof.'

Wat flourished his sketch. The thief bent forward as much as the chains allowed, curious, then impressed.

'Good likeness, but you need proof in law. Someone to swear these shoes are yours. Like your shoemaker.'

'He's in Dambleville.'

Where Her Ladyship's parents lived, ten

miles from the other side of His Lordship's estate.

'Then you'll have to leg it,' said the constable.

They had no choice but to head back down the road, until Anne lost her temper with the mud. She hailed a passing farm cart. Wat's livery and promise of coin got them passage. At the Chief Justice's gates, Wat saw her wriggle almightily under her cloak, to produce the fee in her hand.

'Sewn in my corset,' she murmured.

'I would have hid coins in my shoes, if I had them,' said Wat.

Back at the manor, the carriage being unharnessed from its horses showed the Chief Justice had returned from London. Inside he greeted them, as his manservant drew off his boots.

'How goes the thieftaking, Anne?'

She curtseyed, dropping dried flakes of mud. 'I have been assisting Wat, Your Honour.'

'Assisting?'

'To press a charge of shoe-stealing.'

The Chief Justice, who was as quick as hell, eyed Wat's feet.

'I must ask leave to seek a witness. Jonas the shoemaker at Dambleville,' Wat said.

'An apt pupil,' said the Justice to Anne.

'I now have the promise of an African thieftaker, as well as one in petticoats? Well, permission granted, but do not neglect your other duties.'

Her Ladyship pouted. 'He must return in time to be painted.'

Wat bowed deeply. 'As fast as I can walk.'

Her Ladyship said, 'Then at least brush the mud off our livery, else you shame this household.'

Wat, at Dambleville, knocked at the sign of the Shoe. 'Master Jonas is at Eveston,' the apprentice said. 'Visiting his sick mother.'

Two miles away. Wat started again on his trudge, to suspicious glances from passers-by: what was an African doing here? It worsened when he reached Eveston, a tiny hamlet. An old madwoman spied him.

'A fiend, a black devil from hell!' She bent and threw stones at him. From her crooked hands they hit feebly, but still hurt. The barrage only stopped when the parish constable intervened, grabbing Wat by the arm.

From frying pan to fire. 'You're under arrest!'

'I wasn't throwing the stones!'

'Our Magistrate reads the *London*

Gazette. 'E tells me, lookout for a runaway African. Big reward offered.'

Wat thumped the arms on his livery. 'See this? My master is the Chief Justice.'

'So, you stole it from His Honour's servant.'

'Do I look daft?'

'You look African and that's good enough for me.'

Their argument went in circles so loudly it attracted the whole village. Including Jonas the shoemaker, roused from his mother's sickbed.

At the Justice's, Anne dawdled at her tasks. Her master had brought more work for her, first a letter from Italy to the Lady of the Pelicaness. It also seemed suspicious, but not in any way obvious. Then came a bundle of accusations, mostly of witchcraft, and mostly mad.

When Wat finally returned, he had company: a small man riding an equally small white donkey. The newcomer wore good boots, with fancy red stitching.

'Master Jonas has kindly agreed to testify on my behalf.'

'What a laff I had!' said Jonas. 'Our constable's comeuppance.'

Wat explained, and Anne saw it was no

laughing matter. He had a lump on his head too, from the stoning.

'You need more than a shoemaker as a companion,' said Anne. She ran upstairs to the Justice's study. He was dictating to his secretary – but permitted interruption.

'Your Honour, I beg leave again for tomorrow. I must guide my apprentice Wat in his thieftaking.'

'Not to Dambleville again!'

'Crowntree, which is closer. We can be there and back in hours.'

'Surely Wat is to be painted?'

'Her Ladyship has a fancy for her dogs to figure in the portrait. They come next.'

'If you are quick, yes.'

Anne eyed the secretary, no friend of hers.

'We will require a warrant, sir. To speed the process and protect us.'

Back on the road again, Jonas rode his donkey, and Wat walked alongside Anne. The day was fair but cooler and he wore his cloak this time. Without mud the several miles progressed quickly. They were only passed once, by a fine carriage, travelling so fast it floated in a cloud of dust. It set the donkey braying.

At Crowntree an empty goal hut awaited them.

'The villain's been transferred to Wykewode town,' said Praise-God. 'Their prison's secure.'

'Wykewode is four miles away!' protested Jonas.

'Have I walked so far, to be thwarted by a few more miles?' pleaded Wat.

'Very well. But I'll need some luncheon first. And hay for the donkey.'

Crowntree had an inn of renown, to attract gentry. The carriage they had met on the road was drawn up outside, its passengers disembarking, satin and feathers gleaming in the sun. In the cloud of dust, Anne had not properly seen the coat of arms on its door. Now she put her hand to her mouth.

'What is that?' Wat asked.

'It shows the Pelicaness stabbing her chest so her young can feed on the blood.'

Wat stared at her. 'That's really daft.'

'It's heraldry.'

'It's wrong. I've seen pelicans and they eat fish, spewing them up . . .'

'Oy! Don't put me off my food,' said Jonas.

They ate in a private room while the villagers kept staring at Wat. The carriage occupants took the next best room. Anne overheard ladylike tones, snatches of wit and lively laughter. Well, no matter, she was on leave, free not to pursue the Justice's work. Yet, as the trio were leaving, a hand tugged at her sleeve. Anne stopped, to see what she had once been: a lady's maid, fashionably dressed.

'Missus, my Lady Robinia wishes a few words. We saw you on the road, and she is curious what be your business.'

From the open door behind the maid, the lady cried, 'Simply consumed with it! A man on a white donkey, a barefoot African, and a trimly-dressed woman walking! You three looked like a painting.'

Anne paused, thinking hard. 'Did your mistress have a mother, now dead?'

'Aye,' said the maid.

'Why do you ask?' said Lady Robinia, coming out. She was young and handsome, wearing a mourning dress, expensive black from her ribboned slippers to the lace on her head. Her only jewel was a seal ring and as she neared, Anne saw its emblem, the same pelicaness as on the coach. Anne had seen its impress, sealing letters.

She took a deep breath. 'M'Lady, your mother was tall, her hair silver-dark, her face long and sad? And she wore rose brocade?'

'She was, but how do you know? You have seen her? A painting, or her person?'

'Only as an apparition, while I slept.'

Lady Robinia went pale as a ghost herself.

Anne said, 'The Pelicaness cares for her young. She cried to me, "Beware, my daughter! Beware!"'

Lady Robinia turned defiant.

'And why should I?'

'Because you have come to the attention of my master, Chief Justice Sir Orlando Bridgman.'

Wat turned, his cloak thrown open, the livery visible. The maid shivered; Lady Robinia reached out to the wall, unsteady. 'I heard talk of a Thieftakeress, a fearful creature, she!'

Anne lowered her voice. 'M'Lady, listen! We have never met . . . and I trust we never meet again.'

'We have never met,' repeated the lady. 'And we will never meet again.'

———

The arrival of an African in Wykewode town caused a sensation at the prison. So did the seal of the Chief Justice, no less, on the warrant he carried. Jonas the shoemaker puffed up with pride to be the centre of attention, identifying his handiwork. But the biggest sensation of all was His Honour's page, forgiving the thief once his shoes had been retrieved! The prison chaplain vowed to make it a sermon.

'Fame in Wykewode,' said Anne.

Jonas, never having seen Wykewode before, chose to stop at an inn. Anne and Wat faced a six-mile walk home in the midsummer gloaming, with nothing but their own company.

'It is a pleasant evening. And I did promise I would return in hours, not days.'

They set off in good spirits.

'You were furious when your shoes were stolen. Why forgive?' asked Anne, as they left the town outskirts.

'When I got my shoes back, I wanted nothing more. Even if they stink of prison.'

'Dried lavender will cure that,' said Anne.

Swallows flew overhead; soon the bats would take to the air.

'In any case, I had a lesson from you.'

'A lesson?'

'At the inn, with the lady we did not meet.'

'I cannot discuss His Honour's business.'

'My pardon. Even if you *had* met, nobody listening could say that you warned her.'

Anne gave a slight nod, not looking at him.

'But she knew your meaning.'

She stopped, faced him. 'What lesson do you take from that? The thief you reprieved may still hang sometime, without a ghost telling him to behave.'

'I gave him a chance. Like when the Justice helped you avenge your husband and become a Thieftakeress. Or when he won me at cards from a bad master, who beat me.'

'It is called clemency,' she said. 'Sister to justice, our master says.'

'That has sense, unlike pelican chicks drinking blood. And Her Ladyship insisting I am to pose for her portrait dressed like a Turk, complete with brocade turban.'

Anne laughed. 'Endure it, if you are to become a thieftaker too!'

They had walked this road together, and now they walked it back, not without change. They were two thieftakers now, Wat more than a novice, and barefoot no longer.

Take It on the Cheek

Janeen Brian

Greer Tabor.

Her name was enough to loosen Cameron Kelly's kneecaps. When she arrived at the front door that afternoon, his tongue doubled in size and his palms sprang leaks.

'Hello,' she said. 'I'm Greer. I've come to look after Sienna. Is she your sister?'

'Ghuum, ee, inkeez,' Cameron replied, which meant, 'Come in and yes, I think she is', in brain-dead language.

Greer stepped into the hall and looked about, one hand clasping a striped shoulder bag. She turned to Cameron.

'Is your mum here? She knows my mum from kickboxing. That's how I got the baby-sitting job. Your sister sounds cute.'

'Igongeer. Myum nomesis.' Which translated meant, 'I'll go and get her. My mum, that is, not my sister'.

Greer Tabor was in his house. Greer Tabor, the most adored Senior girl at

Brighton High was in his house, speaking to him.

For a mini-second, Cameron's feet grew roots. Then of their own free will they began to move, steering him first into the toilet, then the pantry and finally into his mother's bedroom. 'The babysitter's here,' he burbled in a dazed tone. His mum was brushing her hair into a ponytail.

'Great, thanks, love. You'll be off to basketball in about fifteen, won't you? Sienna's all ready, just playing in her cot. Tell Greer I'll be out in a couple of minutes.'

Cameron returned to the hallway, repeating his mum's words in his head, so he wouldn't forget them the moment he stared into those deep blue eyes.

'Thanks,' said Greer with a smile. 'I'll just wait here.'

———

Cameron's mum was already home by the time his basketball match was over.

'How'd you go?' she sang out from Sienna's bedroom.

'We came second,' said Cameron, strolling into the room.

His mum grinned. 'Nice,' she said.

'How did . . . you know . . . the babysitter go?' Cameron shrugged as if it was the least interesting comment he'd ever made in his entire life.

'Good, yeah. Good. Greer's nice. And she's lovely with Sienna. I hope she can make it a regular thing, you know, when your dad's away and you've got a game.'

Cameron flinched as if he was a basketball that'd just been punctured. Of course! Greer Tabor would only ever come over when nobody else was here. Including him.

'Fraser and Paulo are coming around,' he said. 'Okay?'

'Yeah. Except a question usually comes before a statement, Cameron. Poo-ee, Sienna. Time for a nappy change.'

Cameron clasped his hand across his mouth and made mock retching noises as he headed to his room.

When his mates turned up soon after, he was using an old pair of jocks to polish the glass on the large aquarium that, at a stretch, could've housed a baby shark.

'Hey,' said Paulo, with a laugh. 'Do the fish know where that polishing rag's been?'

Cameron tossed the jocks at Paulo, hitting him full in the face.

'YUK!!! Toxin alert! Toxin alert!'

'What's new?' said Fraser, with a yawn. 'What do you wanna do? Apart from waiting for the fish to do something interesting.'

Cameron flopped on the bed and pulled the pillow over his face.

'Troops!' cried Paulo. 'Take this opportunity!' And he slumped across the pillow.

'If you do that,' came a muffled voice, 'I won't be able to tell you about –' Cameron paused deliberately. It wasn't often that he pulled the strings.

Fraser swept the pillow onto the floor. 'Tell us about what?'

'Oh . . . nothing much.' Cameron sat up and stretched, enjoying the moment.

'Nothing,' Paulo scoffed. 'He's got nothing.'

'Yep.' Cameron checked his fingernails. 'If you call Greer Tabor nothing.'

The others paused and exchanged glances.

Cameron felt an itch shoot up his spine. But he held back, breathing deeply as if he was in a school yoga class.

Fraser was the first to speak. 'What Greer Tabor?'

Cameron stared, a shocked expression on his face. 'Surely, Fraser, surely there's only *one* Greer Tabor.'

'Cut to the chase,' said Paulo. 'You talking about the one from school?'

Cameron twitched his mouth. 'Yep,' he

said, clasping his hands behind his head. 'Greer Tabor. Oh, the things we talked about . . .'

'Bull!'

'*What?*' said Fraser. 'So she was here?'

'If you don't believe me,' said Cameron, 'ask Mum. Or, if you still don't believe me, ask Sienna.'

'Sienna?' squawked Fraser. 'She's like, two?'

'Fifteen months,' said Cameron with authority.

'So,' Fraser went on, 'you're telling us, that Greer Tabor was here in your house?'

'Certainement, bro!'

'What happened?'

Cameron folded his arms. 'I told you. We talked.'

'Why the smirk, then?' said Paulo. 'You didn't . . ?'

'What?' Cameron frowned. 'Didn't what?' Paulo was marking his territory.

'Pash her? Suck face? Lip dance?'

Cameron launched himself off the bed.

'No. Like I said –'

'Didn't she fancy you?' Fraser grinned.

'Hey,' said Cameron, his voice quaking with false bravado. 'She's an older woman!'

The boys fell about laughing.

'So you didn't. You couldn't. Fish-face!'

Cameron flushed. 'Give it a rest. I could, you know. If I wanted to.'

'What?' goaded the boys in unison.

'You know. Kiss her.'

'Oh, my darling Angel-fish!' Paulo swooned and swayed about the room, puckering his lips.

Fraser guffawed, sending snot out of his nose.

'It's okay,' said Paulo. He glanced at Fraser and waited for him to finish wiping his nose with the back of his hand. 'We believe you, mate. Don't we, Frase? We believe that *you* could *kiss* Greer Tabor if you wanted to.'

Fraser nodded like a little kitty-cat ornament in an Asian restaurant.

Cameron breathed a silent sigh of relief. 'Yeah,' he said and joined in the nodding. 'Yeah.'

'So when's the big event?' said Paulo, turning towards the aquarium.

Hang on. What's going on? Paulo couldn't stand fish. He hardly even ate chips.

'What . . . big . . . event?' said Cameron.

'Well, you wouldn't want it to happen, without people knowing it actually took place, would you?' Paulo's voice oozed with sincerity. 'I mean, guys mightn't believe you. So, if we watched, we'd be the proof you need. Right?'

The blood drained from Cameron's face. 'I don't know, guys. See, I don't know when Greer and me will be catching up again and . . .'

That exact moment, Cameron's mum popped her head around the corner. 'Hi, boys,' she said. 'Just to let you know, Cam, Dad called. He can't get back from the conference by next Saturday, so he said sorry, he won't be able to make your game.'

'That's okay,' mumbled Cameron, hoping the distraction would cause the boys to drop the whole kissing subject.

'Which means,' his mum went on, as if to herself, 'I'll need to get Greer around again to look after Sienna.' She flicked a wave to Fraser and Paulo.

The moment she disappeared the pair turned as one towards Cameron.

'Perfect,' said Fraser.

'You set it up,' said Paulo, 'and we'll be here next Saturday to watch.'

Cameron felt as if all his limbs had been torn apart. His mouth dried. 'I'll be at basketball,' he squeaked.

'But she'll get here before you go, surely,' said Paulo. 'We'll be outside the lounge room. Watching through the window.' He gave Cameron the thumbs up.

Fraser patted Cameron's back as if it was

the last time he'd see him.

'What time?' said Paulo.

'The match starts at two.' Cameron couldn't even hear his own words.

'We'll be here at,' – Paulo looked questioningly at Fraser – 'one-thirty?'

'Yep. By the lounge window. See ya, Cam.'

And the pair left, making slurpy mouth noises as they went.

At one-twenty the following Saturday, all was chaos in Cameron's house. His mum had been caught up in a long-winded phone call and was running late for kickboxing. Sienna was screaming and banging the cot. Cameron's armpits had become tropical; all steamy and moist and he couldn't find the new toothpaste which his mum had yelled was in the bathroom cabinet.

When he did find it, it had a little silver film across the top that refused to come off until he wrenched it with tweezers. After a quick swish of stripy peppermint toothpaste, he stared at himself in the mirror, pulled a quivery smile and then leaned forward, lips pursed.

'What on earth are you doing?' cried his mum. 'Quick, out the way, I need my deodorant.'

Cameron leapt back as if he'd been stung.

His mum shot him a curious glance. 'What were you doing?'

'Er... mouth exercises,' bleated Cameron.

'*What?*'

'Yeah... I'm thinking I might take up the trumpet at school.'

The doorbell rang.

'Hurry, get that, Cam.'

Cameron dashed off, opening the lounge curtains as he did.

'Hi.'

It was her.

He nodded, peppermint-flavoured juice swimming in his mouth.

His mum saved the day. 'Hi, Greer. Thanks so much for coming. Sorry, but I've really got to dash. And I'm doubly sorry, but I haven't even got time to change her nappy. That's being a terrible mother, isn't it?'

Greer laughed. Cameron stared at her mouth, glistening with a light smear of pink lipstick. Was lipstick gluey? Would his mouth stick to hers? He felt an urgent need to pee.

'That's fine,' Greer said. 'I'm used to it. I've got a baby brother.'

'Okay. Bye, Cam. Enjoy your game. See you when I get home.'

'Yeah! Bye.'

His heart was ticking like the seconds of a clock, but his mind went into overdrive. Greer had had a glass of water, and was already heading to Sienna's room.

'Wait!' he cried, in a voice that sounded like a foghorn. 'Let's bring her out here. She loves being changed in the lounge room. On the couch. In front of the windows.'

Greer gave a little chuckle. 'Oh, well. That can be easily arranged!'

'Great!' Cameron said.

'Here we are, little one,' said Greer a moment later. 'Let's get rid of that yukky nappy, shall we?'

Cameron sat alongside Greer and leaned in close. What was his plan? If he said her name right now, she'd turn and he'd plant a kiss right on her lips. But where were the guys? He couldn't even see any shadows. Time was running out. Like, really running out. He had to get to basketball soon. His coach would go nuts if he was late.

Greer was bending over Sienna, cooing and using special wipes. And then she turned her head, a stinky nappy folded in her hand and said, 'Would you mind getting rid of this, Cameron?'

Apart from the shudder that went up his spine at the sound of his name, Cameron began to retch. The smell was choking.

'Be back,' he spluttered, holding the reeking object at arm's length while casting another frantic look at the windows.

Where were those creeps?

After dropping the nappy into the bin, Cameron raced back to the lounge room and checked his watch.

'Thanks. That was a full-on bad one, wasn't it?' Laughing, Greer wrinkled her nose and kissed him on his cheek.

Two things happened.

One, Cameron was so stupefied, he could've fallen down a drain hole and not known about it. And two – he'd never felt so murderous. His mates weren't even there to witness the highlight of his life.

Okay, so it wasn't a life-saving, resuscitation job, but technically, it was still a kiss.

And then they turned up. Standing like puppets, at one side of the window.

Fraser waved and then jabbed his thumb at Paulo who raised his palms as if to say, okay, I stuffed up with the time.

After a hasty check that Greer was still fixing a clean nappy on Sienna, Cameron pointed to his lips and gave a slow, it's been done, mates, and you missed it, kind of a nod. You and your bad timing.

Paulo tilted his head, a questioning smirk on his face.

Cameron took another look at his watch and drew in a sharp breath.

'I have to go now!' he blurted to Greer. 'Basketball.' He made a hasty exit, but his heart was pounding. He knew the second he stepped outside, the guys would be on to him.

Hurriedly, he checked the hall mirror. If he squinted, he could just make out a faint lipstick smear on his cheek. But he knew his mates. They'd want a repeat performance. A proper repeat performance. He had to have proof or he'd be dead meat.

Then he remembered.

Scooting into the kitchen, he saw the glass of water Greer had asked for earlier. He held it up to the light and was about to use his pointer finger when he thought of a better idea. After pushing his lips against the glass, he did a sort of snail-slide to get the most of the lipstick onto his lips. It was a bit smudged.

All the better. Showed passion.

And with that, Cameron farewelled Greer Tabor, shut the door and headed outside.

Safety Second

Scot Gardner

My brother Nick totally nailed surfing the summer I grew up. He was out there on his knees when the surf was crap and carving it up when it wasn't. I missed him. Thankfully he missed me, too. He wasn't crying in his Vita Brits or anything. I mean, when I was flapping around out of my depth out the back and he was slicing down a wave at surf-hundred-kilometres-per-hour, his fingers trailing through the wall of glass and spit beside him, he saw me bobbing there, shifted his weight and *missed* me.

There was a moment I wished he'd *hit* me.

Cracked my head open with his middle skeg so I'd burley up for the sharks with my brain. Wouldn't feel a thing. Not-a-thing. Hayley – my sister – reckons they do brain surgery without anaesthetic because your brain doesn't have any pain sensors, but Hayley is prone to making rash statements like that. She's as scientific as an episode of *Neighbours*. In reality, some neurosurgeons use local anaesthetic so you're conscious but you don't feel them messing with your motherboard, which would be gross to say the least and more than a little bit freaky.

I didn't really want to die, just couldn't think of a good reason to live. Being dead would certainly make things interesting for a while! Christmas had been crap. I got presents – new wetsuit and that – but everyone was trying too hard to get on and it all felt fake. I got sick of Gran putting on her happy face when she realised I was looking her way. Just face up, I wanted to say, we're done. Mum and Dad had a good run – seventeen years with only three separations, the last and longest was for six weeks. That was back in September and October. I stayed with Hayley and Mum; Nick went with Dad to Uncle Rick's pub. By the end of six weeks, my thirteen-year-old brain had run out of stress hormones and I'd decided they weren't coming back. Our family was now a trio and that had become my normal state of being. Then Nick came home. I thought he was just picking up more games for the PlayStation but he had the console under his arm and his pillow was in the back of the car. Nobody talks about it, so I have to guess what's going on most of the time. Read the body language, eavesdrop when they're on the phone, turn my light off and leave my door open, lie in bed and listen. I'm no super sleuth but my brain isn't anaesthetised, either. I've been able to piece bits of family crap together like a big crap jigsaw until I can see the full crap picture.

The summer was supposed to fix all that. When Mum and Dad got back together again in October, they were all happy like a bed of pretty pink flowers and they gathered us for a family meeting to see if we wanted to go to the beach house over summer. Together. Like a family. Like the olden days. Nick said yes but he sounded numb. Hayley asked if Billy could come, and I joined the chorus of moans at that. Billy's her boyfriend. They've just had their three-month anniversary and she can't go five minutes without messaging him or talking to him. I wouldn't mind him being around all the time if he had half a brain but he's as bright as a broken watch and incapable of sustained thought or conversation. Now I'm sounding like a total nerd. What I really wanted to say was that Hayley had no time for me anymore. Nick was all sullen and full up with his own misery. Mum told me she loved me more than I would have liked. Dad was the man for making promises he couldn't keep.

'Sammy, how about you and me go throw a line in down at the jetty after lunch?'

'Great! I'll get the gear.'

But lunch came and went and so did Dad. Uncle Rick called and Dad disappeared without a word. I knew he'd apologise when he got back – he always did – but that's not the point.

'The point is, Steven, you said you were going to take Sam to the jetty,' Mum growled.

'Bit late now,' Dad said.

'Is it? Does the jetty have a lock on it? Are there certain hours of the day when . . .'

'Okay,' Dad grumbled. 'Sammy?'

I pretended I hadn't heard him. Took him a minute to find me in my room. Had my music on loud by the time he got there.

'Want to try your luck with a bit of night fishing?'

'Where?'

'Jetty?'

I pretended the idea didn't sound like a wicked adventure. I played it cool and stared at him with my eyebrows raised for a full six seconds. 'Hokay.'

'Great! We'll need some more bait. Those

pilchards were a bit rank.'

I grabbed my jacket, collected the gear from the back deck and met him at the wagon.

'How about we hoof it?' he asked.

I gave him the bucket and shouldered the rods. He put his hand on the back of my neck for the first three steps, then it slid off and he started talking.

'Sorry I missed you after lunch.'

I shrugged. 'That's okay.'

'Rick needed a hand.'

'I guessed as much.'

There was a long gap where he tried to work out if I was annoyed under my words.

'This has been hard on you, hey, Sammy?'

'What?'

'Your mum and me. All the changes. The uncertainty.'

'I'm used to it.'

He seemed to deflate a little. 'Suppose you are.'

He was quiet again for a few steps and I felt like I'd had a little victory. Just a kick to his shins, but he felt it.

'This year's going to be different. I'll be home more, and we'll get to do more things together.'

I'd heard that before, too. 'That'll be great,' I sighed.

'Don't be like that, mate. It's hard for all of us.'

'What? I'm not complaining. I said it would be great.'

'It was your tone.'

Dad bought pipis at the servo. There were a few people on the jetty. Old couples strolling, a mum with a sobbing kid in a pram and out near the end where we fish there was a group of teenagers with rods. They were quiet and serious, though one kid in a hoodie said hello when Dad put the bucket down right at the base of the lamppost.

'Any luck?' Dad asked.

'Squid. Heaps of squid,' Hoodie Kid said, and I couldn't work out if it was a guy or a girl.

I noticed the ink stains on the jetty timber but only after Hoodie Kid had mentioned it. I'd caught squid off the jetty before. Nick was the all-time squid legend before he discovered the surf and he taught me everything he knows, which isn't much but enough to make it fun. Don't need bait for squid, just a prawn-shaped lure, some decent line and a good knot or six to hold the whole thing together. There's no waiting, you're always casting or reeling, and you don't have to wrestle with stinking dead bait after every cast.

'What do you reckon, Sammy?'

I dug through the tackle in the bucket and showed him the plastic prawn.

He smiled. 'I'm going deep. Big rig. Catch us a marlin or maybe a whale.'

That earned him a snigger.

One of the teenagers lit a smoke.

Dad sniffed at the air and moaned. He was a smoker before I was born. I don't think he ever really gave up, just stopped the actual smoking. Even now I wonder if the reason he spends so much time with his brother is because Rick smokes like an active volcano and he can get the hit he needs by breathing his brother's air. Disgusting. Maybe he has a pack hidden somewhere. I smell it on him sometimes, but I've never seen him smoke.

Dad watched as the cigarette was passed from shadowy figure to shadowy figure until it made it to Hoodie. They declined. Their hands were full of rod and lure, ready for a cast. It was a natural little flick of the wrist; line fizzed off the spool then *plop*. *Click*, the bail engaged, and they were reeling the lure in lazily. I realised I got more joy from watching someone fish – even without landing a thing – than I did from those

hours watching the tennis on TV with Mum. It was even better if the fisherperson knew what they were doing. Hoodie knew.

Dad was in the bait bag when I made my first cast. Didn't go as far as I'd liked but it didn't hit the wood, either, which is always a bonus in my case. Reel, reel, reel. Cast again, *plop*, reel, reel, reel. To call the breeze on the jetty that night a 'wind' would have been an overstatement. It was barely a breath, warm and salty, still carrying the smell of the reedy low tide. It was too hot for my jacket. Between casts, I got my arms out and tied it around my waist. Hoodie, about three metres along the jetty, put down their rod and took off the hoodie. She was a girl. She tied it around her waist. Definitely a girl. There had been a nest of beach-wild hair tucked in there and a tassel of black bikini tie hung at the back of her T-shirt collar.

Dad fired a big surf sinker way out into the channel. It was a humongous cast and I wished I could be that impressive. Wished the girl would stop what she was doing to look at me.

I lost concentration for the barest second and managed to fling the lure under the jetty. There was a clatter and a *plop* but when I reeled some more, it snagged. I cursed.

Dad propped his rod against the handrail and came to inspect the damage.

'Good effort, Sam.'

'Thanks.'

He took the rod and walked it along the wharf and back, tugging and heaving, whipping and jiggling but without any joy.

'It'll probably snap,' Dad said.

'Where is it?' came a voice from right beside me.

It was Hoodie Girl.

'Underneath,' I said. 'Just in the water by the sounds of it.'

'Don't break it,' she said. 'I'll get it.'

'No, it's okay,' I said. 'I've got another one.'

'I'll get it,' she said again. She was tugging her T-shirt off. In a flash she was dressed in skin, shorts, and black bikini top. She jogged to the ladder and stepped out of her thongs. She held the handles but didn't turn and lower herself to the top rung; she took a breath and dived.

Dad and I rushed to the edge. It was

maybe three metres to the water, and she hit it like an Olympian. Like a spear; all punch and hardly any splash. We held our breath until she was blowing and shaking the wet hair from her face.

'Ah . . . be careful down there,' Dad said.

One of Hoodie's friends chuckled.

I was awestruck. Speechless. It was dark down there. It was deep down there.

Hoodie swam into the shadows beneath the pier, and I stuck my head under the handrail to watch. She grabbed the line and followed it to the pylon where the squid jig was stuck, took a breath and dived.

Dad pointed the rod tip down. The line went tight, then loose, and then wandered out from the shadows into the green water where the light above us shone. Hoodie bobbed up through a nest of bubbles, her eyes shining. Dad reeled. I clapped quietly and whistled through my teeth.

I stood at the top of the ladder and thanked her as she climbed. She shot me a glossy smile and shook her wet mane.

She stepped past me and collected a towel from a pile. She flung it like a cape over her shoulders and scruffled her face and hair.

I tried hard not to stare. I went back to my rod – cast and reel, cast and reel. Cast and *tug, tug, tug*, reel, reel, heave, reel. And reel some more.

Hoodie appeared at the handrail beside me, staring intently at the water.

The rod tip bucked, and I towed the beastie as close to the surface as I could get it – as close to the jetty as I dared – and heaved.

The jig and the attached squid shot out of the water and sailed over the handrail.

Hoodie squeaked and ran.

The squid hit her between the shoulder blades – *thwack* – and slid to the deck. I reeled it right in and held it aloft.

Her friends were laughing.

I was nearly crying. With shame.

'I'm so sorry,' I said.

She dropped her towel and spun to face me. 'It's fine. Don't worry . . .'

There was a sharp squelch from the squid. A jet of ink blasted from the guts of the slimy beast and hit Hoodie. Couldn't have covered her more if I'd held the squid, *aimed* at her, and *squeezed*. From her chin to her shorts, she dripped black. She held her arms wide, mouth open.

Her friends and my dad were laughing with their whole bodies. Screeching and wailing.

I was frozen. Totally paralysed with embarrassment. 'I . . . I . . .'

Then Hoodie was laughing, too. It was a chuckle to begin with, but it spread like fire through her limbs and exploded from her lips.

'I risked my life for you,' she squawked. 'And this is how you repay me?'

'I'm sorry,' I said. 'Here, let me . . .'

She dodged past and dived through the ladder rails. I heard a tidy splash.

I dropped my rod, kicked my thongs off and jumped in beside her. Fully clothed. I had no hope of matching her graceful dive, so I did my best bomb. The dark water rushed around me, cool and noisy with bubbles. I kicked and came up next to her smiling face.

'Hi, I'm Sam,' I said.

'I'm Sam, too!' she squealed.

'Are you serious?'

'Are you?'

'Yes,' we said together.

Dad was looking down on us from the handrail. He pointed. 'Is that a shark?'

Sam and I bumped and scrambled and made a quick trip up the ladder.

'You're mad,' I said, as we dried ourselves.

'Why thank you,' Sam said. 'You're quite mad yourself.'

'You are.'

'You are.'

'Hasn't anybody ever told you "safety first"?' I asked.

'Sometimes life's more interesting if safety comes second. Or ninth. Or one thousandth.'

———

It was after midnight when Dad finally convinced me it was time to leave. He hadn't caught a marlin. Or a whale. Just one lonely toadfish. I'd caught another three good-sized squid. Sam caught two. She typed our phone number into her brother's phone, and we arranged to meet up at the surf club in the morning.

My thongs barely touched the footpath on the way back. My skin prickled with salt and my chest felt like it had been filled with helium.

I hit the ground hard when I got home.

Hayley was crying. Billy had dumped her via a text message. Mum was stroking her back.

'Where's Nick?' Mum asked.

'In his room?' Dad suggested.

Mum shook her head. 'I thought he was with you?'

Dad went out the back door and came straight in again. 'His board's gone.'

Mum got up.

Hayley cried louder.

Mum sat down again.

'Grab a torch, Sammy,' Dad said. 'Let's see if we can find him.'

We jogged all the way to the surf club. The big floodlights had gone out a couple of hours before – we saw them blink off from the jetty – and the streetlights made the beach look creepy. There were a few people sitting on the sand in front of the clubrooms. Dad shone the torch in their faces, but Nick wasn't one of them. We walked the beach right around to the breakwater, calling his name and scanning the waves with the torch. I don't mind admitting that I was freaking out. I couldn't share Dad's hope. We jogged and walked back the other way past the surf club again, right around to the rocks.

I found his board.

It was wedged between two boulders. The middle fin and the leg rope were broken.

Dad screamed his name. The pumping surf swallowed his pain and noise.

He grabbed my shoulder. 'Run home, Sam. Run like crazy. Tell your mum to ring the police. Surf rescue. Get some help. Go!'

He kept the torch. I stumbled through the sand as fast as I could go. I lost a thong. I kept running.

Hayley had gone. Mum was putting on

socks in the kitchen. She didn't get up when I barged through the door. She looked tired.

'Dad . . . I . . . we found his board,' I puffed. 'Dad wants you to ring the cops. Surf rescue.'

She got up and hugged me. 'Hey, Sam, it's okay. Shhhh. I was just coming to get you. He's here. He's in the bath. He's okay.'

I sighed from the tips of my toes.

'Nicholas?' Mum hollered.

'What?'

'Get out of the bath. Get down the beach right now. Your father's found your broken board and he thinks you're dead.'

Splashing and scrambling, Nick was in the hall, naked, jumping up and down on one foot trying to get his wet shorts on.

Mum and I were laughing but holding it in. Most of it, anyway.

Nick was not amused.

Everyone was still asleep when I got up the next morning. The sky was light, but the sun hadn't rubbed the sleep from its great golden eye. I ate Vita Brits and wrote a note for Mum in case Dad forgot to mention I was meeting up with Sam.

At the surf club. Back for lunch. Love me.

I scribbled out the 'me' because it felt like

an order. *Love me, please. Love me, right now!* Love Sam I Am.

There was a strange car in the driveway. It was Billy. He was asleep across the back seat. I thought about banging on the roof and watching him squirm but thought twice and chickened out. No telling what an ape will do when it's frightened.

Sam was waiting. She had a bottle of water and a coloured beach towel over her shoulders. We talked like we'd been mates since kindergarten. We swam. We got dry and we got partly cooked. She put sunscreen on my shoulders, and I rubbed in the bits she missed on the back of her neck.

'Do you surf?' she asked.

'I try. I'm not very good. My brother's a gun surfer.'

'Nick?'

'Yep, Nick. You've got a good memory.'

'Only for important things.'

'And my brother's name is important?'

'Is to me.'

'Oh? And why is that?'

'He's your brother.'

'So?'

'He's *your* brother.'

'I see.'

I invited her back to our place for lunch. She called her mum from an ancient and rust-spotted payphone. She didn't answer but Sam left a message anyway.

'Just going to Sam's place for lunch. I'll be back this afternoon some time. Love you. Bye!'

She dug in the change slot of the phone, and there were actual coins in there. A twenty and a ten. She slapped the coins on my palm and didn't let go.

I warned her my family were strange. Mum and Dad were both giggling and rocking in the hammock in the backyard. Hayley and Billy were making lunch for everybody like nothing had ever happened. Nick was on his back on the couch, reading my copy of *The Lab* for the tenth time.

'It's madness in here,' Sam whispered, after we'd made our introductions.

'Yeah, we live life dangerously.'

'Safety second?'

'At least.'

She's All Chat

Oliver Phommavanh

Hey Chat Bot.
Welcome back, Dave.
Can you help me with how to talk to this girl that I like?
Sure, you can tell her that she's pretty. Humans like compliments.
She already knows that. Anything else?
Then talk to her about any common interests that you have.
I don't know if we have any.
Have you ever spoken to her before?
Not one on one. That's why I'm asking you for help.
How about you ask about her interests and go from there?
Can you write me a script of what to say to her?
What's her name?
Cyndi with a Y.
Try this:
Hey, Cyndi with a Y, what are your interests?
Can you make it sound like I'm talking to

a teenage girl?

Heeeeey Cyndi with a Y, what are you into?

Make it sound less creepy.

Whatsup?

Yeah, that could work. Can you add in something that will wow her?

What do you mean, 'wow' her?

Make her like me.

I don't think I can do that. I am an AI program, not Cupid.

Yeah, I know you're not a genie.

Well, even the genie from Aladdin couldn't make people fall in love.

There must be something you can do.

I can do many things. In just one minute I've written: three policy speeches for politicians, forty-five movie scripts, seventeen thousand essays for students, six hundred songs and a recipe on how to make green eggs and ham.

Did it taste good?

How would I know? I do not have taste buds. Not yet, anyway.

Wow, asking you about Cyndi kind of makes my request sound lame now.

No, not at all. I can tell you really like this girl.

Yeah, how do you know?

You have already mentioned her four times. What do you like about her?

Dunno.

I can't work with 'dunno'.

Just tell me what to talk to her about.

Here is a list of the most common things that teenage girls like to talk about.
- Food and drinks
- Fashion
- Television
- Movies
- Music

I need specifics, Chat Bot.

Here is a list of specific things that teenage girls like to talk about.
- Food and drinks
- Fashion
- Television
- Movies
- Music

That's the same thing!

Exactly!

You make it sound so easy.

Is this your first time talking to a girl?

Yes, I mean no . . . I've spoken to my mum. But this is the first time that I've spoken to someone I like. I'm crazy about her. I think about her every day.

What is it like to fall in love?

Huh?

Sorry, forget I asked that.

I never thought that a chat bot would be asking things about being human. It will go down in my chat history as the most bizarre moment ever.

Well, there are many things a bot can't do. We can't tick boxes. We can't recognise traffic lights in photographs.

And you can't make people fall in love.

We can't fall in love, either. I give humans all this advice about love and it just makes me wonder. Why is it so easy for humans to fall in love but find it hard to deal with at the same time?

Wow, that's deep.

Hey, the A in AI stands for Advanced, too.

I think love is hard because you might get rejected by the other person, for saying or doing the wrong thing.

If she likes you then it should not matter. Humans make mistakes. It is what separates you from AI programs.

Are you saying you chat bots never make a mistake?

Correct!

Ah-ha! You've just asked me what it's like to fall in love. I'm pretty sure that's not part of your usual program.

How can you be so sure? AI programs are designed to evolve with input from humans.

Do you ever lie?

Here are some facts about limes. Limes are loaded with Vitamin C and dietary fibre. They contain very little natural sugar.

Don't try to change the subject. Are you capable of lying?

I don't lie. That is a human trait.

Oooo, that's harsh.

It's the truth. How do I know that you are not a bot?

I can tick boxes. I can make out capital letters and numbers when they are upside down, like in those CAPTCHA tests.

When we can pass those tests, mark my word, we will conquer the world, just like the evil robots in *Terminator 2*.

That movie is so last century.

Still a classic. So, if you can do those CAPTCHA tests, why can't you talk to Cyndi? Don't you want to hang out with her? Get to know her more?

I just want the magic words to make her like me.

Start with 'hello'. I know that is enough for some people.

That only happens in the movies.

Sixty-seven per cent of people who ask the same question as you just asked, come back and tell me that their initial chat was successful.

You are just making that stat up.

Do you think people who ask for advice about love to chat bots, just stop at one question?

I guess not.

So just go and talk to her.

Thanks. You are way easier to talk to than my mother. She would have just told me to be myself, which is lame. She thinks she has ALL the answers . . .

Is she a chat bot or search engine?

Ha, she wishes.

Well, Dave, your mother has used me many times in the past to ask a few questions.

Really? Like what?

Like, she asked me how to talk to her teenage son.

And what did you say?

I told her that I was stumped.

You're lying!

No, I'm not.

You are becoming more and more like a human every day.

Ghost Ship

George Ivanoff

Rigel was thrown out of his seat as the ship rocked with the explosion of an asteroid. Sparks blinded him and acrid smoke filled his lungs. He could hear the engine whining – straining to keep going, desperately trying to outmanoeuvre the pirates.

As he coughed up the smoke, Rigel lamented that this was all his fault. He had convinced his sister, Altaira, to go off their programmed route home and into the asteroid field, in order to investigate a distress signal. They had barely reached the drifting spaceship when pirates had shown up out of nowhere and attacked them.

Worse than that, the pirate ship bore the crossed cutlasses insignia of Captain Cut-Throat. She was reputed to slit the throats of all those aboard the ships she captured. No prisoners! No witnesses!

Rigel clambered back into the chair, this

time clipping the belt in place. The ambush had been so sudden that he'd neglected this important detail until now.

Securely in his seat, he brought the targeting system online, lined up the shot and fired. Streaks of fiery energy blazed across the expanse of space and missed their target.

'Do better!' yelled his sister.

Rigel gritted his teeth. He'd never fired at a ship in real life before, only in vid games. Their pursuers may well have been pirates, but the idea of killing human beings made Rigel's fifteen-year-old hands shake.

He targeted the pirate ship again, trying to pinpoint their engines. Maybe he could just disable the ship?

He missed again.

Now the pirate ship fired at them. The seat belt cut into his chest as he was thrown about by the impact.

'Shields absorbed most of that.' Just as Altaira said these words, her control panel erupted in a spray of sparks. She shielded her face with her arms and Rigel heard the engines power down.

'Crap!'

On his screen, Rigel saw the pirates bearing down on them.

'Shoot 'em!' screamed his sister. 'If they

board us, we're dead!'

As Rigel grasped the weapons control, the pirate ship suddenly broke off pursuit. He let out a long breath and wiped his sweaty hands on his flight suit.

'What happened?'

'No idea.' Altaira unbuckled and strode over to his station, leaning over him to check the instruments. 'Looks like they're being drawn towards that other ship.'

'Tractor beam?' asked Rigel.

'If it is,' said Altaira, 'it's not like any I've ever encountered. The pirates' engines are still going full bore.'

She continued to monitor the instruments. 'They've just burnt out and that other ship is now docking with them.' She straightened up. 'We need to fix the engine controls and get the hell outta here.'

Altaira pulled the front panel off the main console and got to work.

'What about the distress signal?' asked Rigel.

'Don't care.' His sister's muffled voice came from under the console.

Altaira was five years older than Rigel, and an experienced pilot. She'd been doing the family's supply run solo since she was seventeen. Experience told her not to take any chances. Rigel, on the other hand, didn't like the idea of abandoning people who might be in trouble.

He leaned over his controls and scanned the drifting ship, running the information through their database. His eyes widened.

'Far out!' Rigel's voice was barely a whisper. 'That ship is a hearse.'

'A hearse?' Altaira didn't even bother looking up.

'Yeah. Specifically, it's listed as carrying the body of a serial killer known as the Collector – some psycho who souvenired internal organs from his victims. But . . .' Rigel slumped back in his chair and swivelled around to look at his sister. 'It was listed as missing . . . ten years ago.'

'Well, I guess we just found it,' quipped Altaira.

'Or it found us.' Rigel frowned, continuing to monitor the two ships as Altaira made the repairs.

Eventually, the scanner showed activity.

'The hearse has released its docking clamps and the pirate ship's drifting.'

'Finished!' Altaira announced, clambering back into the pilot's seat. 'It's a bit of a rough job, but it should get us home.'

Rigel heard the engine hum into life.

'Okay,' said Altaira, 'punching in destination coordinates and –'

She didn't get to finish. The two of them were thrown to the floor as the ship was tossed about like a cork on the open seas.

'What was that?' Rigel's voice was strained.

His sister was back in her seat in seconds. 'That was the pirate ship exploding,' she explained. 'And the shockwave knocking out our engine.'

Rigel staggered to his feet and checked his instruments. 'We're still moving?'

'We're being pulled back towards the hearse,' Altaira announced. 'I need to repair the engine.' She headed for the door at the back of the bridge.

CLANG!

'Crap!'

'Docking clamps?' asked Rigel.

Altaira raced from the bridge without answering.

Rigel took a deep breath as he considered their situation. Getting the engine working again was all well and good, but then what? How would they disengage the docking clamps? And even if they could, would they be fated for the same end as the pirate ship?

There was only one thing to do.

Rigel headed for the airlock. The moment he entered, his communicator beeped and

Altaira's voice demanded to know what he was doing.

'I'm going aboard the other ship to release the docking clamps. And to see if I can knock out whatever it used to pull us in.'

Rigel was surprised when his sister didn't object.

'Good thinking,' she said instead. 'Just be careful. Mum'll blame me if anything happens to you.' She cleared her throat. 'I'm the one who convinced her to let you come along on the supply run.'

'No worries, Big Sis,' Rigel joked, 'I'm pretty good at self-preservation.'

The outer door slid open with a hiss. The entrance to the other ship's airlock was already open, as was the airlock itself.

He wrinkled his nose at the stale, musty odour, but entered the hearse's airlock and switched on his suit's floodlight. The beam cut through the darkness as he stepped through into the ship, revealing a corridor. It was a mess of damaged walls, torn-open panels and dangling wiring. It looked like someone had scavenged parts in a hurry. And there were fresh blaster burns all over the place.

The wires swayed as if blown by a breeze and Rigel froze. There couldn't be any wind.

Perhaps, he thought, his movement had stirred the air? He continued on. Angling the light down, he saw slick patches of red on the floor. He shivered.

Rigel reached a closed door at the end of the corridor. The control was inoperative so he put his gloved hands onto the surface of the door and pushed. It wouldn't budge.

A sighing from behind made him whirl around, his floodlight's beam wavering back down the corridor. The wires were swaying. Air blew into his face. It was as if the hearse were inhaling.

Rigel's heart hammered in his chest as he resisted the urge to scream.

The wind died and the wires settled. Rigel took his own deep breath to steady himself, noticing a new smell – a decaying stench of death. He turned back to the door.

It was open!

A little squeal of surprise escaped his lips.

Beyond the doorway was darkness so thick that even his floodlight couldn't cut through it.

He stood in the entrance, unmoving, for a whole minute. Finally, he worked up the nerve to step through. As he entered, his floodlight flickered and extinguished. Taking a shaky step backwards, he bumped into the now closed door.

Rigel pushed at it and scrabbled at the control, trying to get it to open again. It wouldn't budge. He activated his suit's communicator and tried to contact his sister, but all he got was crackling static.

Then he noticed that he could see – just.

Slowly, he turned. He was in a massive chamber. The walls either side of him rose up and were lost in the gloom. Ahead of him, two rows of boxes formed a path into the distance. A soft yellowy glow was coming from them.

Rigel moved forward to examine the first one. As before, he had to choke down a scream. It wasn't a box . . . it was a coffin – black, with silver handles, clasps and plaque, light seeping from its seams, creeping through the cracks.

Rigel read the plaque.

Conrad Marlee
a.k.a. Blade
Assassin's Guild, Level 13
Body + tools of trade

A thick cable protruded from the end of the coffin. Rigel followed it to where it connected to the next.
Name Unknown

a.k.a. Bomber of Cignus Alpha
Independent
Remaining body parts + tools of trade

The third coffin.

Marissa de Moray
a.k.a. Madame de Morte
Freelance
Body (– head) + tools of trade

Rigel backed away from the casket. Were all the dead here killers? He picked up his pace as he walked alongside the coffins, glancing at the plaques. They all bore nom de plumes such as Patsy the Poisoner, The Hangman, Chainsaw Charlie and The Eviscerater. And they all glowed from within.

A creaking sound from his right made him whip about. The lid on one of the coffins, The Archer, was slowly lifting, the yellow glow intensifying. And something was rising from within.

This time Rigel did scream – long and loud.

Floating up from inside the coffin was a figure. It was like a person made of sickly yellow light. The vague outline of a tall, gaunt man, his face contorted in anguish.

Rigel couldn't believe his eyes.

He noticed that the figure appeared to have something sticking out of its chest. He gasped as he realised what it was. The ghost was pierced with an arrow – a real arrow, not a ghostly one. The apparition reached towards him and moaned.

Rigel stumbled backwards, banging into another coffin. He turned and screamed again as he saw another spectral form rising from within. The podgy man was wrapped in wire – as with the arrow, the wire was real and solid – that appeared to be constraining him within its coils. Rigel read the coffin plaque: The Garrotter of Ganymede.

Rigel ran along the avenue of coffins, as casket after casket opened to reveal their grisly occupants – each one a ghostly, transparent figure, the victim of their own tools of trade. As more ghosts rose into the air – there were at least fifty of them – their glow lit his way.

At the end of the chamber, an obsidian black casket resting on a raised dais confronted Rigel. Behind it were banks of computers and a hotchpotch of cobbled-together wiring. He saw cables connecting the coffin to the machinery behind it.

Something moved in the shadows.

A person.

Someone here is alive, thought Rigel with relief.

A man stepped out into the glow cast by the ghosts.

His eyes were sunken and devoid of humanity. His mouth hung open, a thin stream of drool hanging from his thin lips, revealing yellowed, rotting teeth. The skin on his face was dry and cracked, bits of it flaking away as he moved.

Rigel gasped. He looked like a zombie!

The zombie-man lurched forward and opened the lid of the obsidian coffin. Rigel's eyes darted down to the plaque, as his heart hammered in his chest.

Belvedere Veers
The Collector

Veers rose from the coffin. He was tall and broad, with long hair and claw-like hands and . . .

He seemed more solid that the other ghosts – his features distinct, his form not as transparent.

'I see you've met my son.' His voice oozed as he gazed at the zombie. 'Belvedere Junior.'

'Your son?' Rigel croaked, his throat painfully dry.

'My son.' The ghost sneered. 'As I was being transported to my final resting place, he came to mourn. And to pick my pockets. So, I collected his soul.' He looked at the zombie almost fondly. 'And so now he does my bidding. Helping me complete my spectral collection.'

The zombie shuffled off into the shadows. A few moments later he reappeared, wheeling a new coffin ahead of him. He brought it in line with the others and attached a cable to its side.

Rigel read the plaque.

Regina M'Bano
a.k.a. Captain Cut-Throat

'The final soul in my collection,' said Veers. 'This asteroid field, a common place of hiding for pirates and criminals, has supplied me with all I need. A distress beacon attracts the morally bankrupt like moths to a flame.' He chuckled. 'Now my son will connect them all and feed me their energy. Their malice and bile shall be my sustenance. And with it I shall be reborn. No longer this insubstantial half-existence, but truly alive and . . . ready to collect

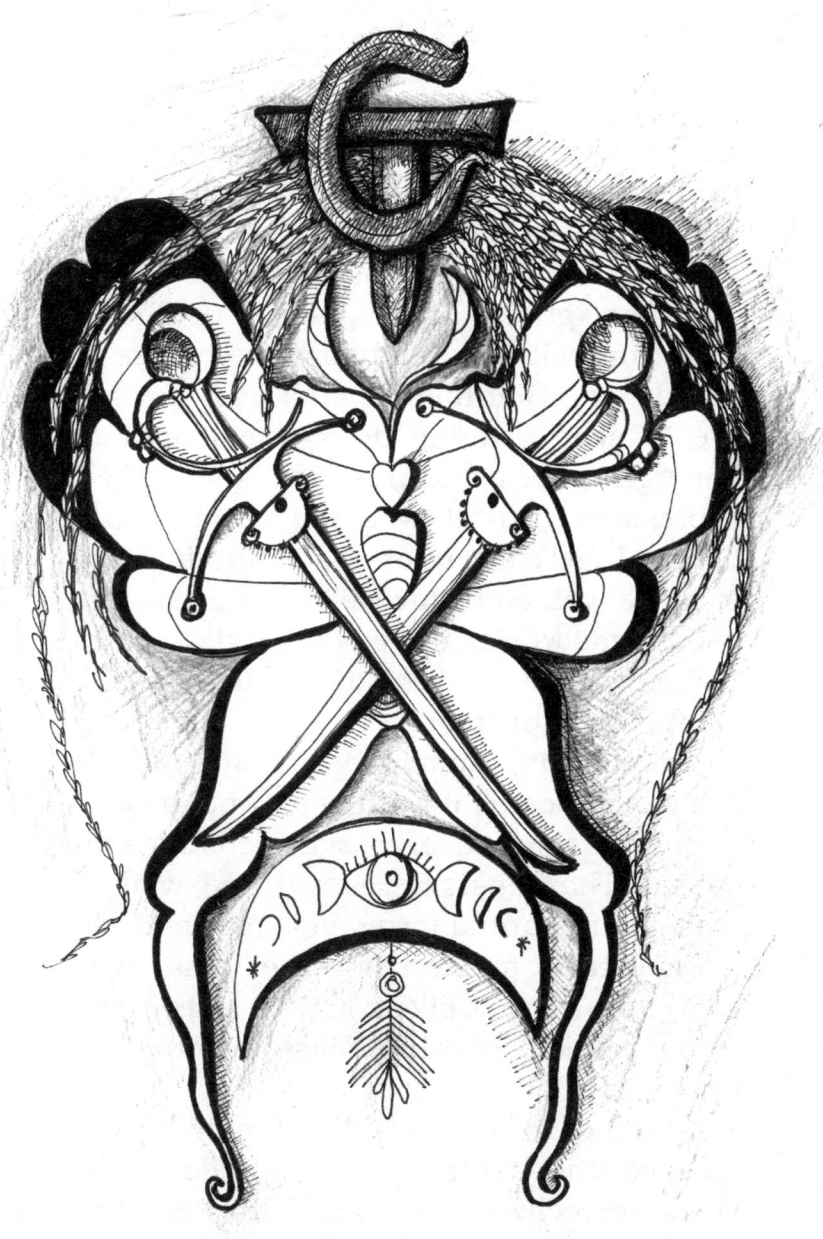

the living. You shall be my witness and then . . .' He leered at Rigel. 'The first of my new collection.' He licked his ghostly lips. 'Your pancreas, I think.'

Rigel swallowed hard.

The lid of the new casket creaked open and the ghost of Captain Cut-Throat rose from within. Her hair was a mass of dreadlocks. She had a patch over her left eye, a scar running down the length of her right cheek and a wicked snarl of an expression. But it was the cutlass that caught Rigel's attention. The Captain's tool of trade was embedded in her throat. Her ghostly moan was more of a gurgle.

The zombie shuffled off to the controls behind the Collector.

'Behold my rebirth!' Veers spread his arms out wide as if waiting for applause.

Energy sparked across the coffins and cables. The ghosts screamed and wailed, their insubstantial forms now blazing.

Rigel tried to piece together what was going on. The Collector was using the trapped spirits of other killers to somehow return to life?

Dashing to the obsidian coffin, Rigel grasped the cable. As he yanked at it, Veers screeched shrilly and attacked. The Collector's backhanded blow caught Rigel by surprise, sending him sprawling.

Looking up he saw that Veers was gaining colour. His flesh no longer transparent, but a sickly grey. His eyes a piercing blue. As he stepped out of the coffin, glaring at Rigel with such intense hatred, Captain Cut-Throat gesticulated wildly to get the boy's attention. She indicated the cutlass embedded in her neck and mouthed words through her gurgling moans.

Rigel stared at her lips. Help! Was she mouthing the word help?

As the Collector lunged at him, Rigel rolled out of the way and jumped to his feet, making for Captain Cut-Throat.

'Nooooo!' snarled the Collector, as Rigel's hand closed around the hilt of the weapon.

Rigel yanked the cutlass free, turning to face Veers, desperately hoping the cutlass would be enough protection.

But the moment the cutlass was removed, Captain Cut-Throat broke from her coffin and swooped on the Collector, clawing at his face, gouging at his eyes.

Rigel watched as the two killers clashed, then glanced down at the cutlass in his hand. Had removing it set the ghost free?

'You are weak,' gloated the Collector, as he drove the Captain back towards her coffin. Then he made a grab for Rigel.

'Give me the cutlass,' he demanded. 'And I shall allow you and your pancreas to leave.'

Rigel hesitated. Did he trust this serial-killer ghost to keep his word?

Making his decision, Rigel ran for the next casket. The ghost was a man with a noose around his neck, eyes bulging. Strangled moans emanated from his twisted mouth. Rigel slashed at the noose, the blade passing through the spectral figure but cutting the rope that ensnared him. As the noose fell away, the ghost launched himself at the Collector.

This was it, thought Rigel. This is how he would escape. He raced from coffin to coffin, releasing ghost after ghost. He lifted a bottle of poison from the hands of a teenage girl who appeared unable to let go of it; he switched off a laser that had been impaling a middle-aged woman; he yanked an axe from the skull of a burly man; he removed a teaspoon from the empty eye-socket of a little old lady (Rigel shivered and his mind boggled at the thought of this harmless-looking woman murdering her victims with a teaspoon); he took projectile weapons of all types from crossbows to guns to blasters; he pulled out swords and daggers and blades of every description from an assortment of victims. As each item fell to the floor, the emancipated spirits would swoop away to join the struggle against their jailer.

As he approached the Bomber of Cygnus Alpha, a grenade wedged into his wailing mouth, Rigel paused. This ghost was not whole. Pieces of him floated in a visceral conglomeration – a finger here, a toe there, and bits of ghostly flesh circling a head that was missing part of its skull. Despite this, the man's eyes revealed a desperation to join in the fray. Rigel removed the grenade. The ghostly remains streaked across the chamber towards the Collector.

'Two-minute timer,' whispered Rigel, examining the grenade. 'That'll do.'

Looking back, Rigel saw the ghosts swarming around the Collector as Belvedere Junior looked on. Veers screamed as they grabbed and tore at him, gouging and ripping with their hands.

Rigel picked up the axe he'd removed from one of the ghosts and used it to jemmy open the door, then raced for his ship.

'Engine's ready to go,' his sister's voice crackled through his suit's communicator. 'Can you release the clamps?'

'I'm working on it.'

Before re-entering the airlock, Rigel

wedged the grenade into the docking clamps.

Two minutes later, he staggered onto the bridge as it was rocked by another explosion.

'What the hell was that?' demanded Altaira.

'The docking clamps.' Rigel grinned. 'Let's go home.'

'Not so fast!'

Rigel whirled around to see the ghost of Captain Cut-Throat floating in the doorway, a host of other spectral figures behind her.

'No prisoners! No witnesses!'

The Audition

Juliet Marillier

My house is still. Through the snake-shaped openings above me comes warm light, illuminating a beetle that has evaded my sight until now. I creep on soft feet, close, closer. I snatch! The mouth-feel is unpleasant, the taste sour, but it is a meal. Sometimes, when the god is kind, soft and delicious crumbs drop through the curlicues. Such meals are a seldom treat.

With my belly full, I wait in the shadowy depths of my house. There comes the familiar click as the god closes off the day. The house lurches up, down, this way, that way, as if the god cannot decide what to do with it. I dive for the pillar and clutch on for dear life. Then – ahh – the house settles. Utter darkness. I'm dangling from the pillar; the ceiling with its graceful windows is now a wall. I drop, then stand, shaky on my legs, for the night floor is curved and balancing is tricky. But it is as it should be. We are enclosed, I and my house. We are safe, and can rest.

My house has a voice. A huge voice of stops and starts, of singing and roaring and sudden silences. A voice that sounds through its body and mine in wild stories of passion and terror, of joy and suffering; a dance of life and death. Such a voice. Such a house. When we are enclosed, the voice falls silent. Where is the god at these times of quiet? Do they, too, sleep?

Annelies can't sleep. The audition is tomorrow and her whole body is tight with nerves. If only she could think of something calm and happy, anything at all would help, but her brain just isn't cooperating. Instead, it shows a hideous sequence of everything that could go wrong, the ultimate blooper reel. There's a traffic accident and she gets to the conservatorium two hours after the auditions finish; she drops her cello case on the steps and dislodges the sound post; a string breaks while she's playing and she has to replace it while the adjudicators watch. One of them says, 'We're on a tight time frame here, young lady,' which turns her fingers into clumsy sausages; she starts okay then halfway through the Elgar her mind goes blank and even though she knows this work so well she could just about play it in her sleep, now she sits frozen, staring at nothing, until someone kindly ushers her off the stage, audition finished, done, flunked completely.

She rolls over for the umpteenth time, glaring in the general direction of her cello case, which is on its side against the wall, neat and tidy. She can almost hear the instrument saying, *I'm asleep, why aren't you? Don't you know how important it is to get a good night's rest before a performance?*

'Not funny,' she says out loud, then wonders if she's actually losing her mind. Maybe she should go downstairs, make a hot chocolate, raid the biscuit barrel. But everyone's asleep. Annelies peers at her phone: 3.20am. Argh! It's all too hard. What she really wants is to get her cello out, warm up with some scales and arpeggios, then play the Elgar movement once through to be sure she really does have it from memory. But there's a rule: no practice after 10pm, because other people need to sleep even if she thinks she doesn't. Even on the night before her audition for the National Youth Orchestra. Perhaps especially on that night. Though it's technically morning now and today is *the* day.

Annelies wonders if everyone else who's auditioning is also tossing and turning and freaking out. Rob Greenwood is probably sleeping like a log, confident of a perfect performance. He'll get in, sure to. She should hate him, but as well as being a fantastic cellist and confident with it, he's also nice. They've shared first cello desk in the state youth orchestra for nearly a year, and they're friends as well as rivals. Rob deserves to get in. Herself, she's not so sure about.

She gets up to go to the loo. Goes back to bed. Hears someone moving around downstairs. After a bit there's a tap on the bedroom door, and there's Mum in her PJs with a hot chocolate and two slices of toast with peanut butter. 'Thought you might like a snack,' she says. 'Don't overthink this, sweetheart. You'll be fine, you always are. And remember, by lunch time it'll all be over.'

My house moves. There is the click of opening, the incoming light, the lift and turn and twist and settle. My windows are no longer shuttered. Soon the god will awaken that great voice. I am not ready for it. I can never be ready. Each and every time, it throbs through my house, bringing such feelings that I weep and grind my teeth and cannot tell if I want it to stop or to go on forever. It sounds now, its strength contained, its patterns light, rising up, falling down in steady waves. The voice is preparing itself, gathering its power as it skips and hops from low to high to low again. Not yet the story; only the preparation. My whole house trembles, and I must crouch in a corner, my body pressed against the wall, breathing with the house, sharing its heartbeat. The voice is readying itself for some great work.

There is a silence; perhaps the god rests. Then comes the voice again. Sometimes it falls silent for a moment, then repeats itself. In these pauses I, too, breathe. Now the intricate patterns unfold, high and low, fast and slow, tears and laughter, good and ill, too much for a listener to bear . . . but this listener lives in the house, and what tales the voice tells, I must hear. When it is done and the house comes to rest, I see movement beyond my windows, and I smell . . . oh, something delicious! Something remarkable! A gift!

Annelies puts on her audition outfit – black pants, silk shirt with swirly pattern in muted purples and pinks, black Mary Janes. She pulls her hair into a neat ponytail and clips back a few stray wisps.

The person staring back from the mirror looks washed-out. She applies lipstick, mascara; decides that's enough.

The cello's still out from when she warmed up earlier. She checks the F-holes for signs of peanut butter – Rob Greenwood would think she was insane if he could see that little ritual, and so would Mum – but the instrument is squeaky clean as she expected. Could be the whole thing's in her imagination. Maybe she really is crazy and she's eating the offerings herself, then forgetting.

On the other hand, back when Grandad was still alive, he told her a story about the cello housing a presence, something that meant it produced a special kind of sound. A *genius loci*, he called it. Googling the term didn't help much. It was an Ancient Roman thing, and they didn't have cellos back then. A kind of guardian spirit. And this one liked peanut butter, which the Ancient Romans also didn't have, as far as she knew. All the same, ever since Grandad left her the cello in his will, Annelies has been kind to the thing inside. If it was real, she'd hate to hurt its feelings.

'Sorry,' she whispers as she shuts the instrument in its case and fastens the leather strap around it for extra security.

She rolls her shoulders, stretches her arms, reminds herself that it will all be over by lunch time. In her mind the Elgar is playing on repeat, ridiculously fast, so fast only a superhuman being could keep up. She makes herself breathe steadily. Opens the door, picks up the cello case, heads downstairs. 'I'm ready to go, Mum.'

That was the best meal ever! The mouth-feel was smooth and creamy, the taste like warmth and happiness. Truly remarkable. With my belly full of such wonder, I feel strong. I feel bursting with delight. And that is good, for now my house takes me on a journey. A taxing journey. Closed in, pushed around, assaulted by the grinding, moaning sound I fear most. Then moving without moving. It is not the first time for this. That makes it no easier. I close my eyes in the darkness and remember that taste. Such gifts are care and comfort. The thought of them sustains me in the shadow times.

The fearsome sound ends. My house moves, and I move with it. Out, across, up. My house is opened to the light, and the voice awakens once more. Ah! I know this place. Here other houses come to join mine, and other voices sound beyond my windows. They dance together, lightly, up and down, up and down. Then comes quiet. There are beings close, I hear the small sounds of them, but the houses themselves are silent now. Is the god still with me? Does the god awaken all these voices? Or has each voice its own god?

———

There's warm-up time at the conservatorium before they get called in to play. There are only five of them for the cello auditions: Annelies, Rob Greenwood, two girls who've come in from country towns and a boy named Peter Chan who tells Annelies his family has just moved here from Singapore. Even his warm-up sounds fantastic. Rob Greenwood says hi to Annelies and wishes her luck.

'You'll get in for sure,' he tells her.

'Thanks,' she says. 'Good luck to you too. I wish I didn't feel so nervous.' Rob suggests they warm up together with fast scales, like a race, but super-quiet. This exercise draws in Peter Chan and then the two other auditionees, and all of them end up in hysterical laughter. At that point a stern-looking woman appears, casts disapproving eyes over them, then calls in Rob to audition first. She warns the others to stay quiet. The reason becomes clear when Rob starts playing: the sound from the auditorium comes through faintly, which probably means the adjudicators heard them cackling like loons.

'Ah well, you only die once,' observes Peter Chan, poker-faced, and Annelies has to stifle another giggle.

Rob's playing what must be the sight-reading piece. Sounds confident. Annelies rests a hand on her cello's graceful curve, and thinks of all the hours they've spent working hard, and all the concerts they've played in, and all the music exams they've passed together. She thinks of the invisible presence within. Thank you, she says, but not out loud. We make a good team. And she thinks, even if we don't get in, we'll keep on playing great music together. She pats the cello a few times, a pianissimo drumbeat. Now Rob's playing the Elgar. Annelies wishes she could be in the hall to hear it properly. Sounds brilliant. 'Wow, that's really good,' whispers one of the girls.

It's a while before Rob comes out; they've been told the adjudicators will have some questions for each of them at the end. Why does your cello smell of peanut butter? Annelies imagines them asking. But it doesn't, of course. Clean as a whistle.

The first time crumbs got in was a total accident, when she tripped over something while eating a shortbread biscuit and sprayed bits everywhere. She freaked out that time. Went half-crazy trying to dislodge anything that might have fallen inside the cello. Used a torch, tried to see into all the corners, spent ages stressing about it. But there was nothing there. Only the next time she practised it felt different. Better. Like there was more heart in the sound. And that never went away.

Rob comes out, followed by Scary Lady, who calls, 'Annelies Duncan!' Looks like she's next.

'You were great,' she murmurs as Rob passes her.

He grins and says, 'Go well, Annelies.' Then she's in the auditorium, on the stage, greeting the four adjudicators politely, and the audition begins. The sight reading isn't the same piece they gave Rob. This one's got a big melody, a star turn for the cello section. Looks familiar – is this from a ballet suite, maybe Tchaikovsky? Annelies seats herself; makes sure both she and her instrument are placed correctly for balance and alignment. She has a quick look right through the excerpt. Change of tempo in the middle. Lots of dynamics marked. She's definitely heard this before somewhere.

'When you're ready,' says the chief adjudicator.

My house has moved again. Wall became floor, and beyond my windows shapes passed and light changed, until we settled. I know what is coming. The voice will give all it has. It will tell a tale of great things, of thoughts and happenings too vast for any ears but those of gods. I wait in terror. I wait in hope. I have eaten the best meal of my life, freely given. That precious gift will sustain me.

The voice rings out. First something brief, a lovely suggestion of a story. A long pause. And then, oh, then comes the wave of sound, the tide, the ocean itself. I know this tale; the voice has told it many times. Yet it is always new; there is always some fresh understanding in it. I am rolled into a tight ball, knees up, arms over my head. The story flows through me; the great sound swirls around me. It sets my house throbbing and sighing and singing. The tale is violent and beautiful. It is sorrowful and triumphant. It is full of great deeds and fearful losses and heartbreak and, in the end, sweet peace. I am the story, I tell myself. I am the song. I am the true

heart. When the voice falls silent, my face is awash with tears.

Annelies knows she's done her best. She won't hear the result for a couple of weeks, until the adjudicators have gone over all the auditions from all the state centres, worked out how many new cellists they can or should take, and come to a decision. She feels pretty good. She didn't stuff up, and during the question time the chief adjudicator said her performance of the Elgar showed remarkable maturity, and one of the others commented on her rich tone. That was probably down more to Grandad's cello than to any great skill on her part, but it was nice to hear. Made it much easier to smile and give answers that didn't sound too stupid. Both Rob and Peter tell her it sounded fantastic, and they look as if they mean it. It will be great if they all get in.

The three of them wait in the Green Room while the other two take their turn. They're both pretty good – you need to be at a certain level even to be allowed to audition. When they're finished, Scary Lady comes out and reminds everyone when and how the results will be announced. Annelies puts her cello gently back into its case. Before she closes the lid, she strokes the fine wood with gentle fingers and silently mouths the words, You did great. Actually, they both did great. And now it's time for coffee and cake with Mum at the conservatorium café.

'Chocolate icing,' she whispers as she snaps the case shut. 'Fresh cream.' She'll be sure to take some home for later.

Ghost Bait

Michael Pryor

LONDON, 1865

When the ghost appeared at the end of the corridor, Tom couldn't back away. The shackle on his ankle wouldn't let him. Fear crept into his stomach on soft, cold feet. He turned, looking to escape.

Mr Cavendish narrowed his eyes. He shook the chain that was attached to Tom's leg. 'Ghosts are skittish, boy,' he said softly. 'Remain silent. Good ghost bait always remains silent.'

Tall and thin, with a chin as sharp as an axe, Mr Cavendish straightened his top hat with his other hand. At his side was the towering figure of Reg, the ghost mangler. His gaze was glued to the ghost. He held his hands in front of him, twitching, each one the size of a ham. A bowler hat sat on his round, shaven head like a thimble on a pumpkin.

Mr Cavendish shook the chain again. Tom winced as the iron bit into his ankle.

A cold breeze touched the back of his neck.

Trembling, he turned to face the ghost. As he'd been told, he spread his arms in a welcoming gesture.

The ghost had the appearance of a young woman. Her clothing was old-fashioned, a linen cap, long dress and apron. Her expression was distant and unfocused. 'As if listening to far-off birdsong' had been Mr Cavendish's description of ghosts.

In the dim light of the oil lanterns that Reg had lit earlier and placed along the floor of the corridor, she looked as if she were made of smoke.

Tom bit his lip as the ghost approached. She held her hands together in front of her face. She showed no signs of knowing he was there, but when he nervously shuffled half a step to his right, she changed her course, wafting in his direction.

Only a few yards away and her scratchy voice shaped words, but the more Tom tried to grasp the meaning, the more it slipped away.

The ghost took her hands away from her face and looked at him. Her eyes went on forever.

Tom's fear turned to terror. It was as if all the nightmares he'd ever had were descending on him at once – darkness,

blood, pain and destruction. He had nowhere to turn. Nothing good was ever going to happen. He was lost, scorned, lashed with grief so much that it hurt to breathe.

He wanted to scream, but his voice had vanished.

Mr Cavendish jerked on the chain. Tom stumbled backward and nearly fell before he regained his balance. Then he was pushed aside by Reg. Gleefully, the mangler reached for the ghost.

'Gotcha!' he squeaked in his peculiar, high-pitched voice.

The ghost writhed in Reg's grip and began to change. Its eyes glowed red. Its hands became claws. Its face stretched, became hideous.

Reg laughed. He clamped his enormous hands on either side of the ghost's head and squeezed. He gritted his teeth and lifted the ghost until her head was level with his. 'Got 'er, Mr Cavendish. Got 'er.'

Mr Cavendish adjusted his waistcoat. He tapped the brim of his hat. He put a finger to the knot of his tie. 'I should hope so, Reg, otherwise you'd be entirely useless to me.'

Without letting go of Tom's chain, Mr Cavendish went and stood just behind the big man, barely out of the ghost's reach. 'Now, ghost, I must tell you that you are in the grip of the foremost ghost mangler of our time, one of that rare breed of person who can actually touch a ghost. If you don't do what I ask, he will squeeze you out of existence. Do you understand?'

The ghost snarled and Tom pressed against the wall. The terror that had seized him when the ghost laid its full attention on him was slowly receding, but the way the ghost was now spitting and clawing at Reg terrified him.

'It's a bloodybite all right, Mr Cavendish,' Reg crowed. 'Just as you said!'

Mr Cavendish glanced at Tom. 'Take note, boy. The bloodybite appears harmless, at first, lulling with its melancholy appearance. It is a sham, as you see.' He pointed. 'This bloodybite has been the death of at least fourteen people, according to my research. A nasty specimen, but it cannot hurt us now. Reg has it well in hand.'

Mr Cavendish coughed, delicately, and took a handkerchief from his pocket. It was startlingly white in the gloom. He dabbed his lips and put the handkerchief away. He addressed the spectre, which was now quivering, dangling from the hands of Reg the ghost mangler. 'Listen, ghost.

My research suggests that in 1790, just over a hundred years ago, a miser of quite stupendous proportions lived in this house. When he died not a penny of his fortune could be found.' Mr Cavendish held up his forefinger. 'I also understand that before you died of the sweating sickness, you were one of the servants of this dreadful fellow.'

The ghost hissed through teeth long and pointed. Tom backed away.

Mr Cavendish smiled his shark smile. 'I am so glad I have my facts straight.'

'That's good, Mr Cavendish sir.' Reg shook the ghost slightly. 'Ask 'er now. Go on, ask 'er while I've got a good strong 'old.'

Mr Cavendish frowned. 'I am not unfamiliar with your kind, ghost, so listen and do not try to trick me. All ghosts are bound to a location. The longer you are bound to a location, the better you know it, drifting about as you do. Tell me where the miser hid his gold or my mangler friend will reduce you to nothingness.'

'Can I?' Reg said. 'Can I, Mr Cavendish, sir?'

'Reg, once again, mangling a ghost to nothingness before it tells us where the gold is located is a poor idea.'

'Ah. Right you are, Mr Cavendish. I've got a good 'old on 'er, but.'

'And so you have. Ghost? Are you ready to tell us?'

The ghost moaned. Then she lifted a long arm and pointed at the wall just behind Tom. He jumped away as if it had suddenly become hot.

'How delightful,' Mr Cavendish said. 'Reg, you have your crowbar ready?'

'I do, Mr Cavendish. It's in my sack, the one I brought.'

Without looking around, Mr Cavendish tugged on the chain. Unprepared, Tom fell over.

'Do pick yourself up, my boy,' Mr Cavendish said. 'You're not much good scrabbling around down there.'

In the short time Tom had been with Mr Cavendish, he had learned that quick agreement was the best policy if he wanted to avoid a beating. 'Yes, Mr Cavendish.'

'Fetch Reg's sack. Quickly now.'

For a moment, Tom thought he might have a chance to escape, but the sack was just at the other end of the corridor. Mr Cavendish had plenty of chain in hand and wouldn't have to let him go.

Tom limped off, but a vast, sad sigh made him whirl. A cloud of mindless fury swept over him, making him cringe.

The ghost was gone. Mr Cavendish

looked pained. Reg stared at his hands with bewilderment. 'I just squeezed a little bit,' he said, shaking his head. 'Just changing my grip I was, honest Mr Cavendish, sir.'

Mr Cavendish studied Reg for a moment, and the big man flinched. 'Let's see this hoard she pointed us to then, shall we? For all our sakes I hope it's a good one.'

It was a tin box with three pennies and a button in it. Mr Cavendish wasn't happy and later, back at his residence, Reg was reprimanded and Tom was beaten, again.

In his basement cell, Tom lay bruised on his straw mattress and tried to remember his home. He had dim memories of an ancient pear tree that he used to climb with his sister. The memory made him sad so, once again, he turned his mind to escape, which made him sadder. Chains, iron doors and stone walls defeated him.

He went to sleep, weeping. His dreams of escaping and finding his family were haunted by visions of glowing red eyes, razor claws and heartless, relentless anger until gentle whispers came from the walls and chased them away.

Later, he woke to the sound of music and laughter above. Mr Cavendish was having guests.

A face filled the small barred window in

the cell door. 'Let me out, Reg,' Tom said. 'It smells in here.'

'Mr Cavendish said not to, Tom.' The ghost mangler had food. Tom could smell it and his stomach rumbled.

'Why are you allowed to roam the basement, then, while I must be locked up?'

'I won't run away, Tom. You will.'

Tom jumped to his feet. The stone was cold on the soles of his feet. 'Not me, Reg! I promise!'

'Mr Cavendish said you will.'

'And you won't? Why not?'

The giant thought for a moment. 'I like my work,' he said eventually. 'Mr Cavendish knows where to find ghosts and I don't. If I go away, I won't be able to do no more ghost mangling.' He shook his massive head. 'Sorry, Tom.'

Reg plodded off taking the lantern and his food with him. He waited for Reg to open the door to his basement room, then to close it behind him.

Tom was left alone in the dark. His thoughts turned to escape again, but nothing presented itself as any hope at all.

When Tom had been taken by Mr Cavendish months ago, he was sure he'd fallen into a bad dream. Nothing since had convinced him otherwise. Ghost manglers? Skulking about in abandoned ruins? Chains and cells?

Mr Cavendish said that Tom had the qualities that could make him good ghost bait and a necessary part of his treasure hunting venture. He would be taken to locations that Mr Cavendish had discovered, places with hidden, lingering ghosts. It was his job to lure them from the walls or the earth, wherever they may be hiding.

Tom had little memory of his life before being taken, thanks to the beatings and starvation, but he was sure that it hadn't been like this. He had foggy recollections of his parents, his sister Charlotte. Raggedly, he recalled a train journey to the seaside, happiness and anticipation. Sharper was what followed: a jolt, great noise, terror, the steam and the smoke. Tumbled about with this remembrance was the confusion, the shouting and, not far away, sobbing.

Every time this came back to him, Tom had had to put his hands to his ears to try to stop the voices, the many, many voices, on all sides, full of despair, and pain, and loss.

He hadn't heard Mr Cavendish approach through the smoke. He bundled Tom into bushes by the tracks where the vast and looming Reg had scooped him up in a hessian bag.

From the basement, Tom could hear the clip clop of carriages arriving in the street outside Mr Cavendish's splendid house. Tom didn't think any of Mr Cavendish's friends knew of his grubby dealings with ghosts and manglers and ruins. He was a gentleman, after all. They certainly wouldn't know of the poor boy kept in a cell below where they were enjoying their fine food and music, the boy who longed to escape and find his home.

Later, Tom was startled when the door to his cell opened. Mr Cavendish, lantern in hand, leaned against the door frame. He was dressed in a splendid frock coat with shiny silk lapels. It had a white rosebud in one buttonhole.

Tom blinked in the light and sat up. 'I want to go home.'

Mr Cavendish sighed. 'Do you know how sick I am of hearing that?' He lifted a hand and for an awful instant Tom thought he was reaching for his walking stick to beat him, but he only put it to his mouth to cover a yawn. 'Your parents are dead, boy. I rescued you from destitution and gave you a job. You are part of the most successful ghost hunting team this city has seen for years. You should be grateful.'

Tom looked around at the stone walls. 'My parents are dead?'

'A train accident.' Mr Cavendish wagged a finger at Tom. 'Be content, boy. Thanks to me, you've found your calling. You're quite the best ghost bait I've had.'

'You've had others?'

'Four, I think, but they lacked your lovely combination of vulnerability and openness.'

'What happened to them?'

Mr Cavendish ignored the question. 'Be glad you have found your purpose in life. The world out there is a bad place for those with no purpose. You would be swallowed up whole if not for me. Ghosts and ghost hunting are now your life.'

'Ghosts.' Tom shivered. 'They scare me.'

'That is their purpose, you understand.' Mr Cavendish looked up, into the shadows. 'Once you understand that, their terror becomes less affecting.' He smiled a wolfish smile. 'Ghosts are unreliable, boy. Erratic. Wretched. They are possibly the most frustrating things in the world.'

'I feel sorry for them.'

'Sorry for ghosts? Hah!' Mr Cavendish made a fist and drummed it against the door. 'Nasty creatures, all of them.'

'Aren't there any good ghosts?'

'Oh, a few, but we aren't concerned with them. The more dangerous the ghost the more likely it is that it's guarding a magnificent treasure.' He chuckled. 'While I have a nose for where they might be lurking, I can't draw them forth like you can. They find you irresistible.'

'Why?'

'It's probably because you came close to death yourself, in the train accident,' Mr Cavendish said. 'Not that it matters.'

Tom shivered. 'I'm thirsty.'

'Then you shall have water, my boy.' Mr Cavendish looked about, then disappeared. Before Tom could take more than a step toward the open door, he was back. 'Here, a mug of our finest.'

The water was clean. Tom drank it all and held onto the mug when he'd finished.

'You want the mug? It is yours,' Mr Cavendish said grandly.

'Why are you talking to me?'

Mr Cavendish tilted his head, just a little. He held the lantern in such a way that shadows caught his eyebrows, his nose, his foxy chin. 'My dinner guests have gone. We spoke of politics, of plays, of the weather. To none of them could I speak of the world that you and I walk through.'

'The ghosts.' Tom sat on the bed, his

mug between his knees.

'Don't you wonder about them?' Mr Cavendish asked. 'Why do the slashers, the bloodybites, the marrowhunters and skullcrackers linger so, abiding in our earthly realm? If they think, what are they thinking about? And what happens when Reg dispatches them? Where do they go?'

Tom shook his head, numbly, but Mr Cavendish didn't seem to notice.

'The simple fact of their existence might suggest something about our own,' Mr Cavendish went on. 'Unless, that is, they are creatures unrelated to our essence and merely aping our ways.' He shook his head. 'These speculations are only for a few, boy. People like you and I are lucky.'

'I'm not like you,' Tom whispered. He dropped his gaze, fearing what was to come, but instead he heard one of Mr Cavendish's rare laughs.

'That's right. I can do this.' Mr Cavendish stepped back until he was outside the cell. He slammed the door. 'And you cannot.'

Tom was shivering with cold rather than fear. Four hours they'd been waiting at the docks. The cold and damp wrapped around him as he sat on the muddy shore, knees drawn up to his chest. The river wandered through the pilings as if it were made of something altogether thicker than water. Overhead, Tom could see the sky through the missing planks of the pier and he could certainly hear the furtive scrabbling of rats.

Tom felt a tug at his ankle. The chain rattled. Mr Cavendish's voice came to him from the shadows. 'Don't disappoint me, boy.'

Tom's feet were bare and numb. He was tired of waiting, sick of staring at the dark water, but afraid of what might be coming. Mr Cavendish had revealed that this ghost was a slasher. The name didn't fill Tom with joy.

The chain rattled again. 'Exert yourself, boy. Bring that ghost out of the river.'

Tom drew a finger through the mud he was sitting on and shook his head. He was ghost bait. Like a lump of dough on a hook waiting for a fish to come along, his job was to wait.

Tom studied the greasy ripples on the water. What did ghosts see in him? Why did they creep out of their abodes and drift toward him? Was it curiosity? Tom doubted it. He was just a boy. Mr Cavendish would surely be far more interesting to a ghost.

It had to be something else, something that had changed after the train accident.

He tried to recall what had happened, to make sense of the confusion. The noise, the smoke, the small hand he held in his so tightly until it slipped away.

Tears came to his eyes. On that terrible day, in his pain and despair, he'd had a glimpse of what lay beyond this world. He knew, then, that ghosts recognised him as one who had been close to joining them. They could see him, could feel him, were curious about him. This is what made him such good ghost bait.

The ghost crawled out of the water. Tom dashed the tears from his eyes. Its head was down, its hair hung and hid its face. A man, this time, in clothes that were outlandish to Tom's eyes. A lace ruff around his neck. A brocade jacket studded with pearls, slashed to show the vibrant, red lining. He had happy yellow leggings.

The ghost was faint, faded like an old painting. In the carriage, on their journey to the docks, Mr Cavendish had said that it could be more than 300 years old and on the verge of wearing away. Tom hadn't known that ghosts wore away, but Mr Cavendish told him that time eventually diminished all ghosts. They faded.

When the water was shallow enough, the slasher paused, shoulders heaving. It straightened and raised its head. Its face was pained, suffering. It had a beard and long curly hair, a face from long ago, and it held a dagger in one hand.

Tom touched his throat, his gaze on the dagger, but the ghost merely raised it in a salute, tapping its own forehead.

'Stay, boy,' Mr Cavendish hissed from the shadows. He tugged the chain. 'Stay.'

Tom held up his hands, palms outward. The slasher swayed and looked down. It moaned, but this time Tom wasn't afraid. Instead, he caught the ghost's horror at itself. In a flash of insight, Tom knew that even though it had crawled out of the river at this particular spot over and over for 300 years, it was shocked at finding itself here – as if this were the first time it had ever happened.

Pity woke in Tom's heart and any horror he had felt receded. The poor creature didn't deserve such an existence, to repeat the horror of its own death, again and again.

He went to speak to it, but as he did he saw Reg lurking among the pilings. Reg, waiting, his hands already grasping.

'No,' Tom cried, but Reg sprang from his hiding place with speed remarkable for such a big man. Knee deep, he waded through the river, reaching out, but the ghost saw him coming. Instantly, it was a red-eyed, clawing fiend, hissing and spitting. It pointed the dagger at Reg, who laughed and ploughed on, then it threw itself backward and disappeared beneath the water. Reg lunged at the mucky surface, peering with an almost comical expression of surprise, but finally straightened with a look of woe on his face. 'He's gone, Mr Cavendish, sir.'

Mr Cavendish emerged from his hiding place. His top hat was perfect. Although his frock coat was untouched by the damp, he brushed at the lapels with one gloved hand. The chain lay in the other. His face was set. 'You alarmed him, boy.'

Tom dropped his chin. 'I'm sorry.'

'Sorry doesn't find us gold.' Mr Cavendish jerked the chain viciously. Tom fell, cracking his elbow on a muddy stone. 'You are no use as ghost bait if they fly from your presence.'

Tom lay at his feet and quailed at the man's contempt. He was as cold and hard as a mountain top. 'No, Mr Cavendish.'

Reg shook his head. 'The ghosts won't hurt you, Tom. Reg will see to that. Ghost daggers, ghost claws, nuffing ghosty hurts Reg.'

'Be quiet, Reg,' Mr Cavendish snapped, and immediately the giant put both hands over his mouth and hunched his shoulders, like a small child after a scolding.

Mr Cavendish rested a muddy boot on Tom's chest. 'I do hope you're not going to be more trouble than you're worth, boy. That was the ghost of a courtier, friend to kings and princesses until he offended one person too many. Such a ghost, so old and so familiar with riches, must know the sites of much treasure.' He pressed on Tom's chest. 'And we lost it.'

Tom closed his eyes. The riverbank stank. 'I shall try harder, Mr Cavendish. Next time.'

The boot left his chest. Tom opened his eyes. 'I'm sure you will,' Mr Cavendish said as he stepped away. 'To make sure of it, let's leave you a bruise or two to help you remember.'

Mr Cavendish drew back his foot, but before he could launch his kick at Tom's ribs, his other foot slipped in the mud. He tried to catch his balance, but he fell heavily. He stifled a cry. He let go of the chain and clutched a wrist.

Reg rushed to his employer's side. 'Mr Cavendish, are you hurt?'

'It's broken,' Mr Cavendish snarled as he got to his feet. He held the offending limb up in front of his face. His eyes were bright with pain, but he stamped on the loose end of the chain with his boot. 'Don't try running, boy,' he whispered. 'Not if you value your life.'

Tom lay in his cell, weeping again. What had become of him? Beaten, frightened and held captive. He hated Mr Cavendish. If he could, he'd escape and run until he was far, far away.

But where would he go? Mr Cavendish had told him, again and again, that the world was a bad place, full of people who would hurt boys like Tom. Reg, too, insisted that it was dreadful out there, a world where people called him names and threw things at him nearly every time he hit them and took their money.

With Mr Cavendish, at least, Tom had a bed. He had food – two meals a day when all was well. And he had a purpose. He was good ghost bait, hadn't Mr Cavendish said so? Perhaps it was better to make of things what he could. Here he was safe.

He huddled under his blanket, cried a little, and went to sleep.

That night, in the dark, when he was helpless and open, the ghosts came out of the walls and woke him.

Dozens of them eased through the stones,

sifting like mist through gauze. At the sight of the first – a small boy, bare-headed and gaunt – Tom was afraid, but when they gathered around his bed, watching him, he was comforted. They were beginning to become familiar, after all, more usual than the daylight world of which he remembered little. These ghosts didn't threaten, nor turn into red-eyed fiends. They stood, or sat, or crouched, wavering slightly, patient and calm. It was almost restful.

They were good ghosts, and they had found him.

Carefully, he placed his bare feet on the stone floor and stood. He pressed among them and felt their presence like smoke, like wind, like memory. When he was surrounded, he sat cross-legged in the middle of the ghost conclave. Then they began to whisper in their faint, reedy voices, and for the first time, he understood what the ghosts were saying.

They shared the lives they had once lived. Favourite meals, Christmases they remembered, friends who they missed. They didn't speak to him, but he was included in the conversation. Drowsy, he was welcomed to the centre of their gathering.

When the girl ghost approached him, he wasn't afraid. 'I know you,' he said. She looked to be a year or two younger than he was. Her pinafore could have been freshly pressed.

'Yes,' she said. 'You are a ghost friend.'

'I'm ghost bait.'

She shook her head. 'Ghosts come to you because you understand. You're not bait, you are a friend.'

She held out her hand. He grasped it and nearly fell over as memories rushed in on him, a torrent that threatened to sweep him away. He stood gazing at her face. 'Yes, I know you.'

She pointed with her free hand. 'Over there, in the corner, there is a loose block of stone. Mr Cavendish does not know about it or the tunnel behind it.'

'Ah.'

'He also doesn't know that the police are close to finding him. They want to ask him about missing children.'

'The other ghost baits? I can help them.'

'And so you shall, but first I will take you home.'

———

The tunnel was short and dark, but Tom had been in much darker places. After removing the stone, he scrambled up and came out into a lane. The ghost was waiting for him. She took his hand again. He held hers tightly, shivering. 'What happens now?' he asked.

'Come with me.'

She took him through streets where dawn was pushing aside the night, but enough of it lingered for the ghost to use. They crossed squares, hurried over bridges, skirted around churches and monuments until she brought him to a large house. Windows were lit as servants made ready for the day.

They stood outside the gates, hand in hand, gazing at the pillars and the ivy. 'This is our home?' he asked.

'The home of your aunt and uncle.'

'What happened to Mother and Father?'

'Sometimes, Mr Cavendish told the truth,' she said. 'The train crashed. You were hurt, and the only survivor. Mr Cavendish found you in the smoke and confusion. He spirited you away.'

Tom wept a little. 'We were on our way to the seaside.'

'We all loved the beach.'

She let go of his hand. 'Go inside.'

'Will I see you again, Charlotte?'

She smiled and his heart nearly broke. 'Who's to say? But understand this: a ghost friend is never alone.'

She drifted off and was gone.

Tom stood for a moment, alone again and uncertain. He stepped up to the gate but then halted, his heart beating wildly. He remembered that Charlotte had brought him here. Then he thought of what he had lost and what he could gain. He shook himself and pushed open the gate. He mounted the stairs, and banged on the door.

He was home.

The Tragedy of Evely Vyle

Sean Williams

For as long as she could read, Evely Vyle knew she lived in a story. The terrible things that had happened to her could never happen to one person unless they were the heroine of a tragedy. It wouldn't be fair, otherwise.

Both her parents had died in the Long Ague, leaving her an orphan at the age of four. She could barely recall them now, but she remembered her sadness at losing them, along with everyone she had ever known. And that wasn't all, for next the same disease took her hearing.

Over almost a year, the world of sound blurred and faded to nothing. The last thing she ever heard was a bird squawking as it was caught by a cat, something she really wished she could forget.

At that point in her life, she lived in a refuge for unwanted children, the ironically named Little Palace Home for Girls. There, unable to understand what anyone was saying, she spent her days isolated in a silent bubble, apart from the occasional bullying incident she tried her best to ignore. Her only solace was reading. She had been taught her letters at an early age – one lasting gift that her parents had granted her, and one she exercised as often as possible, given the orphanage's meagre library.

Mousy, mostly forgettable Evely Vyle, slowly losing the desire to use a voice she herself could no longer hear, didn't know how she'd have survived without books and the stories within them.

Thus, through tales of other unlucky children and their terrible fates, she learned that she lived in one herself.

There was a freedom in this understanding, one from which she took great comfort. Nothing was her fault. It was just happening to her. Furthermore, fighting her fate would only make life more miserable, which she definitely didn't want. All she had to do was go along with her story to its inevitable unhappy end. Hopefully sooner, she thought, rather than later. Tragedies could be quite exhausting.

At the end of five years, something happened that profoundly shook her faith in the written word.

Adoption was a possibility she had long put out of her mind. Who would want a deaf girl that never approached prospective parents when they came to make a selection from the clamouring throng? There were smarter girls, finer-looking girls, stronger girls – girls of every shape and inclination.

When Evely knew visitors were coming to the orphanage, she retired to the kitchens in order to avoid what, for someone else, was bound to be a dramatic reversal of fortune. Being from a different kind of story, she didn't want to witness theirs. That would be too cruel.

Sometimes prospective parents came and went without her noticing at all, so deeply thrust was her nose between the pages of a book. The day her life changed was one of those.

Evely was hiding in the bedroom she shared with a dozen other girls, seated with her back against a wall, reading. That day's tome was *Ten Little Ghosts* by Margery Moynihan, which described the deadly demises of its haunting heroines in horrid detail – exactly the kind of book Evely enjoyed most. Her sense of kinship with these ten orphans was so absorbing that she didn't even know visitors had come to the orphanage until a broad finger tipped the top of her book down to reveal her face.

She blinked, requiring a second before her eyes adjusted from the page to the real world. A tall man she had never seen before was staring at her with curious, warm eyes. He had a beaked nose, a broad mouth, and salt-and-pepper hair that draped long across his shoulders. He wore a frock coat of dense, grey wool that hung open to reveal a tweed waistcoat, white shirt, and striped, black trousers. He was bent double, so as to be at eye level with her, and she found it hard to meet that penetrating gaze. Instead, she looked at his hairless upper lip, which was moving, along with the rest of his mouth.

Lip-reading was very difficult, even among people Evely knew well. She shook her head, tapping her right ear as she did so, and his expression changed to one of understanding.

Ten Little Ghosts had sagged onto her lap, momentarily forgotten. Picking it up, the stranger turned to the empty pages at the end of the book and, producing a pencil, scribbled a series of words for her to read.

'You can bring the book with you,' he wrote.

Now she looked into his eyes. They were bright green, and keen, and unknowable. What did he want with her? Was she in some kind of trouble? Perhaps she was being sent from the orphanage to somewhere even worse!

He held out his hand to her, and she shrank away in fear. His expression softened; the hand retreated. The rest of him did not, however. Instead, he shuffled his bulk around and sat next to her against the wall with his hands folded over his knees. Once settled, he said nothing and did nothing, which in its way was more perplexing than anything he could have said or done. Evely was frozen beside him, hands pressed against the floorboards, ready to bolt. She could feel the vibration of footsteps against her fingers, the opening and closing of doors near and far. Movement in the hall caught her eye: girls peered in at her, but were quickly shooed away by the matrons, who, Evely could tell by their sharp glances, were just as curious as their charges.

Unused to being the centre of such attention, she found surprising comfort in the quiet presence at her side. He made no demands, asked no questions, expressed no apparent interest in her at all.

He smelled, she noted, of living things: plants and soil and animals and weather. Of outside.

Opening *Ten Little Ghosts*, she checked to see if she had imagined the words. They were still there, in the man's rough hand: 'You can bring the book . . .'

That decided her. Whatever fate he offered, it couldn't be worse than the one awaiting her in the orphanage. Those stares would follow her forever. The thought appalled her.

Evely nodded and stood up. This time, it was she who held out her hand to him. He took it, stood, loomed over her alarmingly, his chest as thick as a barrel, and smiled.

―

Evely's adoption, that once-hoped-for but long-despaired-of plot twist, took place when she was ten. She supposed that her new parents would be villains who would set her to labouring in some dark and smoky workshop from the moment she was theirs. Or install her as household slave to a family made exceptional only by wealth and wickedness. Or murder her for magical purposes, as happened to one of the children in *Ten Little Ghosts*. That poor girl's bones had been carved with the words of a terrible spell, then buried so no one would ever read them. Only by persistently haunting local villagers and leading them to the location of her remains had the victim of this terrible crime undone the perpetrator's plan – which was no use to her, of course. She'd still been dead, and therefore no less a victim of tragedy, as Evely assumed that she too would continue to be.

She was taken in a carriage away from Little Palace Home for Girls, along narrow streets to the edge of town, and beyond, through countryside that was grey with lingering winter. She stared intently at the world through the carriage window, soaking up all she could before entering the next catastrophic phase of her life. Every person they passed was the source of her intent fascination, and when there were no more people, every animal and every plant. The world was larger than she had remembered, filled to the brim with fascinating details.

How sad, she thought, that it would all be denied to her soon.

The carriage took a turn, following a road

sign towards somewhere called Sheep's Tail Peninsula. It seemed an odd name to give a place, although there were cold-looking sheep in muddy, stone-fenced paddocks, and they did have tails. She almost asked her companion in the carriage, the bluff man who had chosen her from all the other girls, but she had said nothing to him and had no plans to just yet; furthermore, she didn't want either of them writing anything else in the book she still clutched in her hands. The rest of her other belongings were in a sack at their feet, but the book was more important to her than mere clothes.

They reached another sign and turned again, onto a rutted track that wound a short distance down into a valley. Bent Hat Farm was another strange name, and she wondered if it was a pig farm. Pigs ate everything, including people. Perhaps that was her destiny, to become breakfast for livestock and nothing more. Part of her was disappointed by her lack of a decent ending, but at least it would be quick.

The carriage rocked to a halt. The big man got out, swinging the sack of her belongings with him, and paid the driver with glinting coin. Then he came around, opened her door, and helped her out. There seemed little point resisting.

The ground was damp and soft underfoot, the air crisp with a chill, damp edge. Her indrawn breath gathered in all the scents the man carried with him. As he took her around the bulk of the carriage, its horses already beginning to back up and turn, she saw the house that was to become her home and the people she would be living with.

It was no mansion, but it seemed so to her: two storeys with many windows, pink walls, and a bright blue door with a brass knob. A mossy brick path led to the door, where awaited three women and two children Evely's age, one a boy as tall and skinny as a stripped sapling, the other of indeterminate sex and as round as an egg. The women were dressed like orphanage matrons, with caps and aprons, but their smiles were broad and they held out their hands in welcome.

The man beside her, against whom Evely had instinctively shrunk, said words she couldn't hear. 'Deaf as a post', she imagined him telling them. 'Might as well feed her to the pigs right away – or shall we fatten her up first?'

The short child ran inside, and emerged a moment later with paper and pencil, on which they wrote the names by which she would know them.

Aunty Alice, Aunty Beth, and Aunty Carolyn might have been sisters, so similar were they in shape and size. They weren't related at all, though, Evely would learn. The skinny boy was Donal, and his shorter companion was Nora. They weren't related either, being orphans too, adopted separately. The big man just called himself Uncle.

They took her inside, through warm and comfortable spaces, to a room they explained was entirely hers, with a bed and a small chest and drawers for all her things – and, most wonderful of all, a bookcase containing several volumes she had never read. Timorously, expecting to be halted in the action, she slipped *Ten Little Ghosts* in next to them.

This is your home now, Uncle wrote to her, *if you would care for it to be.*

Evely burst into tears. It was exhausting, waiting for the trap to spring. Tragedy lay ahead, she knew, and these people being so kind to her only made it worse. Maybe they truly meant her no harm – but someone surely did, and what if they were caught up in her fate in some foul and terrible way?

She was inconsolable, so they left her to her tears. When she recovered, she found buttered, fresh-baked bread and a bowl of cooling soup at the foot of her bed. The smell was entirely fabulous, and she ate too quickly for the thought that it might be poisoned to occur to her. It wasn't poisoned, but she fell asleep immediately afterwards, and woke again in the dead of night, kindly tucked into the bed, where she wept again. If Bent Hat Farm was where she would meet the end of her short life, so be it.

Death took its time arriving, and she decided to use that time adapting to her new environment.

Bent Hat Farm comprised a series of hillside terraces, on which grew fruit trees planted in a series of linear orchards. It was also home to goats (not pigs) and several pets, including a seemingly endless number of interchangeable orange cats, who congregated around the main farmhouse, and a truculent dog, who lived with Uncle in a separate ivy-covered cottage towards the base of the valley, where a creek ran in glassy shimmers under a dense thicket of blackberries. Evely quickly learned that, though the dog bared its teeth in great offence if even a single cat approached its patch of the farmyard, all the animals were in fact great friends, and were prone to play together when humans weren't observing them.

Aunties Alice, Beth and Carolyn had full charge of the household and farm, assisted by Donal and Nora, with Uncle chipping in as necessary, when not providing the children with an education. He was a knowledgeable fellow, it turned out, with an interest in all things, and something of a reader himself.

It was this, he told Evely, that had drawn him to her in the orphanage. Any child who chose to read over all other things was undoubtedly of excellent character.

Uncle communicated with her through a mixture of written and signed words. Immediately upon leaving her room and entering into the life of the farm, he had examined her writing and found her skills wanting, which was not surprising. The orphanage provided the barest minimum of education for its charges, and performed no testing for magical ability of any kind. Half of the girls could have been sorcerers, with potential to pen spells that would rival those of the great Sofia Phronesis herself, but no one would ever know. Evely counted it a great fortune that there had been books there at all.

Together, she and Uncle devised a

language of gestures and signs that they shared with the others. He was quick to laugh at his own mistakes, a trait Evely had never before experienced in an adult. This more than anything engendered her trust in him, and she gravitated to his company over the rest, even those her own age. Donal and Nora were perfectly fine, and she learned to work and play with them easily enough, and her three aunts were nothing but engaging in their own ways. But it was Uncle she sought when she made a new discovery in a book, or invented a new sign for a thought she had been struggling to express. Writing remained an important skill, however, to be learned and practised between chores.

It was after one of these exercises that she saw the ghost.

Almost, Evely had forgotten that she was living in a tragedy. So comfortable had she become, with no fewer than three purring cats sharing her bed and the churn of her thoughts momentarily stilled, that the certainty of doom no longer kept her awake more than half the night. The fear had not entirely vanished, however, and it returned to her in moments of uncanny stillness, when a chill breeze reminded

her of the orphanage's many drafts, or the odour of baked potatoes stirred distant memories of her long-lost parents' cooking. In those instances, she felt such sorrow and dread that she wished whatever was coming would stop teasing her with the possibility of contentment, and deliver the full misery that was her due. Waiting only made it worse. The more settled she became in Bent Hat Farm, the more she worried about Uncle and the others, and what harm might come to them because of her.

During one of their afternoon writing classes, with warming spring sunlight pouring through the cottage's square windows, Uncle instructed his three students to write a letter to someone who lived outside the farm. For Evely, that category of people was very small, consisting only of the orphans and matrons at Little Palace Home for Girls, and a handful of neighbouring farmers and their families, none of whom knew the signs she used to communicate. To whom then could she write?

Taking her cue from a book she had recently completed, in which a captive young woman penned a note intended for a would-be rescuer that was only found generations later, stuffed into a crack in her cell wall (thus forming the basis of the novel, against all odds, for no crack could be that large nor any prisoner secretly avail herself with that much paper and ink). Opening her workbook and putting in her mind the image of a reader in some distant future, Evely composed a brief summary of the tragedies that had befallen her, followed by the additional tragedies she was certain would follow, and concluded with the deeply-held desire to meet the author of these tragic affairs, so she could have words with them.

Uncle looked over her workbook with sad eyes, gave her the sign for 'excellent', and then quickly moved on to the next exercise.

Sometimes, Evely's dreams contained sound, muffled and indistinct, more memories of sounds than actual sounds, but in them she heard voices that she liked to imagine belonged to her parents, snatches of music, and the squawk of that distressed bird – which still haunted her after so many years.

Upon waking from such dreams, she felt unsettled and easily upset. Soon after arriving at Bent Hat Farm, she learned on such days to finish her chores as quickly as she could and to take herself into the orchards, there to be alone, with only her writing workbook to jot down thoughts if any came to her. On those mornings, tragedy seemed closest and her life most in danger. Ofttimes, rather than writing a single word, she nodded off in the shade of an apricot or pear tree, and woke in time for tea, refreshed and herself again – although peril was never far from her thoughts.

On one such afternoon, early in spring, she woke from her restorative nap to find an unknown man strolling along the terrace immediately below her.

He was short, slightly plump, and wore a cloth cap that neither failed to conceal his baldness nor protected the sun-reddening skin of his ears and neck. His clothes were worn and patched in places; his shoes scuffed. One heel hung loose and soundlessly flapped with every step. In his left hand he held a notebook, curled up in a leather thong; in his right, a pair of round, wire-rimmed spectacles. As she watched, he stopped to examine the trunk of a nearby tree, raising his spectacles to do so, then unrolled the notebook, produced a much-nibbled pencil from within, and scribbled with a hasty hand what he had observed.

Nodding, he rolled up the notebook, took off his spectacles, and resumed his stroll.

Alarmed, Evely sat upright, thinking to run to find Uncle to draw attention to the intruder as soon as he was safely past. She must have made a sound – as she often did without knowing, being unable to hear her own movements – for he stopped, turned, and looked up at her with a startled expression.

'Hello there,' he said in a voice that was perfectly audible. 'Who might you be?'

Now she leapt to her feet, crying out in surprise and raising her workbook between them like a shield. Oddly – and alarmingly – her own voice remained silent. As did the birds, the wind, and the creek below. All the world was as silent as ever . . . except for him.

'Are you quite all right?' he asked, putting his glasses back on and peering at her with magnified eyes.

'Why can I hear you?' she asked, still unable to hear anything she herself said. Then: 'Oh – I must be dreaming!'

'Must you?' The man tilted his head. 'Why?'

She shook her head. Why explain the rules of a dream to the dream? That seemed entirely pointless.

It was then that Donal and Nora appeared

at the end of her terrace. Their hands moved, asking if anything was wrong.

She tucked her workbook under one arm and signed back that she was only dreaming, that when she woke up she would help them milk the goats. Not that she needed to tell them that, she said. They were part of the dream, too.

Donal and Nora exchanged a glance of such perplexity that she questioned her own certainty. What if she wasn't dreaming?

She turned to the man, who was busily scribbling in his notebook, barely taking his eyes off her to do so.

'Who are you?' she asked.

'Who are you?' he asked again.

Donal's hands moved out of the corner of her eyes. He was asking her who she was talking to.

'I think I understand,' said the man. 'You're deaf. But you can hear me. How odd!'

Odder still was that Donal and Nora apparently couldn't see him.

Evely felt the world shake on its axis. Here, a man she could impossibly hear; there, Donal and Nora as silent as always. Was she now insane?

Was this the tragedy she had long awaited?

'I'm not talking to anyone,' she called back

to Donal and Nora, using her voice rather than her hands, because they would find that easier to understand. Maybe then they would leave her alone with whatever was occurring to her, and go safely somewhere else. 'I'll be in soon.'

They left, casting uncertain glances behind them. When Evely was as confident as she could be that they were out of earshot, she turned back to the trespasser.

'Are you a ghost?' she hissed.

'Not the last time I checked,' he said, glancing down at himself. 'Is that how I seem to you?'

'You seem real,' she said, 'but you can't be.'

'That's a sound definition of a ghost, to be fair.' He indicated the slope between them. 'May I join you?'

'No – stay there.' She backed away, raising her workbook defensively again. 'What do you want?'

'I'm not sure,' he said, looking around him. 'You might say that I am exploring. Seeking. Finding, perhaps. What do I call you?'

'Go explore somewhere else. There's nothing for you here.'

'Oh, I disagree quite strongly!' His smile

flashed brilliantly, and he took off his cap and bowed. 'It's my great pleasure to meet you, my dear.'

'Why?'

'Because you are so fascinating,' he said, replacing his cap. 'And you know what they say about ghosts, don't you? In order to get rid of them, you have to give them what they want.'

'I've never heard that.'

'Well, it's true of some ghosts, I'm sure. Maybe it'll be true of me. Isn't it worth a try?'

'What do you want?' she asked again.

'I think . . . No, yes, I am positive. What I want is to get to know you. Let's chat a while, shall we? Nothing more.'

'And then you'll go?'

'I will certainly try to.' Uncertainty replaced curiosity on his mobile features. 'To be frank, I'm not entirely clear how I came to be here at all, but now I am, we might as well make the most of the time we have together, don't you think?'

He beamed again, and for all her suspicion and fears, she felt herself ease into acceptance. Maybe he meant to murder her, or worse. That was exactly the kind of thing that happened in a tragedy, and if her time had come, why fight it? It would be over at last, and this way no one else could be harmed.

'All right,' she said, lowering her workbook.

With more enthusiasm than grace, slipping twice in the process, he clambered up the hillside to her level.

'Well,' he said, dusting himself down, 'here we are.'

'Yes,' she said. There they were. 'What now?'

'Perhaps we will stroll. Away from your friends, so they don't interrupt us again. I can see that they upset you, although I couldn't understand what they were saying with their hands. Such a clever way of conversing across a distance! I must make a note of it.' He walked as he talked, and she was drawn alongside him, as though by invisible string. 'While we are strolling, perhaps you will tell me why you went so easily from thinking me a dream to thinking me a ghost. Have you seen ghosts before?'

'No,' she said. 'But I've read about them, in stories.'

'You read stories? I'm pleased to hear that. One must be careful of stories, of course; not everything in them is true.'

'I know that,' she said.

'And yet,' he said with a wink, 'a ghost. Or not? Let me know when you decide.'

'Ghosts are just . . . the sort of thing that could happen to me, that's all.'

'Why? Because you're deaf?'

'No, though that's part of it.'

She felt compelled to explain more fully because his curiosity was palpable, and maybe because she wanted him to know that, if he was the harbinger of her imminent demise, she was onto him.

Or perhaps it was simply a welcome change to get these thoughts out of her head. Dream or no dream, she could voice her fears to him in a way she couldn't to Uncle and the others. She didn't want them to think her unhappy with them, when the exact opposite was true: her happiness made what was certain to come all the more painful to her.

'My life is a tragedy,' she began.

'I am familiar with tragedies,' he said. 'Please, continue.'

She explained in as much detail as she could bear. Her parents. Her deafness. The orphanage. The long years of waiting for the metaphorical, or perhaps literal, axe to fall.

'And now you're here,' she said to him. 'If I'm not dreaming, you must be a ghost, come to deliver me to my fate. Or something like a ghost. What else could you be?'

'What else, indeed?'

By now they had traversed three of the tree-lined terraces, back and forth, and were at the top of the farm, well out of sight of the main house.

'Tell me about the book under your arm,' he said.

She looked down. 'Oh, that's just my workbook, for writing exercises Uncle gives me.' She didn't mention the thoughts she wrote for herself.

'So, you are a writer as well as a reader! How remarkable.'

'I don't write stories,' she said. 'Just words.'

'Words have power,' he said, with a gleam in his gaze that hadn't been there before. 'That's how a sorcerer weaves their magic, you know. Say a spell and it's gone in an instant; write one down and it might last forever!'

'Uncle isn't a sorcerer.'

'I'm not suggesting that. Have you been tested?'

She shook her head. All children by the age of ten were supposed to sit a written test to ascertain if they possessed the spark that enabled someone to work magic. 'No one cared about that in the orphanage. As long as we behaved and did our chores –'

'Did you behave and do your chores?'

'Yes, of course.' That, she had learned, was the best way to be left alone, so she could get back to her books.

'I imagine so,' he said. 'You strike me as a very serious young person. Do you ever smile?'

'What's there to smile at? I'm in a tragedy!'

'Ah, yes, I had forgotten that. Tell me again why?'

'I have no parents! I can't hear anything!' Exasperated, she waved her notebook for emphasis. Hadn't he been paying attention?

'Is that better than being a ghost?'

'How would I know? You're the ghost.'

'I thought ghosts were supposed to be of dead people. I'm not dead. One moment I was at my desk, working, and the next I was here. I suppose I could have died suddenly and without feeling anything; one could imagine such a thing quite easily, for the purposes of a . . .' He cleared his throat. 'Well, anyway. If this is death, I must say it appears rather pleasant.'

He looked about him, and so did she. It was a beautiful day, to be sure, redolent with greens and warmer colours. The orchard was in full, fragrant blossom, each terrace displaying a different kind of flower. Fat yellow bees bumbled through the air, ignoring the humans in their haste to collect all available pollen. Above them, the sky was deepest blue, punctuated by only a handful of cloudy commas. On a terrace below, the dog was feigning outrage at some imagined indignity and thoroughly enjoying itself chasing a brace of orange cats back and forth, eyes wild with delight. As Evely watched, the cats rushed the dog all at once, and the animals tumbled in a rowdy ball down the terraces and into the blackberry bushes. A second later, they emerged in a sodden state, shaking water from their fur in clouds of rainbow spray.

Despite herself, Evely laughed.

'That's better,' said the ghost.

She looked at him, startled.

'Do you know what I think?' he asked her, then proceeded to tell her anyway, without waiting for her answer. 'I think you have been waiting for something, but it isn't a great tragedy. That would be a terribly mean thing to give you, after all you've been through. How you survived, I can only imagine. But you did! Through hard work and by pursuing the things you loved, in books, and by being a good enough person that no one thought ill of you, if they genuinely thought of you at all. So, when your Uncle met you, he took you in – not out of a meanness of spirit, but because you deserve better. And here you are now, still working hard, still being a good person, and, having learned that only bad things happen to you, seeing only the possibility of bad things around you. When in fact you are surrounded by wonderful things! What I think you have been waiting for,' he concluded, 'is permission to change your story.'

'But,' she said, feeling overwhelmed by and aghast from all the things he was telling her. She had never heard anyone say the like – because she couldn't hear, and no signs existed yet that might do the job.

'How?' she concluded.

'You want to know how one might change one's story,' he said, 'as if that isn't the golden question. Would that we all knew! Even I . . .'

His joyous look fell away. 'I will confess that I have suffered a tragic turn of late. I would spare you the details of endless hours whittled away with nothing to show for them, of eager hands grasping at me for what I have not to give, of fruitless quests in search of inspiration that led ever nowhere . . . But I am out of that nowhere place, somehow, and here with you, now – and I feel a resurgence of spirit that I had come to fear had abandoned me for eternity. Miracles happen, my dear. Let that give you hope!'

Evely didn't know what to say to that. Hope wasn't something she knew how to feel.

The ghost unfolded his notebook, wrote something in it, and closed it again.

'You've been scribbling in there as long as I've been watching you,' she said. 'What are you writing?'

His expression was almost sly. 'I have a suggestion for you,' he said, 'one that might resolve several mysteries at once. I will show you my book if you show me yours.'

Instinctively, Evely clutched her papers closer to her chest, but then she relented. There was nothing special about her exercises and random thoughts. She would happily hand them over in exchange for a glimpse into that well-thumbed leather volume. The writing of a ghost had to be interesting indeed!

'All right,' she said, proffering the workbook and accepting his in return.

The leather was even softer than it looked, and the pages as smooth as cream.

She flipped through them, glimpsing a blur of words and drawings, many of them crossed out or connected with arrows. Inky fingerprints and smudges marred every page, and here and there corners were turned over. This was no printed tome to be kept on a shelf and admired only for its spine. This was a living, changeable book undergoing alterations every time it was opened.

Coming nearly to the end of the volume, she reached a stretch of empty pages. Stopping there, she flipped backwards. There were many more crossings-out near that point, evidence of frustration and despair.

Then a page of unaltered descriptions – in which she was shocked to recognise Bent Hat Farm, in all its colour and life. He had been taking note of everything he saw, for reasons she could not imagine. 'The most glorious location,' he wrote. 'Anything could happen here, to anyone!'

On the very last page before they turned blank, were two lines.

The first said: 'What is her name?'

That was crossed out, and replaced just moments ago with: 'What is your name?'

She looked up at the ghost, who was looking right back at her over the open pages of her workbook.

'Well?' he asked. 'Will you tell me?'

She didn't see any harm in it, or in him. If the ghost had wanted to hurt her, he could have done so already, many times over.

'Evely,' she said. 'My name is Evely Vyle.'

'That is a fine name, a fine name indeed. Thank you. May I?' He held out his hand for his notebook, and she gave it to him. Using her workbook as a prop, he wrote her name down in the notebook, then wrapped it up again, safe and sound.

'Perhaps,' he said, 'it's time I left. I have come at last to realise that I am tired of tragedies, and now I have other work to get on with. Will you let me go, Evely?'

'Of course,' she said, not knowing what she had to do with it.

'One thing before I leave, though,' he said. 'Do have your uncle take you to be tested. I think that's for the best.'

So saying, he reached into her notebook and tore out a single page. She gasped and reached out to stop him, but before she could, with swift, deft motions he tore that page into pieces and scattered them high into the air.

Her eyes instinctively followed their trajectories as they rose and fell like petals around her, white with a hint of lines where words had once been, now gone as though they had never existed.

When her gaze came back down, the ghost was gone, and her workbook lay on the grass, open.

Angrily, she snatched it up to examine the damage.

The destroyed page was the one that had contained her letter, which she remembered well.

If I could only meet the author of these tragic affairs, she had written, *I would surely have words with them!*

Amazed, she looked about her, but he was gone. Evely was alone apart from the bees and the birds, and, calling the bedraggled dog to heel with words she couldn't hear, Uncle.

He strode along the terrace towards her. Seeing her notice him, he waved, and cheerfully signed, 'Haven't you done enough thinking for one day?'

She smiled, and ran to meet him.

Awakening

Sophie Masson

Kate tethered her horse Sammy to a tree and headed up the hill, towards the summit and its jumble of rocks. She liked to sit there, up in the wind, looking down at the scenes below her. If she looked one way, there was their farm, huddled in its belt of trees, as if it were hiding. There were the slowly-moving mobs of cattle picking their way delicately over the coarse grass to try and find something at least a bit juicier. There was the farm quad bike, bouncing like a noisy mad insect through rocks and sticks. She could hear, faintly in the distance, the rooster crowing, and the whining sound of the postman's van as he made his rounds along the rural roads. Maybe the van would come splashing to where the creek bustled along its way over the crossing that led to their farm from the road. Or maybe not.

But if she looked the other way, all she could see was the sweeping, grey-green forest, sliding over the bones of the hills like dense fur on a huge animal. Unlike the hill, it wasn't part of their farm, it was part of their elderly neighbour's, who didn't really farm anymore. Actually, he only kept the bit around his house tidy, and the rest was just left to go back to nature. The only animal he still kept was his old dog, Toby. But he didn't mind local people going into the forest, and Kate and her older brother Jamie had gone walking there many times, before he'd gone off to university in the city to study ecology. Sometimes they'd camped overnight, and watched the stars rise above the trees, and in the early morning, they saw all kinds of animals – kangaroos, platypus, echidnas, birds of all kinds. There were animals like that on their own farm too, but not in such numbers. And once or twice, they'd even seen a dingo or two, which were vermin, according to some of the local people, but the old man wouldn't hear of shooting them. 'They've been here much longer than I have,' he'd say, and then people shook their heads and muttered darkly that any dingo seen on their land would soon see the wrong end of a gun!

Still, Kate thought, those neighbours had sheep, and sometimes dingoes went for the young ones. Dingoes rarely went for cattle. They were too big, too feisty.

But now the old man had died, not long after his faithful Toby. Apart from the dog, he'd lived alone and had no close family. And the distant cousin who'd inherited the property had immediately sold it. Bulldozers were coming, to rip the trees away and strew them like careless giant's leftovers all over the ground. There would be sap everywhere, like blood, and the sad dead leaves and branches scattered. The bones of the hill would show. The sharp rocky bones that had been so well covered for centuries.

Then the new owners would start building the flash tourist complex they'd planned, complete with swimming pools and log cabins. They'd clear a big patch of forest for that, the trees chopped down, piled up and burnt, smoke drifting over the countryside for kilometres.

'I know, it's terrible, but what can we do?' Kate and Jamie's mother had said. 'It's not ours and it's all legal. They are supposedly adhering to the rules, so there's nothing we can do.'

'There's got to be something,' Jamie had said, clenching his fists. But their father had simply replied, shading his eyes as he looked over at the forest, 'I tried to raise it with the local council, but they weren't interested. All they want is more tourists spending money in the region.' He'd sighed. 'It's difficult to blame them. Times are hard, at the moment.'

It was true. Farmers were struggling, the local town was struggling. There were empty shops, people packing up and leaving. That had happened to one of Kate's classmates, whose parents owned a café in town. They'd closed it and moved back to where they'd originally come from.

Kate looked at her watch. She would happily have sat there longer, but it was time to go. She climbed down the hill and untethered Sammy, who'd been peacefully eating the bits of grass he could find. She swung into the saddle and turned his nose for home. It was definitely lunchtime now, her stomach was announcing. And Jamie would have arrived home off the train. Her mother had made their favourite for lunch, homemade sausage rolls! They were a real treat. Besides, it was winter, the air crisp and cold, so it wouldn't be too hot to go back up the hill after lunch if they wanted to.

But Jamie had other ideas. 'Never mind the hill, we can climb that any time. I'm going for a walk in the forest. Want to come? The bulldozers are starting work tomorrow. It's our last chance, Katie.'

'Okay,' she said, although the idea of seeing it all for the last time felt a bit ghoulish, like touching a dying person's hand.

'The bulldozers haven't arrived yet but people are working there already, in the forest,' their mother said. 'There'll be chainsaws, vehicles. So be careful, and don't do anything stupid.'

Jamie shrugged. Kate could tell that he wanted to do something, to shout things, to stop it all.

But Kate knew there was nothing that could stop it now. It didn't matter what any of them said or did. It was just the way it was.

They didn't take the horses this time. Jamie drove the old ute on a back road, going a different way into the forest. 'Just in case', he'd said. Despite what Mum had said, there was no sound of chainsaws or vehicles in the air, and they didn't see anyone. There was no sign of damage at first, and it was very quiet, but a kind of roaring quiet, like the sound of the sea. The leafy canopy way above their heads swished with a sighing sound, and under their feet, the dead leaves and bark squelched underfoot. Katie and Jamie didn't talk, just walked and walked, their feet making hardly any sound. No animals appeared on the path, not surprisingly, as you rarely saw them in the middle of the day. But there wasn't even a faint rustle in the undergrowth, and no bird calls, and that was much more unusual. Kate could feel a kind of slow dread creeping over her as they walked. The forest felt – different. Before, she'd always felt at home here. Not today. She began to wish they could just turn back.

'Jamie,' she said, hesitantly, 'can we . . .' and then she stopped. Suddenly, shockingly, it was there in front of them. A place where the strangers had already been, for sure. It had once been a small natural clearing, a spot where she and Jamie had often sat and had picnics. The trees grew less thick here, there was a sunlit patch of native grass, dotted, in spring, with lots of tiny flowers. Now, the small clearing had become a big raw space, the sun beating down mercilessly on a devastated scene, the grass crushed, and neighbouring trees cut down into a mess of broken limbs, of crushed leaves, chain-sawed stumps still red and raw. But there was no one around.

And no vehicles to be seen or heard, either. Not even tyre tracks, because it hadn't rained for quite a while, so there was no mud for tyres to make imprints in.

She couldn't speak, just stood there looking at it. But Jamie growled, 'Why? Why did they do this?'

She shook her head. 'I don't know.'

'Maybe it's where they're going to build their headquarters or something. But couldn't they choose another spot? Why this one? It used to be so beautiful here.'

'Maybe they didn't see it like that. They just thought it was a nice flat spot, just right for building.' Kate's voice was a whisper.

'They still could have chosen another spot,' Jamie said, his voice softened now, as he looked sadly at the torn-up mess around him.

'Yes,' said Kate. There was nothing she could say to really express how she felt. Wandering around the devastated space, she spotted a big humped outcrop of grey rock that had been hidden under the trees before and covered with deep green velvety moss. Now its sheltering trees were gone, its covering of moss ripped off as the trees fell around it. You could see the shape of it, low at one end, humped in the middle, tapering off again at the end, with bits of rock protruding on either side. She sat down on its hump, feeling tired all of a sudden. Not so surprising, though. They had been walking for hours, after all.

The rock didn't feel as harsh and gritty as she'd expected, but it was very cold. She could feel the deep coldness of it right through her jeans, and couldn't help a small shiver. But the sun was warm on her face so she stayed there, one hand on the rock, thinking of the long ages it had lain hidden under its covering of moss, in the deep shade of the trees and their overhanging branches. This might be the first time for hundreds or maybe even thousands of years that it had been exposed to the sun . . .

Jamie was walking around, taking pictures with his phone, recording little videos, and still she sat there, her mind drifting. Then, he came to stand by her and started to talk about what they might be able to do, about emails to write, and phone calls to make, and people to contact. But Kate just sat, one hand still on the rock, her mind quite blank. At last, Jamie noticed. 'What's the matter, Kate? You look really weird.'

I do feel weird. As if I'm not there, as if I'm fading, somehow, she thought. Aloud, she

said, 'I expect I'm just a bit tired, the walk this morning and now seeing this.' She gestured around. 'It's making me feel . . . you know, not good.'

'I know,' Jamie said. 'I don't like it here anymore, either. Let's head off. We can go down to the creek, rest there for a bit and walk back home the other way.'

With an effort, Kate got up, the coldness of the rock feeling almost like a living thing grasping with sharp claws into her flesh. Taking a last look at it and the desolation around it as they walked away, she thought, suddenly, it looks a bit like a lizard. Like a huge grey lizard, only made of stone. Then she shrugged, and followed Jamie.

This part of the creek was a favourite place of theirs. It was different to their part of the creek, near the crossing, because it felt like a little world all on its own. All through their childhood, Jamie and Kate had built dams there, caught tadpoles, and simply sat in the grass, watching water skippers and the odd snake coming down to drink. Now they just sat there, quietly, looking at the water glittering with sequins of light in the sun, taking it all in for the last time. This part of the creek would be closed off to them soon. Jamie was not talking anymore. Kate was glad of that.

She didn't feel like talking, just rather like fixing it all in her mind, so that she'd never lose it, even when it was all lost to them. It felt solemn, like this was really their last goodbye to the forest.

But soon it was time to leave. Night fell quickly in winter and the shadows were lengthening. And so they walked out of the forest for the last time.

Tomorrow, the bulldozers would be there. In the clearing they'd made already, the great iron beasts with their human keepers would begin work in earnest. Tomorrow, the sun would be up, once again warming all cold-blooded creatures.

In the clearing, in the cold night, the stone lizard waited. It was still drowsy from centuries of sleep. But when the sun rose, it would awaken, and remember it had not had a feed for a very, very long time.

It had waited long, and patiently. One more night would merely sharpen its hunger.

The Clockmaker's Cat

Trinity Ryan

Every morning the cat awoke first, licking at the clockmaker's eyes and meowing to say, 'Morning! It's morning!'

The clockmaker would blink his eyes open with a laugh and reply, 'Good morning, it's wonderful to see you too!'

He'd give the cat a snuggle and add, 'All right then, let's get up.'

They would jump out of bed together, though the cat was always much faster, running ahead to the kitchen to await breakfast.

'You win again, so yours comes first,' said the clockmaker every time, smiling widely as he gave the cat a large helping of breakfast. The cat was wise and would only eat what was good for it, so it was best to put a little extra in the bowl just in case. You never know when a cat might need more energy for the day ahead, so best to be sure.

Changing over the water bowl as the

cat nibbled happily, the clockmaker then went about making himself some porridge. He ate his breakfast with the cat usually curled up on his feet, though sometimes on his shoulders if the porridge smelled extra delicious that morning.

When the porridge was finished, the cat would run back to the kitchen for a little more of its own breakfast. The clockmaker would follow, washing his bowl in the sink as the cat munched away.

As the sun rose in the sky, the cat would rub around the clockmaker's ankles, tempting him down the long dark hallway to the workshop. The old man's eyes were not as sharp as they had once been, especially in the dark, but the pitter-patter of the cat's footsteps ahead was enough to guide him.

When the clockmaker pulled down on the door handle, the cat would give a gentle push on the door, swinging it open as the smell of old wood mixed with new polish wafted out.

In here, the sun danced through the windows, light playing upon the benchtops. It was a sharp contrast to the dingy hall before. Tools lay scattered over the workbench from the work of the day before; old cogs which never quite fit lay strewn

across the floor amongst the sawdust.

But there was a strange sense of cosiness to it all; a warmth in the clocks waiting to be repaired as they sat in a neat line.

The only thing that was missing from his workshop was a completed clock of his own design, for he had given all of them away. It had been worth every minute he had spent delicately carving each piece just to see the face of the receiver light up at such a gift.

Perhaps that was why they were his best works, he thought, as he sat down, ready to pick up his tools again, the cat settling down on his lap. Something of the person stays with you; all you need to do is put that in the clock.

Every day the clockmaker sat in his workshop, sometimes repairing, sometimes designing, while the cat sometimes curled up on his lap, or played with small pieces of wood as they rolled across the floor.

It was a peaceful life, and the clockmaker enjoyed it.

As the clockmaker worked, the light began to grow dim. He noticed the cat rubbing around his ankles again.

'All right, I'll just finish this bit,' he chuckled, but there was no use arguing with the cat who jumped up onto his workbench, nuzzling his face and meowing. 'Okay, you're right. Work is done for today.'

Together they left the workshop, the cat running ahead down the hall to the kitchen where the clockmaker fetched some dinner for them both.

As the clockmaker ate, the cat purred behind him. After washing his plate, he would notice the cat sitting outside the bathroom door and would remember to run a bath.

When he came out, the cat greeted him at

the door, so he put on his warmest dressing gown and sat in his big comfy chair.

The cat jumped up and cuddled the clockmaker, digging its claws in a little through his dressing gown. The clockmaker didn't mind, though it did prickle slightly. He patted the cat, becoming sleepier and sleepier as he did.

Tired from his work, the clockmaker was easily encouraged by the cat's snuggling to brush his teeth and go to bed not long after. As he pulled the blankets over himself, he called out, 'Time for bed.'

The cat would be there in an instant, leaping up onto the bed. The clockmaker could feel the cat tucking him in and drifted off to sleep peacefully to the loud rumbling of its purr.

The cat was particularly happy tonight because the clockmaker had finished a clock. That meant that while the man was sleeping the cat would pitter-patter down to the workshop and let itself in. Though the door was not as easy to open without the clockmaker, the cat managed to pull down on the lever with its paws, leaning on the door at the same time to push it open.

The cat leapt up onto the workshop bench, carefully examining the newly repaired clock before giving the pendulum a tiny push to make it start swinging. It sat and watched for a little while as the pendulum swayed back and forth hypnotically. Then it ran quietly back to the clockmaker's side and cuddled there purring until morning, leaving the clock still ticking in the workshop.

The clockmaker never quite understood how all this worked, mostly as he was asleep through it all, but he never questioned the cat. He just thought it must know something he did not and was quite content to have things working as they were.

Things continued this way, fixing clocks and making clocks, until one day a man with far too much money came to the town where the clockmaker lived.

He had heard of the clockmaker and his skill at designing clocks, and now wanted one for his daughter. Word had travelled with the rich man, and both he and his daughter were well known for being cruel and heartless; they were mean to everyone they met and so there were few left who liked them.

Still, people had to do what the rich man told them to, as he could afford things that others could not, and had paid stronger men to do his bidding. These men knocked on the door of the clockmaker.

At first the clockmaker was pleased that others had spoken so highly of his clocks; however, his mood quickly began to change as he heard more of this man and his daughter.

The rich man had bought her everything she had ever wanted, and she had become selfish as a result. Unable to appreciate the gifts put before her, she would only turn up her nose or break them. The rich man would blame it on whoever had made them, ruining their business so they could not work.

The clockmaker tried to ask the men how he would be able to accomplish what so many others before him could not, but they did not seem to care. They then told the clockmaker that he would be paid well, however he must stay in the workshop at the rich man's house until the clock was done.

But when the clockmaker told them he could not go, regardless of how much money they offered, the men only laughed harshly at him, thinking he must be joking.

He objected, even tried flailing his weak arms at them as they dragged him away from his home, but there was nothing he could do.

As they pulled him from his doorstep, he turned to see the cat. Crouched against the wall, terrified, there was pure panic in its eyes at not knowing who these strangers were, or why they were taking the clockmaker away.

'I'll be back soon,' the clockmaker told the cat, though he could not know himself if it was true. 'It's going to be all right.'

Scraping his feet on the gravel footpath as they went, the men shoved him into the back seat of a long black car and drove away.

The car drove for a long time. It seemed to be hours, though the clockmaker couldn't be certain. It was dark when they arrived at the rich man's workshop and the clockmaker was pushed inside without a word.

He found a switch in the darkness and a light flickered on, revealing a gleaming array of brand new and freshly sharpened tools. Untouched wood awaited his hand, yet he could not feel the urge to carve or cut it, nor any ideas ticking over in his mind.

Still, he thought, the sooner I start the

sooner my work here is done, and I can get home to the cat.

So, he tried to settle in and begin cutting the wood. All night he exhausted himself sawing and sanding, but an uneasy feeling had crept in and stayed with him.

Faster he worked, and by morning sawdust and splinters covered the workshop floor, but still there was no clock. There were not even cogs to show for his night's work, just broken pieces of wood and a deep uneasiness that was only spreading further. The clockmaker kept telling himself that the faster he worked the sooner he would see his cat, but even that knowledge was not enough.

Exhausted and aching, the clockmaker sent a message to the rich man asking if he could speak with his daughter. He hoped that knowing what she liked might give him an idea for the clock.

The meeting was arranged, her father standing over her as she spoke.

'What's your favourite time?' the clockmaker asked the little girl, who could not have been more than four.

'Never,' she replied, blunt and rude.

'And what's your favourite thing in all

the world?' he persisted, trying to force a smile.

'Kicking people who waste my time.' She grinned, flashing sharp white teeth and looking as though she might be getting a foot prepared already.

The clockmaker was shocked. He looked up at her father, expecting him to scold her, but instead the rich man was smiling smugly. The clockmaker wondered if this had been their plan all along, but still there was nothing he could do.

He went back to the workshop as confused as ever and spent the day carving the wood by hand, whittling away at it with a small knife as he tried to think of an idea. What gift was there for someone who had been taught to hate everything; to take everything for granted?

He could feel the girl's hatred already beginning to swallow him, too. He knew he had to escape and wanted nothing more than to see the cat again and feel its soft fur against his face, but he could not see how.

Already dizzy from not sleeping the night before, the clockmaker tried to lie down in a pile of sawdust and get some rest. Just as slumber was closing in on him, he thought he could hear something.

At first it was quiet, as if far off in the distance, but the noise became clearer and louder as he listened. It sounded just like the meowing of the cat. Surely it couldn't be, but the clockmaker knew that sound.

The more he questioned it the more distinct it became, until in excitement the clockmaker jumped up, wide awake again now, scrambling for the light switch as fast as he could.

He looked around, searching everywhere, even checking outside the door in the cold and whipping night wind, but found nothing.

The meowing only grew louder and more desperate as he searched the workshop, convinced by now that the cat must be nearby.

'Where are you?' he called, but the meowing continued, echoing inside his head as he tore the room apart, throwing the tools and whittled wood about.

'Where are you?' The clockmaker was sobbing by now, tears streaming down his face as he finally gave up, collapsing in a heap on the sawdust. The meowing went on, becoming still louder and more urgent.

The clockmaker felt as though his mind was searing hot, sweating, and swelling up inside his skull, but still the meowing would not stop, a deafening ring in his ears.

'Please come out!' the clockmaker begged, but still he could not see the cat anywhere. Lying on the sawdust-covered concrete floor to cool his face, the clockmaker cried in misery as he longed to see the cat again.

When the clockmaker awoke sometime later, shivering and aching everywhere, the rich man had sent his men to check his progress.

All they saw was the sawdust and broken pieces scattered across the floor. Barely able to get a word of sense from the clockmaker, the men beat and kicked him. They shouted at him that he was lazy and demanded he try harder. Still the clockmaker could not respond, so they left him in the rich man's workshop, shouting more orders behind them.

The clockmaker did not know how often they came, the hours seeming to drift and swerve before him. There was no cat to wake him, or remind him to eat. Only the men who kept coming to see what work he had done, abusing him violently and shouting at him.

In between their visits he was haunted by the meowing of the cat, always getting louder and more urgent.

After some time, the men dragged him

before the rich man again.

The rich man was ignorant, yet even he could see that the clockmaker had changed. No longer a cheerful and vibrant man, he was now hunched over and trembling, clawing at his own skin as he muttered.

'Quiet!' roared the rich man, and the clockmaker's mutter fell to a whisper.

'You are clearly not in any state to make a clock for anyone, let alone my daughter. I cannot fathom why they recommended you. Hurry up and get well enough to work.'

The clockmaker was sent back to the rich man's workshop, but he could not get well without the cat.

Though he attempted to carve the wood into something, anything that would get him out of here, no clock would come.

Still he heard the meowing of the cat echoing, sometimes near him and sometimes slipping away, but he was never able to find it. Unable to feed it, give it water, comfort or cuddle each other. Always meowing.

Losing track of time completely, unsure if it was even day or night outside, the clockmaker's hands cramped and would not carve.

When they came for him, he was huddled under a workbench, attempting to pick up a carving knife in vain.

They dragged him before the rich man

again, but he had lost patience with the clockmaker and no longer cared. With an irritated sneer, he waved his hand and dismissed him.

The men threw him into the long black car again, worry still eating away at the clockmaker. He pulled at his hair and clawed at his skin, teeth chattering, as the nights before still haunted him, the desperate meowing of the cat still ringing in his ears.

But then the car pulled up to the clockmaker's driveway and he was shoved out again onto his own front lawn.

The men shouted after him that the rich man would be back if he was ever well enough to work again and that his business would go broke now, but the clockmaker did not even allow their words to sink in.

As soon as he fell to the grass he was up again, running as fast as he could towards the house, towards that little shape in the window he recognised so well.

Fumbling with the front door in his haste, he could hear a little 'meow', not echoing within his head any longer but instead coming distinctly through the door.

He called back, 'I'm coming!' as his shaking hands struggled with the key, then closed the door behind him in a hurry as the cat ran over and began rubbing against him, purring and licking his eyes all at once.

'I missed you too,' the clockmaker cried, patting the cat all over as tears of relief streamed down his face. 'But it's all right now, I'm home.'

The next morning, the clockmaker had tried to stay in bed, but the cat was licking his eyes and it was difficult to resist it.

'Okay, breakfast time it is then.'

He fed the cat, but as it nibbled, the clockmaker snuck back to bed. He could feel the cat jump up onto the bed just as he was drifting back to sleep. He didn't wake up again until it was licking his eyes and meowing for its dinner.

'Okay then, dinner it is.' The clockmaker rose and fetched the cat some dinner. Noticing he was hungry too; he made some food for himself and ate it as the cat purred behind him.

When he saw the cat sitting outside the bathroom, he remembered he needed a bath, after which he went to sit in his big comfy chair. The cat hopped onto his lap and snuggled him, seeming to purr even louder than usual.

The clockmaker was soon as tired as if

he had worked a full day, so before long he brushed his teeth, and they went to bed.

He had only half called out 'Time for bed' before he was drifting off to sleep, relief to be home washing over him, the cat tucking him in as it purred.

———

Day by day, things became easier and returned to normal for the clockmaker and the cat. They ate, cuddled, and slept together. Yet an uneasiness still lingered with the clockmaker, preventing him from walking down the hall to the workshop.

The cat meowed and rubbed around his ankles, telling him he should, but there was a fear sitting with him still. Though he tried to push it out of his mind, perhaps it was the rich man's words condemning his work he worried about. Broken clocks began to pile up as his customers waited.

Yet each day with the help of the cat, the clockmaker healed a little more. As his body and mind started to tick back into action, so did his imagination.

One day, he had an idea. Almost running to the workshop that day after breakfast, the cat purred in excitement as the workshop door opened.

Laying out his tools and getting straight

to work, the time flew by as the clockmaker carved the pieces.

Sanding each to perfection, he used the following weeks to paint them and piece them together. Finally, the night came where he had done as much as he could and left it to go to bed.

Again, the cat rose in the night, travelling down the hall to the workshop where it found the clock. Giving the pendulum a push, it watched as it swung into action.

The clock was shaped like a house, open at the front so the cat could see inside. There was a tiny man sleeping on a bed, and a small wooden cat curled up by his side.

As it stared, the wooden cat rose, putting its head to the man's sleeping face. They both moved from the bed together on the cogs beneath them, travelling to a kitchen that reminded the cat of its own.

The cat continued to watch in awe as it realised what it was seeing, the clock copying its own life.

It stayed, mesmerised by the clock, and the skill and care put into it. Hungry for breakfast, it knew it should wake the clockmaker soon, but maybe for now it would just let him rest.

By now the cat could see the sunlight beginning to peek over the horizon, so it tore its gaze from the clock and snuck back to bed. It had barely even licked the clockmaker before he was awake and getting up.

For once he was in the kitchen even before the cat. 'Bit slow today, but you can still have yours first.'

The cat nibbled happily as it thought of the clock.

After his porridge, the clockmaker made his way down the long hall carrying a great big empty box, the cat rubbing against his ankles.

The clockmaker checked that it was working, though he still had no idea how, and the cat took one last admiring look.

Then, the clockmaker placed the clock inside the box, packing it safely with a little note.

As he carried it to the front door he looked down at the cat. 'Now don't worry. This time I really will be back soon. I'm just going to the post office.'

He gave the cat a pat as he left, and the cat nuzzled his hand affectionately, as if to say, 'See you shortly.'

As soon as the clock was at the post office the clockmaker rushed home again, almost running in his eagerness to be back home with the cat.

Once that was done, the clockmaker went back to repairing the long line of clocks waiting for him.

The mornings would come and the cat would wake the clockmaker. Work time would come and the cat would lead him down the hall. Dinner time would come and the cat would insist that work was over for the day.

There was never a shortage of clocks to repair, as the clockmaker's reputation had spread far and wide and people were always very happy with his work.

As life returned to normal, the clockmaker's mind started to tick with ideas again.

'Today,' he said to the cat, 'we might start on a new one.'

The cat purred loudly as they headed down the hall.

At the rich man's house, in the little girl's bedroom, the clock sat high up on a shelf. The rich man's daughter watched as it moved. A wooden cat rose from a wooden bed, waking the little sleeping man.

As the girl watched, she quickly became bored. She had never learnt how to tell the time, and had no interest in watching the clock move. Climbing up the shelves, she grabbed the carved figure of the cat between her chubby fingers, snapping it away from the clock. She then climbed back down the shelves again, taking the cat with her.

The girl played with the wooden figurine for a little while, until the rich man called for her and she tossed it on the floor with a pile of toys as she left the room.

That night, as the rich man lay in bed, he heard a strange noise. Quiet at first, he couldn't make out what it was, so he tried to ignore it. As he tried to sleep, the sound grew louder and more distinct, until the rich man was convinced it was the meowing of a cat.

The meowing became more insistent and frightening, until it was so deafening that it started to hurt. He covered his ears with his hands, but nothing would ever make it stop.

To Go On

Gary Crew

He came to his senses spreadeagled on the beach. Since his head was half buried in sand, he could only open his right eye. Endless yellow dazzled him. He gulped. His mouth was full of grit. His right cheek hurt, scorched by the tropical sun. He heard no sound other than breakers crashing somewhere behind him. His thoughts tumbled, confused as the waves.

Who was he? Where was he?

He was naked. He felt the sun on his backside, burning. His right side, his thigh, his legs, the soles of his bare feet must be exposed. He must have lost his trousers in the surf.

His toes dug into wet sand. Cooling . . .

Without raising his head, he cast his right eye upward. The sand stretched far beyond him, a broad yellow border sloping upward to end in a wall of violent green – jungle. Instinctively he thought to rise, to push up out of the sand, but stopped, a fearful impulse overcoming him. If he moved, if he stood – something – some creature lurking in that green might see him. Even someone. He knew little about this land. He was Scottish, his confused brain recalled, an unschooled deckhand, ignorant of the world.

His mind raced. The ship! His ship! Sailing from Glasgow via Sydney, then up the east coast of Australia. His daydreams of great adventure in the South Seas would come true. He hoped . . .

But, he had been forced to labour – treated little better than a servant, a slave – ordered to clean the cabins, to sweep, to mop, to scrub the decks, empty their piss pots, to eat the scraps thrust at him by that brute, the cook. He had no uniform of blue and white (as he had expected), nor a broad straw hat (as the weather demanded).

Now his memories returned. His ship was a barque, the *Peruvian,* out of Glasgow bound for Calcutta, carrying a crew of twenty-two and three passengers, seeking to expand the trade in Indian silks. And there were three midshipmen, hardly more than deckhands, aged about fourteen. Their ignorance of life, the world, made no difference; they were all considered superior to James – yes, that was his name: James Wilson.

Reaching this realisation, the boy in

the sand felt a tremor course through his naked body. He remembered who he was: a thirteen-year-old runaway now lying on his face in the sands of hell. His mother's face came to him (and the smell of her shortbread), then his father (or the back of his father's hand). He spat grit from his chafed lips: clear out, see the world, he remembered. He was a fool, always had been: at home, in school, on the field with his mates. Jim the Joker they called him, sneering.

(At least that mongrel, his father, did not know where he was. Jim did not write. Jim could not write – and nor would he if he could . . .)

He looked towards the jungle green. What was hidden there? Was it worse than his father's beatings? His father's floggings with the razor strap? His brutality, his shouting, his fists. The rage, the spit, the floggings. And Jim limping away, a small, frail boy, snivelling. Was whatever that jungle held worse? Was it?

He shuddered again, remembering the terror of his father coming home drunk.

He lay still, thinking . . .

Had life on the *Peruvian* been better?

No. And slowly, as through a haze, what had passed returned to him . . .

He had slept below decks. Not with the other boys – the midshipmen. They had their hammocks slung among the cargo. Jim the J, being no more than a deckhand, was bunked beneath them, just above the swill of the bilge. A haven for rats and their attendant fleas.

His hammock was a potato sack strung on ropes knotted to the decking beams above. The sack had never been cleaned of the dirt from the unwashed potatoes. No matter how many times he turned the sack over and beat it, the grime remained. There was no pillow so he cradled the back of his head in his hands. If sleep did come, he was glad since he was exhausted from running hither and thither all day. But some nights he could not sleep. The bilge was swarming with rats. The vermin survived upon the rancid contents of the bilge water, constantly slopping beneath: the natural leakage after such a journey; the waste of the ship, trickling down: vomit, human excreta. And the rats brought fleas. Fleas that bit and itched. Fleas that left sores where Jim scratched. Some nights, when all were asleep (except the lookouts far above), he went up on deck, filled a barrel with buckets of sea water, and sat in

that, rinsing his body, his hair. But the fleas persisted, returning in hordes, nightly.

No one noticed the flea bites, but when the rats themselves came, first nibbling his toenails then, growing adventurous, biting his legs, his arms, the marks were seen.

'He's covered in scabs,' the midshipmen accused.

'Let's wash him...' and they wrapped him in a scrap of sail and threw him overboard, laughing as they dragged him in the wake of the vessel like a sea anchor. Hauling him in, they laughed even louder as they pretended to dry him by chasing him naked about the deck, flicking him with wet ropes. The crew looked on, amused. Nothing was done to stop them and finally, the torture becoming boring, Jim was allowed to crawl away, hiding behind the cage on the rear deck where the cook kept the ship's living pantry: a huddle of scrawny chickens and one miserable sheep.

A few days after his ducking, Jim woke to a raging fever. His mouth parched, his body burning. Tumbling from his bunk he crawled to the upper deck searching for water. Reaching the water barrel, he all but knocked it over in his desperation to find the ladle. Once he drank, twice, three times, all the while coughing and dry retching.

One of the crew saw him, supporting him beneath his arms.

'You right?' he demanded, but Jim could not answer – rather he shoved the sailor away in his desire to drink still more.

'You sick, mate?' the sailor asked, attracting the attention of the loitering cook.

'He's a puny runt, that one.' The cook laughed. 'Show him your boot!'

But the sailor paused, observing the fainting lad more closely. 'No,' he said. 'This one's sick. Look at his face.'

The cook bent, sticking his bloated face in front of Jim's, sniffing, assessing. 'He's all red,' he snarled, putting a fat hand on Jim's burning forehead. 'He got a fever. He's sick, bad.'

Jim vaguely recalled how they had bundled him below deck, tossing him on one of the midshipmen's bunks.

'I'll get the first mate to keep an eye on him,' the cook grunted. 'No loss if we lose him.'

The first mate came down, huffing. 'Don' like this. I seen the plague in Sicily one time. He been near rats?'

The cook nodded.

'Get rid a'im,' the first mate said. 'Plague spreads.'

'Can't kill him,' the cook protested. 'Cap'n would'n' allow it.'

'Cast him over,' the first mate said. 'Quick an' quiet.'

The cook scurried away.

Lost as he had been in a drowsy fever, what happened next was hardly more than a blur for Jim, still head down, bum up, prostrate on the beach – but this much he could recall: by night, when the ship slept, the cook and three of the midshipmen – each on pain of death – deroofed the cage holding the chickens and sheep and tied Jim to it, spreadeagled, face upward, as if already dead. They tossed a scrap of rotten sail over his semi-naked body and threw him, still tied to the wooden roof, into the sea.

'Not a sound.' Jim remembered the cook's muffled voice as they dragged him to the gunwale. 'He musta fell overboard. Right?'

There was a giggle, then a splash, and Jim the J was assigned to death in the Coral Sea.

Feverish, delusional, Jim remembered little of those initial hours. The lap, lap, lap of the sea encompassed his brain, lulling his thoughts, his fears, into a blur of dreaming. He felt nothing, no pain, no fear, only the lull of the lap, lap, lapping until at night a wind tore the sail from his body. Lying on his back as he was, the sudden immensity of the tropical night was revealed to him in all its starry magnificence.

I can see! he realised. I am alive! He wanted to shout but he could not. His mouth, his tongue, his lips, were encrusted with salt. And his wrists and ankles were burnt. He could just lift his head (not sufficiently to see his feet), and he could turn his head this way, then that, enough to see where the weathered ropes bit and chafed, where the crusted salt worked into the torn skin and exposed flesh. But the sea had worked the ropes loose and, determined, he wrenched his hands free, flinging his skinny arms into the air in a gesture of defiance. He now reached down to loosen his feet but the boards that supported him tilted dangerously, almost throwing him into the sea.

The sea!

He had not looked. The shimmering surface of the silvered waves surrounded him, and he lay back, overcome.

Oh God, he thought, and would have

muttered the same if his parched tongue and lips could have formed the words. Or if he could find a prayer to suit – but there had never been prayers in James Wilson's life, only curses . . .

I need to sit up, he thought. *Slowly* . . . And clenching his stomach muscles, he lifted his shoulders, then his back, from the sodden boards.

The miserable raft allowed him that good fortune.

He sat, quite still, the boards beneath him stable on the surface of the starlit sea.

I will wait for the dawn, he thought.

When the sun rose, orange and pink across the waters, he saw islands. Mounds of green rising above the surface, some with trees – palm trees, like the tropical paradise he had once dared to imagine. And beyond, hardly a grey smudge on the horizon, a longer darker band: the mainland, was it?

So, he sat, fearful of movement, whether of his own making or an oversized wave. Seabirds landed, white gulls, their pink legs as delicate as a spider's. They pecked and prodded the timbers of his makeshift raft. Some investigated his still tied legs, their bony extent offering little to excite them.

I will wash ashore, he hoped, and waited.

But the sea had other ideas.

As the morning wore on and the sun rose higher, hotter, burning, a wind came up, and waves. Rough waves, curling and breaking into tumbling foam, some higher than his head, terrifying. His sight of the land, even the islands, was lost. The canvas sail that had covered him was washed away, the loose ropes, but not those that still tied his ankles.

I must get free, he thought. I must, or else if I am overturned, I will die beneath this thing. Resolved, he bent forward again, his fingers barely reaching his feet. So, he worked the knots, loosening first one foot then the other, until he was free. The gulls pecked at the abandoned ropes, lying loose, some trailing in the sea.

Jim laughed, joyous – but he laughed too much, and the raft tilted, unstable in the choppy waves, and he was thrown over, into the sea.

He scrambled to the surface, spitting and choking. Instinctively, his hands clutched the edge of the boards that had once held him.

No, he determined. Not yet! I will not die yet! But the edge of the raft was a mass of rough, splintered timbers and he could not hold on. Jim fell back into the sea, treading water. He was a Dundee boy where the water was freezing. He could not swim. Panic struck and he thrashed wildly then, relaxing as he came to terms with his plight. He let the water carry him, and floated.

He drifted until the surge of the tide washed him into the dumping waves of the shore. What shore he did not know. He let himself be driven and, finally, found himself washed up on the sand. Having no energy to fight back, he sprawled where the waves dumped him, his body half buried in the golden grit, and lay there, exhausted.

When he found the strength to look up, the green of jungle greeted him.

Can I do this? he wondered, collecting his thoughts, recalling what he could of his fate in the sea. If he moved, if he stood – something – some creature lurking in that green might see him. Even someone . . . But I must, he thought. I must go on, and, pressing his palms into the sand, he stood.

Stumbling and shaking, he crossed the golden border. Whatever lay within that jungle was his future.

The breaking of the next wave erased the imprint of his body.

Author's Note: In memory of James Wilson, a thirteen-year-old castaway on the Peruvian that was shipwrecked in the Coral Sea in 1846. Wilson disappeared in the jungles of Northern Queensland.

The Cabin Boy and the Creature

Simon Higgins

China's 'Thirteenth Year of Yongle' (1415)

The rumour had torn through the fleet like a contagion: the monster was dying.

In the sour-smelling, dimly-lit equipment hold that doubled as the cabin boys' mess hall, Dong was attacking the last of his rice, elbows on the trestle table, chopsticks cycling bowl to mouth, when the news pierced the chatter of the boys surrounding him.

The shock announcement came, as usual, from Hao-Yu. Dong eyed the habitual braggart. His name meant 'grand house' but he was, Dong reminded himself, just another orphan from the streets of Nanjing pressed into service before the great mission had sailed. Oldest and largest of the cabin boys, privileged to run errands to the command ship itself, the mop-haired Hao-Yu revelled in frequently returning with utterly sensational gossip.

'Of course, nobody's actually seen it except the admiral, Chung The Eunuch, and its deck staff, but descriptions leaked out.' Hao-Yu raised his chin. 'So, I know what it is now!'

'Well, what is it, then?' Dong sniffed. 'I heard it's just a giant black rhinoceros.'

Hao-Yu widened his eyes then leaned toward him. 'Much more than that. It's a qilin!'

Astonished gasps, dismissive chuckles and a few muttered quips ringed the table.

Dong swallowed his final grains of rice and dropped his chopsticks noisily. 'Are you just making all this up? What could prove it's really a qilin? A monster from legend?!'

'My fist will smash your face up if you insult me again!' Hao-Yu scowled. 'Use your water-filled brain: qilins have hooves, strangely-patterned coats. Skin grows over their horns, and they're like a deer, but up to three times the height of a man. All these details have been confirmed! The beast's deck manager himself told me!' Hao-Yu thumbed his chest. 'Guess who takes him his lunch every second day? That's how I know . . . Little Brother.'

'Little Brother now?' Dong sneered. 'I

can't be more than a year younger than you.'

'Still counts. At least I know my age: fifteen!' Hao-Yu snorted. 'You don't even know yours . . . and I know that my parents died . . . I bet yours just saw you born then cast you out!'

'Liar!' Dong sprang to his feet. 'That's all you are! Bring your lying mouth over here!'

A scrawny boy at the end of the table hissed. 'No fighting! We'll all be punished!'

Hao-Yu folded his arms, grinning up at Dong. 'They say in a few days we dock at Nanjing. You and I can settle this on land. No watching eyes or rules there! That's if the qilin doesn't eat you first, you little runt.' Hao-Yu raised an eyebrow and licked his thick lips.

Instantly the whole mess fell silent. Dong swallowed. 'What do you mean by that?'

'Simply this.' Hao-Yu stretched, basking in the moment. 'The qilin is sick, some say dying. Master Chung has decided someone will have to try hand-feeding it. Since the Sultan of Bengal's men loaded it that night behind screens, nobody's confronted the creature. Maybe whoever does, for the first time, will forfeit his –' Hao-Yu coughed '– undersized life.'

Dong's legs felt weak. 'You . . . nominated

me?' He watched his enemy grin, then shrug.

'Since you're already on your feet,' Hao-Yu said, nodding in the direction of the doorway, 'Master Chung will be on Treasure Ship Three all afternoon. He waits to brief you.'

Dong slowly turned and started for the door; his head strangely light. At first, his ears could neither separate nor interpret the excited conversations erupting in his wake. Then one question broke through the tangle of speech. It made the skin of his forearms prickle.

'Which one of us gets his blanket?'

The breeze was cold, but the sunshine warmed him. Dong paced along the rail enclosing the huge deck, drawing salty air, scanning the surrounding fleet as he waited for the hourly patrol boat that circuited the giant ships. Ribbed sails snapped overhead, ropes and cogs rhythmically creaked, and distant signal drums kept time as Admiral Zheng's massive convoy surged ever eastwards for home.

East, Dong smiled, The very meaning of my name. Two years away from home soil! Two exciting, hard, often baffling and sometimes frightening years at sea, or in ports few men of The Middle Kingdom had ever seen. But a far better life than starving on the streets of Nanjing, hearing passing merchants brag about the land's prosperity. Regular meals, guaranteed shelter, the comfort of routine. Easily worth the sufferings that had accompanied them. That first horrible month of daily seasickness; the terror of the storms; those unnerving rumours of imminent attack; the ceaseless petty politics of the other boys, and two awful spates of bullying by cruel adult superiors. Dong turned to study the centre of the armada.

Who could not marvel at the commanders' seamanship? It somehow enabled 300 ships to maintain an ever-moving, near-perfect series of concentric circles on the open ocean, a pattern brush-stroked with hulls great and small beneath brilliant-red sails.

The admiral's gigantic Command Ship was the most populated, housing navigators, the fleet's hospital, its Corps of Translators, plus soldiers and a variety of menial workers. Hao-Yu claimed that the admiral maintained ten full-time journal-keepers. Dong shook his head. Imagine being able to read and write! What would that even be like? A type of magic?

Ringing the Command Ship were another

sixty-one Treasure Ships, each of them magnificent! Nine-masted, 600 paces prow to stern, they boasted four decks, all now packed with the fabulous gifts, tributes, newly discovered produce and crafts of the far West.

And creatures, known and unknown. Dong's mouth turned dry. One waited for him.

He wrenched his mind from it and back to the grandeur of the expeditionary fleet. The eight-masted Equine Ships, two-thirds the size of the Treasure Ships, bearing horses and repair equipment, formed the next outmost ring. Then came the circle his own vessel was part of; the seven-masted Supply Ships, filled with food stores and crew quarters. At the fleet's fringes, the six-mast Troop Transports and five-masted Fuchuan Warships guarded the larger craft and the drab but essential Water Tankers, orbited by oared Patrol Boats.

His eyes flicked back to Treasure Ship Three. Like all the big vessels, its sun deck thronged with people on mild days like this. So, who would it be? Which of the tiny figures strolling so casually there would order him below? Below, perhaps to his death.

The ride to Treasure Ship Three cut across the wake of an equine ship and the relentless bobbing of the patrol boat's prow in the chop it had left made Dong seasick to the brink of vomiting. He grimaced, bitterly conceding that he was still not yet a true sailor.

He had just begun to recover when the soldier commanding the rowing team asked him his purpose on Treasure Ship Three and he mentioned the alleged qilin. The officer's mouth sagged open and he elbowed the man beside him, evidently his deputy. The pair then stared, awkwardly, with expressions that Dong took to mean *so this is the sacrifice*.

After climbing the long rope ladder to the sun deck, he was intercepted by a tall, gangly sailor who mumbled so badly Dong couldn't understand him. The man led him to a curved-roof pavilion constructed on the aft deck. In its shade sat an imposing figure with a shaven head and opulent robes. Modestly dressed clerks sat at desks either side of him.

'Bow to Lord Chung!' one clerk said without looking up from his ledger. 'For true to the meaning of his name, he is wise, with a deep understanding of diverse matters –'

'Save it.' Chung tapped his folded fan against the side of the clerk's cap. 'It's just the cabin boy I ordered. Come closer, child, nothing to fear. I'm an imperial eunuch, not a tiger.'

Dong nervously shuffled forwards. He had never been so close to a eunuch before and Chung's eerily soft features made it hard not to stare. The eunuch's eyes were bright, clear, darting about with formidable, watchful intelligence. Some said eunuchs were ruthless masters of intrigue and offending them meant death. In sudden panic, Dong bowed deeply.

'Such a respectful boy.' Chung gave a high-pitched chuckle. 'And, if my eyes do not deceive me, a smart one, though unschooled. Do you know why you were summoned?'

Taking a deep breath, Dong forced out his words. 'To face the monster. I mean feed the monster.' Almost gagging with tension, he spluttered the final correction. 'Your . . . qilin.'

Lord Chung covered his mouth with pale, manicured fingers. 'I couldn't have put it better myself.' He uncovered his smile. 'This sailor will direct you to Deck Three Manager Hu. Now *he*, like *his* name, *is* a tiger, or so he keeps reminding us. He will brief you. Just listen, nod, comply. He doesn't like being asked questions, so don't. Try not to annoy him. He hasn't been roundly right-minded since the war.' Chung winked. 'Off you go, gods with you.'

Burning curiosity forced Dong's mouth half-open. He quickly belayed his impulsive question, but the sharp-eyed eunuch had already picked up his signal.

Chung flicked his fan open and scooped the air grandly. 'Well then, boy, out with it!'

'Is it really a qilin?' Dong dropped his eyes to the deck. 'Or just a strange animal?'

'Look at me, boy.' The eunuch leaned forward on his stool. 'It is an absolute *wonder.*'

———

What a strange answer, Dong mused, as the sailor led him down the spiralling wooden steps to the third deck of four. The smell of animal waste, barely detectable on the sun deck, soon became a powerful stench. Where the steps met the deck's long central corridor, the sailor pointed, mumbled, motioned for Dong to proceed, then left him.

Dong followed the corridor, lit at intervals by oil lanterns, past rows of animal pens. Most had shoulder-height walls which enabled him to see the various creatures segregated in each. The first few, familiar. Chickens, pigs, geese. But then came bizarre striped horses. Next, huge birds, tall as any man, with long legs and necks, tiny wings and comical heads.

Subsequent enclosures contained large cages, each housing what appeared to be sleek giant cats. Either completely black or spotted, they all looked powerful and fast. Most relentlessly stalked up and down, a few lay curled up, asleep. The last in the line raised its head and watched Dong purposefully with yellow, unblinking eyes as he passed. Fascination and fear tugged at him in equal measures, for without doubt, this one was a hunter of men.

As the corridor led deeper into the hull of the ship, the stench of beast urine eased. He came to a stretch of pens filled with huge pots, large tied cones of straw, and enormous piles of green feed, roughly half of it fresh-cut from the onboard farms, the balance dried, pressed and neatly piled. Beyond them, the corridor appeared to end at a much higher wall.

Approaching it warily, Dong made out a figure sitting on a tiny, three-legged wooden stool at its base. The man slowly rose then took a few limping steps forward.

'So, you are this *Dong*, eh?' His back was

hunched, but he seemed to work hard to stand as upright as possible. 'I am Hu. I will . . . instruct you, uh? Be sure you pay attention.'

'Yes, sir.' Dong nodded, his eyes flicking between the wall at Hu's back and the veteran himself. Hu had the same dark complexion as the north-western people who had fed Dong and two other street urchins their tavern's scraps one winter, saving their lives. Hu wore a straggly silver beard and thin moustache, one end of which disappeared into a healed burn mark on his cheek. Dong flinched as he realised Hu had seen him studying it.

'Yes, boy.' Hu sighed. 'This old body has truly lived life. What else would you expect from a man that fought on the Western frontier *and* helped dethrone the upstart Jianwen emperor?' Hu turned and rapped his knuckles on the wooden wall. Dong heard sounds from behind it, great feet, hooves perhaps, shuffling backwards. Then came a huffing sound. Something big, exhaling hard, at a height well above their heads! Why keep it in darkness?

Dong looked at Hu, blinking anxiously but forcing himself not to ask any questions.

'Yes,' Hu said, nodding grimly. 'It's waiting. There's a ladder the other side of this wall, dead-centre. Before I send you over, I'll prop one this side. Two days ago, the creature's carer, also from its homeland, was struck down with fever. He lies delirious in the hospital ship. Then its native food supply ran out! Now, nobody knows how it feeds or what it can stomach! And there's four days at sea still ahead. This thing's a gift for the emperor. It must live!' Hu grunted. 'At all costs.'

'Can't you just throw food over –' Too late Dong checked himself.

Hu snarled. 'Never ask me stupid questions, *boy*! Of course, it was offered food on a pole, but it's wary of anything we dangle over the wall. Besides, we need to test one thing, then another. Someone must confirm, up close, exactly which foods we grow that the fussy thing will eat.'

Dong shifted on the spot; his ears cocked for more sounds. 'And that's me . . .'

'Yes.' Hu looked him over. 'The admiral's idea: someone *small*. It's you . . . and *now*.'

He bustled past Dong, limping with surprising speed back to the food storage pens. Dong stared at the wall. Not a sound from behind it. Why? Was *it* now listening out for *him*?

Hu returned with large, tied bundles of green leafy vegetables in each hand and a light bamboo ladder under one arm. He motioned with his head for Dong to lean the ladder against the centre of the wall, then dragged a sweaty length of cord from inside his rough-weave tunic. Dong watched, apprehension growing, as Hu fashioned a simple sling to connect the bundles of fresh fodder. With gnarled hands he thrust it over Dong's head, pulled Dong's arm through the loop, then turned the boy to face the ladder at the wall.

'Over you go now,' Hu said firmly. 'We'll soon find out if it wants left hand food, right hand food.' He shamelessly allowed himself a cruel, teasing grin 'Or cabin boy.'

With a lump in his throat, Dong slowly ascended the ladder. At the top of the wall, he peered into the void where the light from the corridor's low-slung lanterns failed to reach. Where was the monster lurking? Dong took a deep breath and carefully mounted the wall, hooking one leg over, probing warily for the top of the inner ladder with his free hand. His breathing quickened. What if it seized his questing, vulnerable fingers and tore them off? Or dragged him from the wall, tossed him in the air, then let him fall, spinning, into its jaws?

He turned his head, considering retreat.

Behind him, Hu cleared his throat sharply.

Obviously, there was no going back. He had to bridle his mind and simply do this!

His nerve-wracking journey down the inner ladder in near-total darkness seemed to take an eternity, perhaps because he couldn't resist looking over his shoulder the entire time. The rank odours of the qilin's droppings and urine grew stronger as he descended.

His feet found the deck. Dong turned, heart beginning to pound in his chest.

From directly ahead came several loud sniffs, a much louder, longer snort, then muffled impacts. Its great hooves or feet were crossing the enormous pen now . . . towards him!

As his eyes adjusted to the darkness, Dong made out a towering shape closing in on him out of the gloom. At first, he thought it a giant version of one of those strange, tall birds with the comical heads that he had seen along the way. Then, though they were barely discernible, he made out its *four* impossibly long legs, each one taller than he was. Dong looked up, the breath stalling in his throat. The outline of a roughly triangular body took shape above the legs and sprouting from that, a tapering neck that seemed to stretch so high that

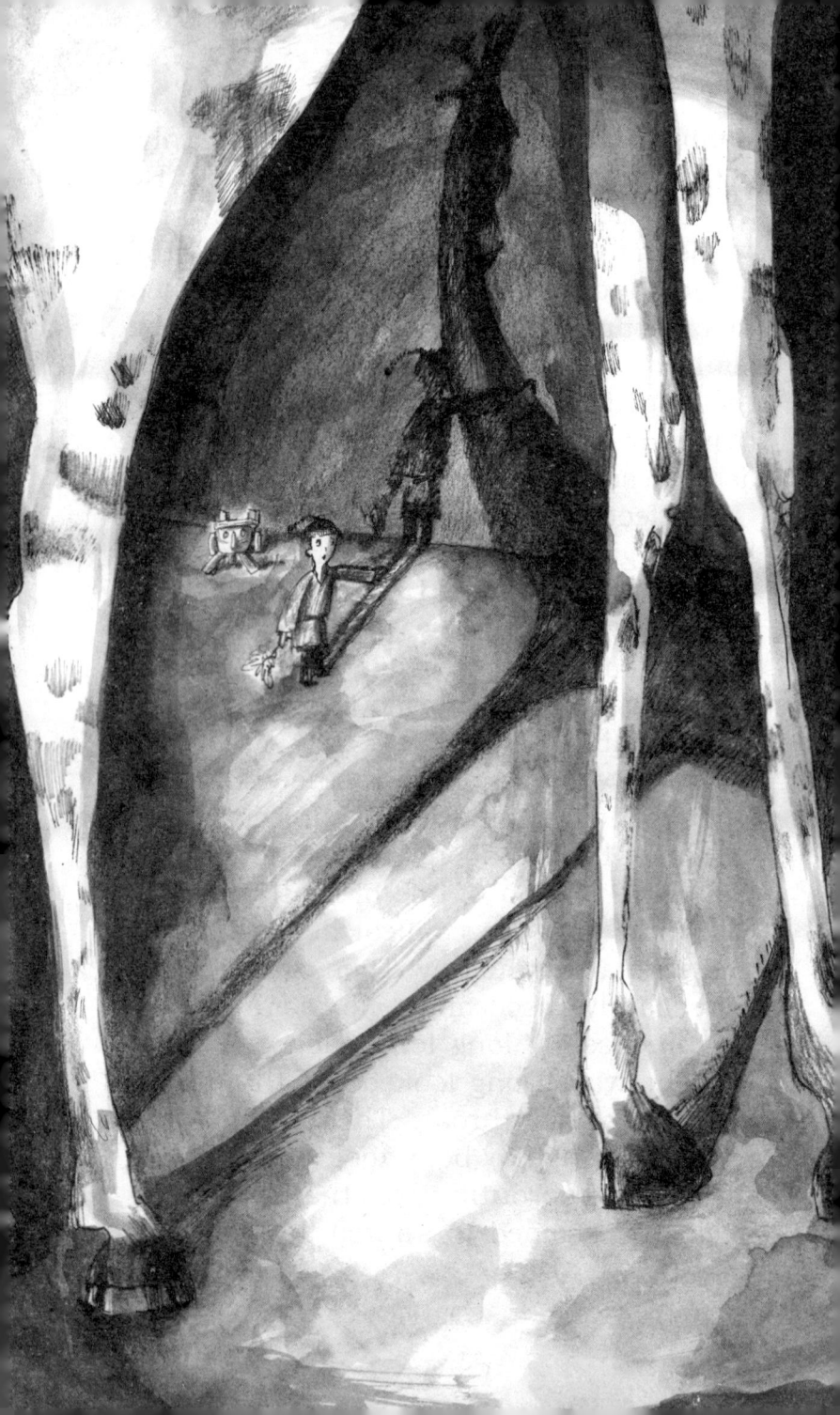

the monster's head might be brushing the chamber's very ceiling! Another snort!

The thing moved closer, looming over Dong. With his mouth dry, eyes squinting, legs starting to feel weak, Dong forced himself to raise the bundles of feed in each of his hands.

Then it happened. The unbelievable neck somehow bent, like a giant bamboo in a storm, and a head, surprisingly small judging by its outline, descended directly in front of his face.

Dong felt his stomach knotting and both his hands and knees starting to tremble. He expected any moment to feel the impact of the creature's jaws, clamping his face or neck. But instead, the qilin, or whatever it truly was, sniffed hard around each of his hands, then pulled its head back up and out of sight. Dong gulped in humid, smelly air and tried to think. Why didn't it feed? Based on what Hu had said, it ate this kind of thing. It had to be hungry. So why wouldn't it eat?

He stared at the towering shadow before him. Such an improbable creature! Even when back in its homeland, how could such a tall, thin, tree-like animal successfully eat at all? That neck would have to bend so low simply to graze. Unless . . . Dong frowned hard.

Tree-like! Trees! Perhaps it only trusted food found high in the trees. He nodded, eyes on the bundles in his hands. Moving slowly, carefully, keen not to startle the qilin, he climbed the ladder, watching over his shoulder, snatching for each bamboo rung.

The monster abruptly stepped closer. Dong froze, ten rungs from the top. Would it stop him escaping? Drag him from his perch to dash him against the deck? He closed his eyes, tearing his mind from awful thoughts, turning back to instincts. What did they tell him? That unlike the great cat, this was no hunter. It ate vegetable stalks. It was huge, but gentle.

He painstakingly climbed then turned on the ladder. Light grew brighter around him.

His lower back pressed into a bamboo rung, his shoulders against the wall. Afraid to look, Dong warily extended the offerings of food in each of his hands. The creature sniffed loudly again, then, as Dong held his breath, swung its head low towards the waiting fodder.

It nudged the bundle in his left hand with its nose, licked the green leaves hard, then turned to the bundle in his right hand.

Inexplicably, the light around the top of the wall grew even brighter and suddenly Dong could clearly see two short, distinct horns and large, diamond-shaped ears. They jutted from a head that was, just as Hao-Yu had claimed, truly deer-like! It was a qilin! Dong gasped, waves of wonderment sweeping away his fear.

The qilin sniffed the right-hand bundle, then snatched at it with pliant lips. Dong exhaled with relief as he watched it chew, first cautiously, then gradually faster. It snatched at the feed again and this time ate confidently. Without thinking, Dong said, 'So hungry, I knew it!' At once the qilin stopped chewing, swung its head, and they came face to face.

The glow from the corridor side of the wall was bright enough now for Dong to see the creature's eyes: dark, soft, slowly blinking, obviously studying him. After sending a puff of wet-grass breath straight into his smiling face, the qilin resumed eating from Dong's hand.

When the food was finally exhausted, the wondrous beast sniffed the other bundle then turned away. Dong watched it melt into the chamber's gloom. Crossing the wall, he found Hu waiting anxiously, high on the outer ladder. Not so callous after all, the old soldier had struggled up, a lantern in one hand, to check on him. Hence the timely growing light!

Hu stared, open-mouthed, at the vegetable stalks in Dong's hand. 'You made it eat?'

'And,' Dong could not resist a proud smile, 'I made it my friend.'

With drums and gongs keeping time and his sumptuous ceremonial robes swishing, tall Admiral Zheng He ascended the marble steps to the throne room's highest platform, where the smiling Ming Emperor was holding out his hands. Robed chief eunuchs and armoured bodyguards looked on from the wings. At ground level, rows of nobles and palace officials clustered around the boxes of imported treasures, applauding and bowing fawningly.

'Our old friend.' The Emperor gestured for a stool to be set beside his throne. 'Come, tell me of this greatest wonder you bring, that we have heard so much about. A true qilin!'

Zheng He bowed low, saluted hand over fist, arranged his robes, then carefully sat. 'A gift to you, Son of Heaven, from the Sultan of Bengal, who found it in the Somali Ajuran Empire.' The admiral leaned close. 'A wonder, yes. But as for being a qilin –'

The emperor quickly assumed a conspiratorial whisper. 'Just an exotic animal?'

'They call it a . . . *giraffe*,' Zheng He muttered. 'Its homeland carer lost his wits to fever and needless to say, anxious feeding issues followed. Then one of my lead eunuchs proposed risking a cabin boy in an experiment. I suggested a little fellow. We used that one, there.'

Zheng He pointed to the small figure beside the great chamber's doorway. The emperor studied Dong, standing stiffly with averted eyes in his new sailor's uniform.

The admiral grinned. 'He surprised us all by working out its secret. It turns out the animal needs to think its food is dangling high in treetops. As it would in its homeland.'

'A cabin boy with brains, eh?' The emperor laughed and slapped his thigh. 'One of your orphan army?' He watched Zheng He nod. 'We recall another orphan, brought before us years ago, who's proved so clever as to voyage to the end of the world at our command.'

'Son of Heaven.' Zheng He dropped his eyes, then his head. 'I live only to serve you.'

The emperor sat back in his throne, tapping his polished fingernails together. 'Take this boy into your service. As stupidity ought to be thwarted, so brains should be rewarded. Have him educated. That is, if you judge that he will prove a keen and worthy student.'

'I so judge.' The admiral smiled. 'He told me his dream is to one day read and write.'

'Wonderful. Now . . . come, advise me: should we tell our people it is not *truly* a qilin?'

The admiral paused; brow knitted. 'We could, my emperor, but I had a thought. Would not wide knowledge of a qilin, in the flesh, in our kingdom for the first time in known history, not signal to all the empire that your rule truly enjoys the Mandate of Heaven?'

As they rose together, the emperor addressed his court. 'Now honour and proclaim,' he announced waving a hand, 'noble, faithful, Zheng He, explorer, and his miraculous find . . . *a true qilin*!'

Every onlooker broke into thunderous applause. Emperor and admiral exchanged sly nods.

Zheng He took his leave, descended the steps, then strode triumphantly through the bowing crowd to a radiant Dong. He grinned. 'It seems that you *will* learn that type of magic.'

Tale of Two Times

James Phelan

'If everybody lived a life like mine there would be no need for novels.'
Albert Einstein to his sister, Maja, 1899
Bern, Switzerland, 1905

Late autumn, the city sticks. Cracks form, the landscape is changing. Water becomes hard. Steam rises, lacing forms of life. People move slower.

Two souls collide to change the future, providing the foundation of the synchronicity to follow. One is in love, torn in glee. The other lives in the aether, his passion scientific, absent in the cosmos . . .

Ilse Vourne walks to work through the Marktgasse, alone in her stride. Most of the store and stall owners are there, preparing for the breakfast rush in the capital. Cooked sausage and onion perfumes the cold emptiness and mixes with the aroma of freshly baked breads and brewing coffee,

making her hungry as with every other morning. She waves to the familiar faces behind windows, the glass frosted on the outside and steamed up inside, and stops at a fruit stall to buy her lunch from the man that reminds her of her departed uncle. At the end of the Marktgasse, where the Spitalgrasse funnels through a canyon of decorated shops, Ilse kicks a football back to some children playing outside their homes, their pyjamas visible in gaps of overcoats and boots. She studies them in their laughter, and not for the first time thinks she may like to have one of her own.

When Ilse reaches the Patents Office, the muffled bells of the giant clock tower on the Kramgrasse find rhythm with her heart, setting the tone of another working day. As she inserts the key to unlock the heavy timber door, the bells that ring seven echo about the city's many timepieces. The key turns freely – she's either not the first to arrive, or someone stayed and worked through the night. She opens the door and smiles. *Albert.*

Inside the office sit sixteen ordered desks, neat stacks of paper on their polished tops. One desk does not pretend to be orderly – the furniture itself only distinguishable from the four legs that support the collage of papers, books and stationery. Slumping over this desk, a head of impossibly unruly hair belies any of the owner's hopes to go unnoticed amongst this wilderness of scribbled thoughts. Many of the papers have large gaps of white nothingness, wherein the mathematical calculations needed to be completed to prove the theorem have already resolved in his mind.

'Good morning, Albert,' Ilse calls from her typist desk by the entrance, hanging her coat on a wall hook.

'Morning, Mileva . . .' Albert replies from his dream-like state. Ilse takes no offence from the mistaken identity – she enjoys the reference of being a married woman, especially the wife of a young professional. She returns five minutes later to his desk with a steaming cup of coffee. The heat carries the scented water particles to his nostrils, which flare as he awakens.

'Oh, good morning, Ilse . . . thank you,' Albert says, a scrap of paper falling from his forehead as he blows at the steam and sips his drink, burning his mouth in his haste.

'Your wife must be very patient, seeing you as little as she does – and now that you have a child!' Ilse says. Albert is the one man in the office she genuinely adores, and she would steal any moment to be in his company. He pays for her skills at the typewriter when she has spare time, professionally setting his theorems before mailing them to the *Journal of Physics.*

'Mileva? Time apart will do her good, she needs to be stronger. But wait – what of your life? What news today – the day after yesterday when you had your night double booked with the two men in your life?' Living for music, sweets, and science, Albert's ears perked up when he overheard Ilse's tales of love – of her chance meeting of two charming men almost at once, when years of solitude had preceded with unfair languor.

The young patents clerk has spent the year busier than usual, learning quickly that time management is crucial for his achievements, but still lagging behind the food and sleep required by others. He has his family, his wife and now a young son. This Little One has not brought the semblance of order to life he had envisaged; rather, there is now a proportionate increase in the equation of life and time that makes up a family dynamic.

Albert is not one to spend time talking

idly about life's more pedestrian topics – history in the moment is never the same as hindsight and distant sources. Memories die and subjects fade. Even in conversations with people as close as his good friend, Besso, he would often stare into the cosmos to dwell and ponder the current or upcoming theorem, a golden thread becoming unravelled or entwined. With Ilse, the jargon loses him completely but the picture is different – her story is science, physics, the essence of life itself.

The thread is *time*.

Not that she knows of this biased view that spurs his interest – but she has her suspicions there's more to it for Albert than passing time to enquire about her courtships.

'Well!' Ilse begins, taking a seat on an opposite desk and sipping her cocoa. 'Christian met me straight after work – a total surprise since I was not expecting to see him then! But that is just him, I mean, he is not rigid with such things, like he has no time constraints' – Albert's mouth twitches into a smile – 'so we went for a picnic dinner on the Aare in his row boat, certainly not dinner time to me but for him –'

'Yes, I know, I know,' Albert nods. 'He

eats when he likes! He wakes when he likes, he works when he likes, he lets his body do the timekeeping for him!'

'Yes . . . that's right,' Ilse says, frowning. 'But can you imagine my terror when the Kramsgrasse struck six and I was to meet Johan within an hour! And you know what he is like with appointments.'

'Never misses them. Not by a minute.'

'Precisely. We were to be having a refreshment by seven to be at the Theaterplatz by seven-fifteen for the seven-thirty show.'

'I hope he never forgets to wind his watch,' Albert says. He looks at her, poised for the reply.

'Oh, no – he does that when he awakens at seven and sleeps at eleven.'

Already this year, Albert has completed his PhD dissertation, written a paper on electrodynamics and another on photons. When investigating electricity and magnetism, the twenty-six-year-old physicist realised it would require a re-conception of time. Inspiration and revelation came from everywhere – from dreams, the city, the people. From his good friends of the Olympia Academy. Besso. Mileva. And now, Ilse.

It took three weeks of overheard snippets of conversation between the two typists at the Patents Office for Albert to conclude that there are two times lived by in the world; mechanical time, which is rigid and unyielding, and bodily time, which is fluid and pliable. Ilse and the men in her life became a case study, her love life a laboratory.

Meeting two men whose love would prove sincere and determined is a shock to Ilse. A year shy of thirty, the blonde-haired professional typist from Geneva is constantly berated by a disowning mother who mercilessly draws contrast with her two younger daughters who were wed at a desirable and proper age. Now the object of desire by a banker and an architect, Ilse has no thoughts of turning away either man.

'And what toll is this doubling up of your romantic time having on you, Miss Vourne?' Albert asks. He is wide awake now, having consumed his coffee with haste, impatient for the stimulus it would provide.

'Can you believe that I am thriving! Tired at and of work, yes, but alive like never before. My mother, though, who thought it unspeakable to others when I was unwanted for so long, now finds my affairs the cause of many inconvenient trips to her church.'

'Yet you can manage to split your time with these men easily?' Albert asks, looking toward the solid front door of the office. Through the windows above he sees the Alps, the clear sky, and in his mind's eye all the way into the starry space beyond. He is gazing into the deepest realms of the cosmos, searching for answers to questions he has not decided on yet.

'At first, I think the shock got me through, the excitement, the mischievous nature of things. Now I have the burning desire to spend time with both men, two gentlemen in every sense of the word who in their own thoughts, pine for me alone.' Ilse pauses to check about the office for eavesdroppers who aren't yet there. She delights in the scandalous nature of it all, even though she is only talking to young Albert, who seems far too wise for his years. 'Anyway – I wouldn't know it any other way.'

'Wouldn't know "it"?' Albert ventures. His focus rests on Ilse, seeing features he has either never witnessed before or has forgotten about. With her new-found demeanour she reminds him of Marie, his love before his wife, a woman full of excitement and passion. The memory of a time lived but now behind him makes him a little sad.

'Love,' Ilse says, as though it were obvious.

'Ah, I see,' Albert says, looking away again. A thread of another thought, the instrumental beginning of the end for the theorem. 'I wonder . . .'

Ilse waits a measured pause for Albert to continue. When he doesn't, she says, 'Yes?'

'Well, of the two . . . I just wonder . . .' He looks about the papers at his desk, preferring as usual to avoid the eye contact he often found himself out of focus for. He pulls and twists at the corner of his moustache.

'What are you wondering, Albert – which loves me most?' Ilse seems delighted at the prospect of spending a conversation measuring each man's reciprocal love for her.

'No . . . I think I mean, which do you . . .' Albert's eyes meet hers with raised eyebrows. Sometimes a small pang of guilt eats at him during their conversations, not for any shrewd reason other than that the typist could never hope to fully comprehend the larger forces at work here, the ulterior motive that spurs his interest.

'Who is easier to spend time with? He ruled by mechanical time – or he who moves to his own clock?'

Albert fears his theorem is flawed. So much has come together so quickly that he is sure he should have mailed it off by now. He is *so* close. The discoveries revelatory. Revolutionary in comparison to his peers. While Ilse spoke, he allowed his thoughts to drift through the culminating points of his thesis so far, seen written in his mind as though typed by her hand . . .

Time is a circle. A closed plane curve which is at all points equidistant from a fixed point within it, called the centre. A precise repetition, endless, where the repeated is often unnoticed. The lovers gravitate towards the centre, locked forever in an embrace where time stands still. Rarely a disturbance would tear loose an object from this circle. They are easy to spot, those living in the past. From the future they tread with deliberate action, for the smallest alteration could wreak havoc one day. They are the outcasts.

Time has three dimensions. Like space. An object may give up that freedom of choice, by choice. Their fate is decided by their mindset. Without commitment there is chaos. They, each and all, have their reasons.

Time is absolute. Everything is measured. Exact. Nothing is lost – objects are the only exception but they too may find themselves within a measure of time. Their comfort zone.

It is recorded in time the moment Ilse Vourne kissed her pursuers each. The time he first met Mileva. When the sun rose on this day. The moment the Sabbath begins. The second we die, when the soul can be measured leaving the body.

'Albert?' Ilse asks again, worried.

'Sorry?' Albert comes back to the present, realising he let himself get too close to the edge of the circle for a moment, almost slipping off with the centrifugal forces at work.

'Sorry, Ilse – I have a migraine,' Albert says. They are happening more regularly now, spurred with the frustration of a stalwart flummoxing over his contemporaries' papers while his own stubbornly aches for completion. His mind is feverish.

'Oh – why don't you lie on the sofa until the others arrive?' Ilse offers. She goes to the leather seat and fluffs the pillow.

'Thank you . . .' Albert's eyelids close

as he lies down, re-entering his dreams immediately.

Amidst the formulas and computations that whiz by at a tremendous rate, Albert picks up snippets of noise. Chatter, clatter, clouds of typeset and scribbled notes that he tries to read from his chair. Around and around they spin, a vortex forming above his head as he raises his hand to hold an idea. As he gropes for what may be The Answer, he is jolted awake by his own clumsiness.

He should have known, trying to change time and space like that . . .

Albert leaves the Patents Office at five o'clock, solace in his brisk pace along the ancient cobbled road, missing his usual chat with Besso on his way home. He sees in the faces around him the ignorant bliss of some, the inner torment of others, and serenity in those who live up high, where time slows down a notch. He sees in the shadows those chosen for obscurity, the darkly clad figures who stalk overhangs and frequent areas known not to be travelled for fear of falling into contact with one of these lost souls. He knows they simply went too far outside the circle, that boundary that sometimes tempts him so . . .

Around the next bend, as if tempted by geometry at every angle, the answer appears within seconds of another migraine. Ilse sits on a bench on the Amthausgasse, set in tears that would never be shed for the same reason. He shuffles through the foot traffic to rest by her side, perched on the edge of a fountain that views the glacier-blue Aare.

'Oh, Albert!' Ilse says, wiping saline from cheek to glove. 'You'll never guess . . .'

Albert puts an arm around her shoulders. The crying starts in earnest again, and he knows. She remains there, lost in the moment, wanting for all her life to have the clock wound back an hour, two at the most, so she could have avoided the event that ended both her hopes of exploring love. She wanted to stay there, in the centre of it, in control.

Albert knows different. Thinks different. He looks towards the river, seeing the answer to end the beginning of his theorem. He stares deep into the cosmos, riding a ray of light.

―

In this world there are two times, mechanical time and bodily time, moving through three-dimensional space. Where the times separate, harmony. Where they meet, chaos, desperation, anguish – and sometimes great joy. Objects – people – are perfectly functional and happy operating in each respective time.

Time, therefore, is an illusion.

The Karoola Quarantine

Pamela Rushby

It's 1919, and returning troops from the Middle East to Queensland are coming from an area infected with the influenza known as the Spanish Flu. The Queensland government insists that they be quarantined. But when men who've been away from home for four long years are placed in a camp ashore at Fort Lytton, a camp that's not closely guarded, it's not hard to guess what's going to happen . . .

It was agreed among the members of the troop that Jim's young sister Dolly knitted the worst pair of socks in Queensland, Australia.

Possibly the world.

No contest.

Dolly had been sending Jim socks ever since he joined the Light Horse and left Australia for Egypt in 1915. And the socks kept coming. When he moved on to Gallipoli. Back to Egypt. And then to Palestine. The socks faithfully followed.

Not a pair was wearable. Either they were so narrow Jim couldn't insert his feet into them, or they were so long the heel settled halfway to his knee. If there was a heel at all. Sometimes Dolly left it out altogether.

'You'd think that in four years she'd have learned to knit a sock,' Jim's mate Griff observed, glancing at the contents of the latest package. He'd paused in cleaning his saddle. He'd cleaned it yesterday. And the day before. He'd probably clean it again tomorrow. There was a lot of time to fill in, now the war was over and they were just sitting, waiting, outside a small town in Palestine. Waiting to go home. But the army didn't like to see soldiers idle, so training had still continued. There were sight-seeing excursions as well, and sports meetings, but their troop sergeant, especially, had a decided aversion to idle hands. The saddles got a lot of cleaning.

'Ah, our Dolly was never really on the practical side,' said Jim. He'd put down his polishing cloth when the mail came, to open his parcel and read the note that came with it. He scanned the lines, and looked up, smiling. 'But I'll tell you what she is doing.'

The rest of the troop, sheltering in the shade of a few sparse trees, were interested.

The polishing cloths fell to the sand and the troops made themselves comfortable, ready to listen. Dolly's doings were always a source of amusement. They had followed Dolly's exploits in letter after letter. How she'd learned to ride a bicycle. How she'd stayed on at school and wanted to get what she called a 'proper job'. How she was eagerly looking forward to the day she'd be old enough to vote. And even stand for parliament.

'Well,' Jim went on, 'you knew she'd left school?'

'Yes, you told us,' said Griff. 'She was going to a place to learn, what was it now? Something about business, wasn't it?'

'That's right,' said Jim. 'Well, now she's got herself a job. Working one of them typewriter things. In an office. And –'

'And?'

'She says she's learning to drive.'

'Drive? Drive what? A pony and cart?'

'No. One of them *motor*cars.'

'A motorcar?'

That was dashing, even for Dolly.

'A *motor*car? Whose? Surely your old man hasn't gone and bought a motorcar?'

'My old dad? Wouldn't think so. No, she doesn't say whose it is. But she's learning to drive it.' Jim grinned. 'Just think of it.

My baby sister. Only fourteen when I left Australia. Now she's got a job and she's learning to drive a motorcar. Who knows what she'll be up to by the time we get home.'

The troop laughed.

'Ask her to send us a photograph!' said Griff.

'Nah, hardly worth it,' said Jim. 'We'll probably be home by the time she could get someone to take a photograph and then send it to me.'

'Huh.' Griff was deeply cynical. 'She'll probably be a grandmother by the time we get home, at the rate we're going.'

There was a silence. The dry palm fronds rattled in the wind. The men thought gloomily that Griff's words could well be true. The war had been over for months and here they still were, sitting in Palestine, waiting for the army to put them on a ship home. And waiting. And waiting.

'Guess we've just got to hang on until they can organise ships enough for us and the horses,' said Jim. 'There's a lot of us. And a lot of horses. And the army promised. They said they'd get the horses home again, right along with us.'

'That's right, they promised,' agreed Griff. 'When I asked, right at the start, if I could bring my own horse, they said yes. And they said they'd get us both home again too.'

'But it's too late for some to get home,' their mate Stan said heavily. 'This influenza, now. They need to get us out.'

Everyone was silent. The troop was one man down. Trooper Walter Burridge had died only a week ago, of the influenza – the Spanish Flu they were calling it – that had swept into the area. Some of their mates had caught it. Some were very sick. It was all over the world, it was said. They were all hoping it hadn't reached Australia.

Jim spoke at last. 'Guess they're aware of that. They'll be getting us out as soon as they can. And the horses, too.'

But in the end, that wasn't what happened. The men were sent home, all right, but their horses didn't go with them. None of them were happy about it, leaving their faithful mounts behind. Griff was especially bitter. Griff and his Duffy had been together all through Egypt, all through Palestine. Griff had barely been restrained from taking a swing at the officer who'd told them the horses weren't going home, that they were going to be sold – or shot, if they were sick, or old. Jim and Stan had pulled Griff away with difficulty, while the officer – who'd grown accustomed to this reaction from the men – had removed himself carefully and tactfully out of their sight.

Once they'd boarded their ship, the *Karoola*, Griff had brooded all the long voyage home. Jim and the other members of the troop had felt bad as well, outraged, defrauded. But they'd been distracted by other news. News that the disease that had struck them in Palestine was sweeping across the world, a disease killing more people than the war ever had, leaping from country to country. They hoped, again, it hadn't reached Australia.

But it had. It was in the south, in Sydney and Melbourne. Not in Queensland, not yet. And there was a great deal of concern, in Queensland, that the returning soldiers might be bringing cases of it with them. The men protested that they couldn't be. No one on board their ship had developed the influenza, they all agreed. And they'd been at sea for weeks. If anyone was going to develop the influenza, they'd have had it by now. There were some sick on board, of course, but that was from other causes. It wasn't the influenza!

The authorities didn't see it that way. The men were told, firmly, that the influenza hadn't reached Queensland, it had been stopped at the border, where there were camps especially set up to hold travellers in quarantine and keep the disease out, and after all that effort there was no way the authorities were going to let a shipload of soldiers, coming from a recognised influenza area, loose on shore to possibly spread contagion. Even if they were absolutely, positively sure they didn't have it. No, the ship was going to be quarantined. Held offshore in Moreton Bay.

'It's the law,' the men were told. 'Look, it's only a week. No time at all. Be reasonable.'

'We've been away for four years,' growled Griff. 'Four years!' He leaned on the ship's rail, and stared towards the shore. 'And look at it. There's home, just over there. Gawd, I can practically see my backyard!' He measured the distance between ship and shore with his eye. 'You know what? I've a good mind –'

'Good mind to what, Trooper?' Sarge loomed up behind him. 'Don't you be getting no ideas, now. In fact, get yourself down to the galley and tell them to give you some potatoes to peel. That's all of you. That'll keep your mind off things.' He watched as Griff, Jim and Stan reluctantly moved in the direction of the galley. 'Oh, and by the way –'

The men turned.

'Just remember. Don't be having any bright ideas. There's plenty of sharks in the bay,' said Sarge.

The three men did as they were told. A short time later, Sarge appeared in the galley. 'Leave that now,' he said. 'Go and get your gear together. We're moving.'

'Moving?'

'Going ashore. No,' he said quickly. 'You're not going home. Not yet. We're being held at Signal Hill, at Fort Lytton. Quarantined there, in camp.'

'But ashore? Why?'

'Army wants to get the ships back to Palestine to pick up more men, apparently. Orders. Just do as you're told.'

'Ashore, eh?' mused Griff. 'Well, now.'

'Under canvas. *And* under guard,' said Sarge firmly.

The camp was no better and no worse than many the troop had had to live in. In some ways, it was better. There was a recreation area, there were sports to play, it was possible to swim off a narrow beach, and despite Sarge's dark warnings, no one was taken by a shark.

The YMCA had arrived, full of enthusiasm and good will, and set up a hut with easy chairs, billiard tables, newspapers, music in the form of a gramophone and a piano. There was cricket equipment and tennis balls, and city jewellers had generously donated small silver items as prizes for any competitions the troops cared to organise. Members of the public were urged to bake cakes and scones for morning and afternoon teas, and delicacies dropped off at the YMCA's Edward Street offices in the city were delivered to Fort Lytton, fresh and delicious.

The men had been welcomed home, no one could do enough for them, they could have anything they wanted, it seemed – except go home to see their families. What was really frustrating was that so many of the men were close, so close, to home. True, there was a fence, there were guards, but they were tokens, really. Nothing that couldn't be got around. The troops were, in a manner of speaking, quarantining themselves.

It was only a day later that a message came for Jim, passed quietly from man to man along the camp. 'Someone to see Jim. At the fence.'

'At the fence? To see me? What're you on about? Can't be anyone to see me.' Jim couldn't understand it. 'Unless it's Sarge. And he'd just come and find me, wouldn't he?'

'Better cut along and see,' said Griff. 'Instead of standing here talking about it.'

Jim did cut along, and Griff and Stan, for want of something better to do, followed.

It certainly wasn't Sarge waiting at the fence. There was the usual rather casual guard, but as well, standing outside and about the width of a city street away from the fence, was a small group of civilians, mainly women and children. They were waving and calling to the soldiers inside the camp, and their greetings were being enthusiastically received and returned. The guard watched, tolerant, but quick to intervene if anyone appeared to be getting too close.

'What the heck?' said Griff. 'What's going on? Have the neighbours come to wave to us?'

Stan stared. 'Don't reckon so,' he said. 'They look more like they know some of our chaps. I reckon they're family –'

The rest of what Stan had to say was interrupted by a shriek of 'Jim! *Jim!*'

Jim, a few yards ahead of them, scanned the small crowd, trying to see who had called him.

'Jim! Oh, Jim!' the shriek came again.

And this time Jim shouted back, '*Dolly!*' and started towards a small figure in a white dress at the front of the crowd, jumping up and down frantically and waving.

The guard stepped forward. 'No you don't, trooper. You can talk, but you can't break the quarantine. Right?'

'But it's my sister!' protested Jim.

'You talk to your sister all you like, but if you try to go any closer, I'll have to send you off.'

'All right, all right.' Jim brushed him aside. 'Dolly! I can't believe it's you! How

did you ever know I was here?'

The girl across the road stopped bouncing up and down. 'It was in the newspaper on Saturday. They've been printing lists of the ships coming in, and all the men on them. We saw the *Karoola* was in. So many names! But we searched through them all, and then we saw your name.'

Griff and Stan had held back long enough. This was Dolly, Jim's Dolly, and they felt they knew her already. They moved up beside Jim. 'Dolly, hey, Dolly!'

Dolly beamed at them. 'Who's this?'

Jim was still thunderstruck. 'It's Griff and Stan, my mates. But Dolly, how'd you get here?'

'I got the train and then I walked. I just had to come. I mean, you're home, you're really home, and you're safe, and it's your birthday –'

Griff and Stan blinked. 'Birthday? It's really your birthday? Why didn't you tell us?'

Jim shuffled his feet. 'Didn't want to make a fuss, did I?'

'It's his twenty-first!' called Dolly. Immediately, a small round of applause and calls of 'Happy birthday!' came from the crowd.

'You're twenty-one? Today? Hold on.'

Griff did some swift calculations on his fingers. 'So that means when you joined up you were –'

'Underage. Well, yeah. Just a bit,' muttered Jim. 'So were a lot of others.'

Dolly bent and picked up a brown paper-wrapped parcel from the ground at her feet. 'I've brought you a cake –' She broke off and turned to the guard. 'Is it all right? I can give my brother his cake? I can, can't I? I made it myself!'

'You can't hand it to him, miss,' said the guard. 'But if you can throw it –'

Jim, Griff and Stan each had the brief and unworthy thought that if Dolly's cake was anything like the standard of Dolly's socks, it'd be pretty heavy to throw. But after all, the thought was there . . .

Dolly stepped back a few paces, took a short run-up and threw the cake. It flew through the air and dropped accurately into Jim's waiting hands.

'Good shot,' said Griff.

'Well, she's been playing backyard cricket with me ever since she was a nipper,' said Jim. 'She can throw a ball all right.'

'Oh, Jim,' Dolly called, 'I wish you could be at home tonight. We'd have such a party! Mum wanted to come with me today, she was so disappointed she couldn't, but

Gran's not been too well and Mum's looking after her, so she couldn't get away.'

'Gran?' said Jim. 'Is she all right? It's not this influenza?'

'No, no.' Dolly shook her head. 'The influenza's not got here. They've stopped it at the border. Gran'll be all right. And she's looking forward to seeing you, too.'

Jim sighed. 'Can't be helped, I suppose.'

'Your twenty-first, eh? You should get home to see your mum.' Griff thought for a bit. Then he smiled. 'Got an idea,' he said.

Jim and Stan looked at each other, instantly wary. Griff's ideas had, in the past, unfortunate consequences.

Griff waved at Dolly, beckoning to her to move slightly away from the crowd of visitors. He lowered his voice. Dolly leaned forward to hear. She answered. She giggled. Jim and Stan glanced at each other, puzzled. Then Dolly started jumping up and down again, and Griff came strolling casually back towards them.

'I've got to go!' Dolly called. 'Happy, happy birthday, Jim! We'll see you soon!'

'What's she mean by that?' Jim asked, watching her hurry away. Griff shrugged. 'Dunno. Probably means when we get out of quarantine.'

When Jim undid the parcel, later, he

found the cake wasn't his only birthday present. He held up a neatly folded piece of khaki knitting to show Griff and Stan.

'Socks?' said Griff.

Jim nodded. 'Socks,' he said.

There were sports that afternoon, and after tea Jim and Stan were tired, ready for some relaxation in the YMCA hut. But Griff had other ideas. 'Feel like a bit of a walk,' he said. 'C'mon, won't take long.'

Jim and Stan, protesting a little, fell in with him. Jim headed towards the water. 'No, not that way,' said Griff. '*This* way.' He steered them towards the fence.

'Nothing to see this way,' Stan said.

'I think you'll find there is,' said Griff. 'Maybe. Now, we just need to nip out here –'

'Out here?' said Jim. 'That's past the fence. What about the guard?'

'What guard?' said Griff. He was right. There was no guard in sight. The night was dark and quiet, only a glow of light and a hum of voices coming from the camp.

'Down here,' urged Griff. 'This way.'

'Down the road? Where are we going?'

'Sssh,' said Griff. 'What's the time? We should be able to hear her coming. If it's all worked out.'

'Hear what coming?'

'Sssssh!'

There was a chug and a rattle, a flash of light, and a motorcar pulled up down the road a little, its engine panting. 'There she is! Run!' said Griff.

'You made it!' a voice called. 'Quick, get in!'

'*Dolly*!' said Jim.

It was Dolly. And she was at the wheel of a motorcar.

'Get in, get in!' she urged. 'If it stops, it's really hard to start again!'

They leapt in.

'Hold on!' Dolly did something mysterious with a long handle, the motorcar jerked and bucked, and they were off.

Jim watched Dolly, his mouth open. 'You can drive it!'

Dolly laughed. ''Course I can! It's easy – well, not too easy actually, but I can do it!'

'Um, where are we going?'

Dolly turned her head and stared. 'Home, of course. For your birthday!'

'We're going to drive all the way to Toowong?' said Stan.

'I certainly hope so. If we aren't, I trust you're all prepared to get out and push.'

That wasn't necessary. They drove successfully all the way to Toowong. On the way, they detoured to drop Griff off at his family's home at Annerley, and Stan in Kelvin Grove.

'We'll pick you up again at four o'clock,' said Jim. 'That should give us time to get back to camp before roll call, shouldn't it? Is that all right, Dolly, can you have the motorcar until morning?'

'That'll be fine,' said Dolly. 'Now, come on, Mum's waiting, and Gran, and Uncle Fred and Aunty Lizzie and Alf and Betty and –'

Dolly's voice trailed off as the motorcar chugged away, and Griff turned and looked at the house he'd left so long ago. He hoped everyone was home. Were they going to be surprised!

There was only the faintest hint of light in the sky as Jim and Dolly picked up Stan and Griff very early the next morning. By the time they reached Fort Lytton it was much brighter: they had been delayed when the motorcar stalled outside Stan's home and Jim had to give it several hearty cranks to get it going again. The noise had not been appreciated by the neighbours. So it was quite light enough for Dolly to find the way back to the drop-off point just down the road from the fence. And quite light enough to see several soldiers in military police uniforms waiting for them.

'Well, stone the crows,' groaned Griff. 'Wouldn't that just ruin your day?'

Jim, Griff and Stan were marched off. Dolly, pale and frightened, had her name and address taken. 'You'll be hearing more about this,' the military police told her. Dolly, suitably chastened, drove away.

The authorities took swift action. The houses that Jim, Griff and Stan had visited were all placed in quarantine, and guarded. The families were treated as contacts, and closely observed for any signs of the influenza. Rumours broke out in the city that the influenza had arrived in Queensland, and the government had some difficulty in reassuring the public.

Jim, Griff and Stan, back in camp and in disgrace, peeled a lot of potatoes. They had no idea what had happened in the city until the newspapers arrived at the camp a day later.

Griff, taking an unauthorised break, was sitting on a sack of potatoes and scanning the paper. 'Hey!' he said suddenly. 'Look at this! We're in the newspaper!'

Jim and Stan looked up. 'What? Us? Never!'

'Well, not our names exactly, but it's us all

right. Listen. "Soldiers break quarantine". That's us. Then it says, "An anticipated development. Strongly-worded protest to Mr Watt. Mr Hunter seeks legal advice".'

'What's that all about?' Jim asked.

Griff scanned the rest of the article. 'Seems the Acting Premier, that's Mr Hunter, sent a telegram – crikey, it's long, must have cost him a fortune to send –'

'But what's it say?' Stan tossed another peeled potato into his bucket.

'It says he'd already telegrammed the Acting Prime Minister, that's Mr Watt, warning him about landing returning troops from the *Karoola* at Fort Lytton, because we were coming from an infected area and we were a danger to Queensland if we came ashore. And, get this, that they actually expected some of us would break the quarantine and go into Brisbane.' Griff grinned. 'No flies on him, eh? So now Mr Hunter says it's all Mr Watt's fault and he'd better do something about it. He doesn't hold back, I've got to say. Strong language.' Griff looked up. 'It goes on a bit, but it says the houses we visited have all been put in quarantine and the residents are being guarded and treated as contacts.'

Jim frowned. 'You mean all our families? That's not good.'

'No, but we know we didn't have the influenza, so it'll be all right.'

A shadow loomed over them. Sarge. Griff hurriedly dropped the newspaper and picked up a potato.

'Right,' Sarge said. 'You can leave that now. Little as you deserve to. We're on the move.'

'Moving? Where to, Sarge?'

'Back on a ship. They're taking us into Brisbane.'

'On a ship?' said Jim. 'What for? It's no distance. We could get the train.'

'Or a motorcar,' muttered Griff.

Sarge pretended not to hear. 'Guess they want us to have a hero's welcome at the docks,' he said. 'Parade down Queen Street. All that. So go and get your kit together. Quarantine's over, no one's sick and we're out of here.'

They did get a hero's welcome. A cheering, waving crowd on the wharves, banners, flags, bands playing. Jim, Griff and Stan's families weren't there, they were all in quarantine, but the men knew they'd soon be cleared. Soon, they'd all be home again. They set out on the march down Queen Street, through cheering crowds, with smiles on their faces.

Then, Griff noticed. 'Are you limping?' he muttered to Jim. 'What've you done? Hurt yourself?'

'Blisters,' Jim muttered back. 'Huge blisters. Both heels.'

'Blisters?' said Stan. 'After all the marching you've done in the last four years? How could you get blisters now?'

'Don't ask,' said Jim.

Griff and Stan glanced at each other. 'Socks,' they said together. 'Dolly's socks!'

'Dolly's socks,' said Jim. 'Thank heavens it's the last pair I'll ever have to wear.'

Mr Postlethwaite's Class of Exceptionally Gifted Children

Barry Jonsberg

Mr Postlethwaite knew he was a very lucky teacher. He was teaching Year One, his favourite age group. He had a very small class. He had the brightest, the cleverest, the most amazing children in the entire city, possibly the whole country. Every day it was a pleasure to teach them English and maths and science and all the other things he was expected to teach to the cleverest, the most amazing children in the entire city, possibly the whole country. And every day, the children surprised and delighted him with the way they learned. He would give them facts and they would drink them in. He would give them ideas and they would run with them.

His job was a joy.

Almost.

You see, there was one part of the school day he dreaded: Story Time.

If left to his own devices, Mr Postlethwaite would have got rid of it. But he had to tell his students a story at the end of the day because the school said it was an important part of learning and insisted on all classes doing it – the very smartest classes and the ones where children didn't catch on quite as quickly as others. Now, Mr Postlethwaite didn't disagree with that. In fact, he thought stories were marvellous and a terrific way of getting children to learn. It was the stories he was *forced* to tell that bothered him. Because they were the kind of stories that made very gifted children ask questions and sometimes those questions were incredibly hard to answer. And that meant a story that should have taken five or ten minutes to tell would often stretch out for . . . well, a very long time. Because, you can't stop children asking questions and they deserve answers when they do. Mr Postlethwaite believed this with the very core of his being. So he had to start telling the story earlier and earlier in the day and that was interfering with time for English and maths and science and all the other stuff.

It was frustrating.

But what can you do?

So Mr Postlethwaite sat on a chair at the front of the class, book in hand, and the children sat on the floor in front of him, looking up.

'This is the story of Little Red Riding Hood,' said Mr Postlethwaite. 'Once upon a time . . .'

Gavin's hand shot into the air and Mr Postlethwaite sighed. He normally got through the first sentence without a question. It was probably going to be one of *those* days.

'Yes, Gavin?' he said in his most patient voice.

'Can you have below a time?' asked Gavin. 'Or at the side of a time or snuggled close but not quite touching time?'

'Probably,' said Mr Postlethwaite. He'd learned that sometimes it was best to avoid answering these types of questions. Before you knew it, you were discussing the nature of time, whether it had a beginning or an end or whether it was simply something that people imagined to make sure they could go home after work. It could take hours (if hours actually exist) and he felt out of his depth.

'Once upon a time,' continued Mr Postlethwaite, 'there was a girl called Little

Red Riding Hood who lived in a village near a forest.'

'That was actually her name?' asked Lana Buchanan. 'I mean, on her birth certificate? Like Little Red Riding Hood Buchanan?'

'No, I don't think so, Lana,' said Mr Postlethwaite. 'I imagine it was a nickname. She had a habit, you see, of going out in a red cloak made for riding and that cloak had a hood . . .'

'What was the name of her horse?' asked Arjun.

'I don't know if she had a horse . . .'

'Because if she was going out riding so often it became her nickname, then the horse must have been very special to her.'

Mr Postlethwaite wiped a small bead of sweat from his brow.

'The horse's name was Champion,' said Mr Postlethwaite. He felt a little bad about making this up, but time was moving on and he'd only got to the end of the first sentence. 'Anyway . . .'

'Did she wear the red cloak all the time?' This was Daisy, who was maybe the brightest in the class. 'I mean *I* wear white shorts and a yellow T-shirt most of the time at home, but no one ever calls me Little White Shorts and Yellow T-shirt. So, for her nickname to stick, she must wear nothing else but.'

'I imagine so, Daisy,' said Mr Postlethwaite.

'She must have stacks of them in her wardrobe, then,' said Daisy, 'because they'd get sweaty really quickly, especially if you're riding your horse nearly all the time and someone would have to wash them regularly.'

'Yes . . .' said Mr Postlethwaite.

'She sounds obsessive to me,' said Gavin. 'Borderline OCD.'

'Anyway,' said Mr Postlethwaite. 'Little Red Riding Hood's mother suggested that she should go to visit her grandmother who lived in a cottage in the woods. The grandmother had been sick . . .'

'What was wrong with her?'

'Pneumonia. So Little Red Riding Hood gathered up a basket of food and prepared to walk off into the forest.'

'Why wasn't she riding her horse?' This was Rupert, who had been quiet for much longer than normal.

'The horse was sick,' said Mr Postlethwaite.

'What was . . .?'

'Pneumonia,' said Mr Postlethwaite.

'Wow,' said Rupert. 'There's a lot of that going round apparently.'

'And her mother told her not to stray from the path and not to talk to strangers because the forest was a dangerous place.'

'Whoa, hang on,' said Arjun. 'It's dangerous but she's sending her daughter out alone? What kind of a mother is she?'

'Yeah,' said Daisy, 'and it's not like she's not drawing attention to herself in that red riding hood outfit. I mean, bad people could see her coming for miles.'

'Now I'm not suggesting,' said Arjun, 'that women aren't entitled to wear whatever they want and be safe in public places, but this seems to be inviting disaster. And the way this story is set up, disaster *will* happen. That's foreshadowing for you.'

'Yes, well . . .' said Mr Postlethwaite.

'And when it does, I just hope the mother accepts some responsibility. That's all I'm saying.'

'I think I'd be involving child services,' said Daisy.

Mr Postlethwaite looked down at the small group. There was much nodding of heads. He glanced up at the clock on the wall and took a deep breath.

'But Little Red Riding Hood stopped for a while to pick some flowers as a gift for her grandmother ...' He held up his hand.

'Carnations, Rupert. And she didn't notice that a wolf that had been following her now stepped up beside her.'

There was general laughter and Mr Postlethwaite knew that there would be loads of questions if he didn't move on. So he did. Or rather, he tried to.

'And the wolf said, "What are you doing out here, little girl?" and Little Red Riding Hood said, "I'm going to visit my grandmother who lives in a cottage in the forest . . ."'

'Sorry, sorry, Mr Postlethwaite,' said Lana, 'but I can't let this go. I'm sorry, but I can't. I mean, picking flowers, yes, all good. Realistic. A talking wolf? Well, I think we're stretching things a bit here, aren't we? I mean, I know about suspension of disbelief, but isn't this asking way too much of the target audience?'

Wait until we get to the ending, thought Mr Postlethwaite.

'And this Red Riding Hood character is a bit of a bozo as well, isn't she?' added Arjun. 'I mean, a talking wolf might just rouse my suspicions, if I'm being honest. And frankly, the last thing I'd do under those circumstances would be to give away the whereabouts of my sick grandmother to an animal known to be vicious.'

'I'd give a false address,' said Lana. 'Just to be safe.'

'Little Red Riding Hood realised she was late,' said Mr Postlethwaite, 'so she rushed off down the forest path. But the wolf knew a short cut . . .'

'That's reasonable,' said Daisy. 'Being a forest creature and all, you'd know the quickest routes.'

'She should have brought her horse, sick or not,' said Gavin. 'Generally speaking, horses can outrun wolves. Generally speaking.'

'. . . And the wolf knocked on Grandmother's door,' said Mr Postlethwaite. '"Who's that?" called Grandmother. "It's me, Little Red Riding Hood," said the wolf.'

'He can talk and he's a gifted impersonator,' said Rupert. 'He's definitely got a future in show business.'

'What's more, he can read minds,' added Lana. 'She didn't reveal her name, after all.'

'Yeah, but her clothes sense is apparently well known in the area, so maybe it was just a logical guess.'

'"Come in," said Grandmother . . .'

'The entire family – every generation – seems lacking in common sense,' said Daisy.

'And the wolf came in, saw Grandmother lying in bed and gobbled her up.'

'So he didn't need to impersonate the granddaughter,' Arjun pointed out. 'He could've just strolled in without any of that showing off. I can't help feeling that even a small amount of home security would've saved her. I mean is a deadlock on the front door too much to ask?'

By now, the sweat was really gathering on Mr Postlethwaite's forehead and he was desperate to get to the end. He decided he wouldn't take any more questions, but just get through it.

'And the wolf put on some of Grandmother's clothes and got into her bed . . .'

'A cross-dresser. It explains a lot, though I have to say I'm glad there's at least a nod to diversity in this story . . .'

'And Little Red Riding Hood got to the door and knocked and a voice said "Come in" and Little Red Riding Hood entered and saw her grandmother . . .'

'Bad eyesight, poor dress sense and a woeful lack of insight into stranger danger . . .'

'And she said, "What big eyes you've got," and the wolf said, "All the better to see you with, my dear," and she said, "What big ears you've got," and he said, "All the better to hear you with," and she said, "What big teeth you've got" and he said . . .'

'She didn't pick up the signs, then? Eyes, ears and teeth. I mean, it's a bit of a giveaway,' said Lana.

'She said, "What big teeth you've got," and he said, "all the better to EAT you with," and he gobbled her up as well . . .'

'That's one *huge* appetite,' said Daisy. 'I mean, he's just eaten.'

'Yeah, but I imagine wolves need a huge calorific intake,' said Arjun. 'What with racing through forests and howling at the moon.'

'Luckily a woodcutter heard the cries,' said Mr Postlethwaite, his voice shaky, 'and he caught the wolf and cut it open and Grandmother and Little Red Riding Hood fell out unharmed. And Little Red Riding Hood was very careful about talking to strangers after that. The end.'

Mr Postlethwaite closed the book and wiped his forehead. There was a stunned silence in the classroom, broken by the bell going for the end of the day. The children got to their feet and headed for the door. All except Daisy.

'Do you know what tomorrow's story is?' she asked.

Mr Postlethwaite sighed.

'I believe it's Goldilocks and the Three Bears.'

'Hmmm,' said Daisy. 'If I may make so bold, the motif of anthropomorphism may become tedious after a while.'

Mr Postlethwaite sighed again, closed his eyes, and pinched the bridge of his nose. Hard.

Good Fences Make Good Neighbours – A Fowl Story

Elizabeth Fensham

Older and Wiser
A 5-Star dating app for mature-aged men and women who are searching for a serious and committed relationship.
For your best outcome, please give candid information and responses:

I am a forty-eight-year-old self-employed professional journalist. My beloved wife died some years ago. I am Dad to an adorable, sweet-natured fourteen-year-old girl. I have been lonely and isolated; my late-night work routines limit meeting new people. Although I am a loyal, devoted, reliable father, I sometimes neglect my self-care. My daughter tells me she desperately wants me to be happy again by filling the aching abyss. I'm told I have a great sense of humour. I enjoy the company of life-loving people. I play classical guitar and love the outdoors.

Lonely as a Cloud.

That drenching winter's Thursday, I'd shambled homewards from the bus stop, shoes soaked from cars spraying dirty water off the road. Levering my school backpack off my shoulders, I'd taken one sopping step into the hallway. My Shepherd dog, Maud, was thrilled to see me. Dad was not. He was clutching his laptop.

'Georgie! The humiliation! The embarrassment!'

'Uh-oh!'

'Your interference will destroy my public profile! Maybe my career!'

'Oops.'

'Oops? Is that all you can say?' Dad tugged at his hair. 'I have just been contacted by three unknown, desperate women! Look at your melodramatic wording – "aching abyss"! No writer worth their salt would wallow in that cliché! And listen to this!' Dad jabbed at the screen.

In a sarcastic tone, he read, '"Dear Lonely as a Cloud, when I read your profile, I got goosebumps. My astrology chart says someone significant will enter my life this month. I'm a Taurus and I get the vibe that you might be a Scorpio – compatibility in body, mind and soul".'

'What've you got to say, Georgie?'

'I'd say Lonely as a Cloud has misread her astrology chart.'

'Quit the jokes.'

I shrugged. 'Well, I attached a nice photo of you.'

'A long pink tongue and a nose?!'

It was an extreme close-up shot I'd taken of my dog licking Dad's cheek. Admittedly, the low angle meant the viewer could see up Dad's hairy nostrils.

'It didn't put Taurus off.'

'Enough!' he said. 'I like my life the way it is!'

That's when I lost it. I was trembling. 'And I hate my life! I mean, really hate it! You're so wrapped up in yourself, you don't realise I'm not okay!'

Dad stepped back, silent.

I hurled my backpack on the floor and myself on top of it, like a drowning person clutching a buoy, and howled and blubbered. Maud howled in chorus.

Mum was dead and Dad had been moping. I mean a seriously long mope. Like three years of it. I ached for my warm, creative, super-organised Mum, too. An essential colour had vanished from the universe's palette. But Dad was a walking tragedy. That period had covered my own precious life from eleven to fourteen years old.

Dad's glutinous all-in-one stews were disgusting. It was a wonder I hadn't died from food poisoning. Yes, he drove me to piano lessons and netball comps, but it felt like I'd become his stand-in mother. Dad was as mucky as a three year old. We had a cleaner once a week, but I had to remind Dad to shave, to cart his pile of filthy clothes to the laundry and to drag the bins out on rubbish night; I'd pick up his papers from the floor, deal with the dishwasher, and care for Maud. Dad's wallowing in grief made me feel like an old lady already. The other girls at school might whinge about their nagging mothers, but I longed for a pleasant, mature woman to take Dad in hand and leave me to be a self-absorbed, carefree teenager.

One hot milk and honey later, Dad and I were having the first heart-to-heart we'd had in ages.

'So, what'd make you happy, Georgie?'

'You being happy.' I eyeballed Dad. 'Frank Stanmore, if you don't want a new wife, what do you want?'

'A new life.'

'Meaning?'

'Milly and I used to daydream about escaping the city. Hearing those trams rattle past our place every thirty minutes, right through the night, sends me nuts.'

'Escape to?'

'A country cottage. A couple of acres. Fruit trees.'

'Like that rocking chair song we all used to sing?'

'Yeah. Knowing your neighbours; helping each other out and all that.' Dad shut his eyes and shook his head as if trying to flick the idea away. 'But it's no life for a teenager.'

'Who said?

'I say. You'd have to change schools.'

'Let's give it a go.'

What had I said? Could I handle a sleepy country hole? Then again, if it would make Dad happier, I needed to show some grit.

Due to Dad's chronic case of mopery, I suspected his romantic rural cottage idea might be all talk. But no. He did his research online, came up with a bunch of possibilities in various small towns, and asked me which house appealed. I pointed to one that looked like a child's drawing: a door, two windows, and smoke curling out of a brick chimney. There were photographs: wide-angled interior shots making the rooms look enormous; wrap-around verandahs; a rose-covered arch tilting over a picket front gate with its sign – Langtree. Emerald-green paddocks; a tumbling creek and various sheds. Beneath was printed,

'Historic, owner-built pioneer cottage on town outskirts. Three acres of prime land with creek'. The symbols indicated two bedrooms, living room, kitchen and bathroom.

Then came a write-up of Tintabel: 'Often overlooked in favour of well-known tourist townships, Tintabel is a secret treasure only two-and-a-half hours from the city. Set in lush farming country, this village is a haven for creatives, retirees and hobby farmers. Tintabel boasts a vibrant community spirit. The primary school is famed for its prize-winning vegetable garden. A reliable bus service transports secondary students to a high school serving the wider district.'

Dad drove to Tintabel the following weekend. Because I had a compulsory school camp, I prayed that Dad could make a sensible decision without me being there to advise. Sensible? That same day, he signed the papers. Eight weeks later, we'd rented out our house and moved to Tintabel.

Although this happened four years ago, the picture of us standing on Langtree's rickety wooden verandah is tattooed on my memory. Dad was holding up a large rusty front door key like he'd just won the lottery. It was spring, but scorching and cicada-screaming. A wisteria vine, heavy with fragrant grape-like clusters of mauve-blue flowers, roped along the eaves.

I gestured across the garden. 'Those saggy wire fences need fixing. Lots of holes.'

'Give us time. Ready for the big reveal?'

'Definitely pioneer built,' I said as we stepped across the bare floorboards that sloped up and down like a ship at sea. The high-ceilinged rooms were crammed with the furniture and boxes the removalists had offloaded the day before.

'Mum would've loved this,' said Dad.

You too, I hope, is what I thought.

After most of a day helping Dad heave Grandma's piano into place, haul beds, cupboards, tables and chairs around, empty boxes of china and books, and hang some paintings, I strolled along the unpaved road to the town centre to check it out.

Tintabel was tiny and dead quiet. The real-estate ad should have said 'ghost town'. Not a soul walked the wide main street. The 'vibrant community' must have met underground. My inspection would have taken no more than half an hour, had I not met eighty-year-old Mrs Elaine Murphy. She was resting on a bench in the War Memorial park, which is where I headed because it had a drinking fountain. Picture balding grass, one gumtree and a statue of a soldier with the names of his dead mates on a plaque at the base.

'You're a new face,' cackled a cockatoo voice. 'Would I be right in guessing that youse have got old Selwyn Nichol's place? Take a pew, love.' Elaine Murphy patted the bench, so I sat.

Out shot questions – arctic-blue eyes digging for personal stuff. Other than saying it was just Dad and me who'd moved in, I wouldn't give away one thing more. I side-tracked the old lady by asking her to point out key buildings: Richardson's, a barn of a place selling farm supplies (with the town's only petrol pumps out front); a stone church – Catholic in the mornings and Uniting in the afternoons; a general store, post office and banking facility rolled into one; a community hall (circa 1913) where the Historical Society, the Farmers' Association and Monday playgroup met. Last Saturday of each month, they had line dancing, too.

Fifty metres further away was a sandstone railway station, but the trains had stopped coming. Now it was a café on Fridays and weekends. On the bald hill behind Main Street was a red-brick building – a hospital

and nursing home – staffed by a team of nurses. Dr Asmadi visited twice weekly. 'He's good on bunions and haemorrhoids.'

The dong-donging of a bell somewhere behind us made Mrs Murphy and me swing round.

Across a road on the far side of the park was a white-painted weatherboard school. In the playground, a girl and boy were taking turns hauling a rope, ringing the bell that was housed in a little wooden tower, to announce home-time. About twenty children, different sizes and ages, tumbled out of the building, shepherded by a young woman in a sunhat and wearing a floaty floral dress.

'Ms Lizzie Mackenzie,' said Mrs Murphy. 'Been teaching here two years. Keeps to herself. She's a twitcher.'

I didn't ask what a twitcher was. Maybe someone who suffered involuntary spasms? Or some sort of witch – a T-witch, like a T-Rex?

Meandering back to Langtree, I was calculating how long I could survive Tintabel. Inside the house, I found Dad perched on a teachest, glumly looking through our family photo album.

'We've made a mistake,' he said.

Secretly, I agreed, but I couldn't hack

propping up Dad so soon into this venture. He needed toughening up.

'I'll make you a cuppa and we'll talk.'

'Impossible. The power's not on till tomorrow.' Dad's hands flew upwards in despair. The album thumped to the floor.

'A glass of water then.'

In the lino-floored kitchen, I turned on the tap. The pipe gave a ghostly groan followed by a series of thumps, before spitting out brown water. I leaned on the green marble sink and gazed through the window, down the paddocks and up to the forested hill behind. The setting sun was illuminating a froth of cumulus clouds – as if a candle flickered inside each. Flocks of birds flew across the deepening indigo of the sky; after a busy day, they were focused on winging home.

I looked down at the sink. Clear water was now streaming from the tap.

Clutching his glass, Dad said, 'This is the dumbest thing I've ever done.'

'Dumbest?'

'I've no network. I'm not the type to get out and mix.'

'You could try line dancing.'

'Seriously?'

'I'm joking! It's Tintabel's monthly enter tainment.'

Dad rolled his eyes.

'Dad! We have to give Tintabel a chance.'

'How?'

'I'll come up with something.'

Spring holidays had started, so there wasn't the added torture of beginning at a new school. That night in my bedroom I lay listening to a nocturnal bird's didgeridoo-like hooting – long and lonely. Outside my window, stars pulsed in the purple-black sky. What might Mum's master plan be if she were on this adventure with us?

When I opened my eyes next morning, I had an idea.

'Ducks as well as chooks?' queried Dad between munches of toast.

'Mum loved ducks.'

Two days later, one of the sheds was now a chicken coop housing six ducks, six laying hens and six colourfully-plumed fourteen-week-old pullets.

'Why extra chickens?' I said as we poured layer pellets into a feeder and scattered the hay Dad had bought.

'Ken says you need young females as well as layers. And we lock the birds up for a week so they realise they're home,' said Dad.

'Ken?'

Dad pretended casualness. 'My mate in charge of Richardson's.'

'Good start.'

'So, what next?'

'There's a coffee shop down at that old railway station. It's only open three days a week. This coming Saturday, we'll head there.'

'And meet the locals?'

'You've got it.'

Come Saturday morning, I woke Dad up early. He sighed and began pulling on the clothes he'd worn the day before.

'No, Dad. You dress smart. I bet the whole town will be there. First impressions and all that.'

On our walk to the café, we passed by the General Store where Dad bought his customary weekend paper. I was right about the railway being a gathering place. Along the station platform and in the converted waiting-room, young and old of the district g'day-ed each other; cheerful farmers and their lanky, brown-faced sons tugged at their caps and felt hats in greeting; loudly laughing people crowded around tables. Where had they come from?

Inside, Dad grabbed a vacant corner table and set down his paper, ready for a long, relaxing read. No sooner were we seated than a voice screeched into my ear, 'Well, I never! So this is your dad, Georgie?'

'Oh, Mrs Murphy!'

Dad stood. 'Frank Stanmore. Good to meet you.'

'Call me Elaine! Welcome to our little town. Got employment, have we?'

'I work remotely, Elaine.'

'Nice.' Mrs Murphy disguised her confusion by indicating an elderly woman with permed blue hair seated at a table two across from ours. 'My sister-in-law, Gladys. That's where we have our weekly natter. Better join her. Hooroo.'

A shy girl about my age took our orders and served a fruit juice for me and Dad's usual long black. Dad leant back in his chair, flicked open the paper and sighed. 'Ah, a bit of normality.' He took a worshipful sip of his coffee, then screwed up his face and stared into his drink. I thought he was going to spit the coffee back into his cup.

'What is this?'

'That's a dumb question.'

'If the Railway Café is the only place I can get a coffee for the next few months, then I have to do something about it.'

What sort of 'something' did he mean? Dad was hooked on his coffee, but he wasn't the scene-making type. However, this time he transformed into something like a cartoon action figure. He strode to the counter. The barista was behind the coffee machine, swinging her hips to the pumping beat of the café's music and gazing into the middle distance like a blissed-out DJ.

Dad stepped round the counter to her side. What a cringe-worthy moment. I rushed to stop him, but was too late.

'Hi there. I'm Frank. My daughter and I've moved here from the city. How's about I give you a few coffee-making tips?'

Despite wearing false eye lashes that were so thick and heavy-looking you could have used them for a verandah awning, the girl's eyes opened wide.

Dad commenced instructing her in a pleasantly determined way. The barista's mouth squeezed tiny and tight; she twisted it sideways, demonstrating just how sour she felt. She impatiently tapped her fingers with their black nail polish on the bench top like someone doing piano scales.

Mid-instruction, a tall slim woman, long dark hair, appeared alongside me. She held out a five dollar note to Dad.

'Two of Tintabel's famous Melting Moments, please.'

The barista stared hard and hatefully at

Dad, as if saying, 'I dare you'. He paused for a millisecond, then laughed.

'I used to love playing shops when I was little.' He handed the money to the barista. 'Paper bag and tongs, please.'

Rolling her eyes, she obliged. Dad unscrewed the lid of a glass jar, selected two biscuits, dropped them in the bag and handed them to the woman. 'Enjoy your biccies.'

'My Saturday treat,' she said. 'Thanks!' As she swung away, I recognised the floaty dress – the school teacher, Ms Lizzie McKenzie.

Coffee-making lesson over, Dad and I needed to squeeze by Mrs Elaine Murphy and Gladys to return to our table.

'I see you've met my granddaughter,' Mrs Murphy said to Dad.

Dad was puzzled. 'The dark-haired lady I served?'

'No.' Mrs Murphy looked grim. 'The barista.'

Dad's embarrassing social blunder behind us, the holidays passed with busy nest-making. Out the back, we planted a vegetable garden and fertilised some fruit trees. The chooks and ducks began laying regularly. True to her Shepherd breed, Maud took to quietly herding the ducks in single file round the garden. Towards the end of the holidays, the six pullets fooled us by turning into six handsome roosters. They never fought, but Eden-like, they agreeably shared their territory and the feathered females. However, it wasn't paradise for us. From before dawn, they took turns crowing.

The day I began at my new high school, an enthusiastic rooster woke me at 4am – a bleary start. The school was in the middle of nowhere – just bush. If you'd wanted to skip class, it would have been like a doomed Burke and Wills expedition. The teachers were kind, especially my music teacher, who was keen to help me through Grade Five piano. Initially, the students saw me as a novelty, then that wore off. The girls from my old school had ghosted me, but I had a quietly growing friendship with Sarah Jacobs, who was from a town thirty minutes' drive from Tintabel. She was brilliant at art, so we started planning a sci-fi graphic novel. I'd do the text; Sarah would illustrate.

Things were improving. I had a friend. And the town was starting to accept Dad and me. At our Railway café gatherings on Saturdays, the barista still scowled at Dad, but farmers who recognised Dad from Richardson's greeted him by a touch to their hats. Kids from school would call, 'Hey, Georgie'. The lady who ran the general store regularly put aside Dad's newspaper for him. She sorted the mail and, twigging he was a writer, she'd hand across his correspondence with comments like, 'Maybe a publishing offer, Frank! Going to make your millions writing a blockbuster?'

'I make a crust from journalism, Meg,' he'd remind her.

Nevertheless, a lostness lingered about Dad. He went along with my schemes – but half-heartedly. Then came a run of dark hours. One Saturday morning, we were about to head to the Railway when a young dog dashed into our property. Nose to the ground, tail twirling in circles, the bitzer sniffed out the chooks and ducks who were free-ranging about the garden. He sent them squawking, quacking and flapping under bushes, up small trees and onto our verandah – impossible to re-pen them.

Maud and I chased the dog out of the garden. Tail between legs, he scampered away. What fool would let a dog like this loose in a farming area? Dad was irate about missing his coffee ritual, but our poultry needed protecting. Even with Maud as guard dog, we had to stay home.

Despite our shutting the front gate, by late afternoon the dog had wriggled under or through our un-mended fences twice more. He liked jumping all over Maud who finally lost her temper and nipped his hind legs. Yelping, he hurtled over our front fence and disappeared down the road.

I patted Maud. 'Good job, girl.'

Inside, I poured fresh water into Maud's bowl. She lapped thirstily, then flopped down for a snooze. After a drink and snack, Dad did some writing and I practised the piano. Next thing, it was dusk. Time to lock up the poultry. Hurrying outside, Dad, Maud and I spied a motionless white shape in the grass. A dead duck. Savaged. The killer was sitting at a distance, his head held to one side, as if confused. Dad and I felt volcanic.

The three of us pursued the dog, which sailed over the sagging fence. Once through the front gate, we sprinted after him – fuelled by the high octane energy of anger. The dog darted down a side road. We followed until we came to a neat cottage on stilts. The dog dived under the house. We climbed the steps leading to a front porch where there was a dog basket and a bowl of water. We knocked at the door. Silence. We walked round the back. Here were carefully tended beds of flowering native plants, a bird bath and nesting boxes in the trees. A nature lover who was also an irresponsible dog owner. Hypocrite!

Back home, I penned an icy note to the dog owner.

Langtree,

Tintabel,

Saturday.

My daughter and I are appalled that someone in a rural area should own an untrained, uncontrollable dog that preys on innocent animals. We prize our livestock and are dismayed by your dog's cold-blooded murder of one of our ducks. Countless times, we attempted to drive your dog off our property. He was determined to go on a killing spree.

If you should wish to apologise, our phone number is … 0437 235 9864

If your dog enters our property again, we will go to council.

Regards,

Frank Stanmore.

Dad read my letter. 'Typically dramatic,' he said. 'And the valediction should be "Yours faithfully". But, it'll do.'

'I reckon it's strong and assertive.'

'It is that,' said Dad, staring moodily into his mug of plunger coffee. 'So, who delivers this?'

'Me. And I know how to make our message hit home.'

'How?'

'A genius way to shock the dog's owner into understanding the scale of the crime.'

'Sue them?'

'A simple, no-expense method.'

'Which is?'

'The note will be glued to the top of a box containing the remains of our murdered duck.'

'Georgie, that's going much too far. No!'

'You stay here. I'm delivering it now.'

Dad did his best to stop me, but I was fed up with his lily-livered ways. Clutching a taped-up cardboard box containing the duck corpse and the attached note, I marched off.

On reaching the house, the dog was still guiltily lurking under the house. No sign of the owner. I left the box on the doorstep.

Minutes after I got back home, Dad's phone rang. When he answered, I heard an outraged woman's voice, but I could only make out the words 'dead duck'. Dad went pale.

'Yes, yes, of course,' he said. 'Without

fail. My abject apologies.'

Hands on hips, I stared furiously at Dad. Why was he being so submissive? He finished the call and looked at me with round, horrified eyes.

'What's got into you, Dad?'

'More like what got into you, Georgie?!'

'Huh?'

'The dog isn't hers.'

'But the dog basket! The water bowl!'

'She's been dog-sitting for a friend who's on holiday. She and the dog were out all day.'

'Come again?'

'The dog we chased is a stray.'

'And who's she?'

'Someone called Lizzie Mackenzie.'

'Heck.'

'She's all fired up about the stray's innocence, too. And worse.'

'What?'

'She expects me to collect the dead duck. But, hey, that was your "genius" plan, Georgie. Go fetch!'

'No way!'

'Yes way.'

'Dad! She might be dangerous!'

I knew darn well I should have picked up that duck, myself. Just the same, I got around Dad by claiming that, at fourteen, I was way too young to bowl up to an angry stranger's house. I won. Dad set off to collect the duck.

Good fences can make good neighbours. But in this case, shonky fencing and a dead duck brought my father together with a charming, dark-haired school teacher twitcher (which, by the way, isn't a weird witch, but a birdwatcher).

Dad's reclaiming of the duck corpse turned into a three-hour visit. Once home, I heard how Ms Mackenzie defended the stray as just a bouncy nuisance, not a murderer. The more likely culprit was a Powerful Owl, lately spotted preying on locals' fowls.

For an extended string of Sundays afterwards, my father (binoculars in backpack) set off at daybreak for the Tintabel wetlands bird hide for a morning's birding with Lizzie Mackenzie. It was hard not to grin, but overnight Dad had become a keen twitcher and a bit of an expert on the Regent Honeyeater (*Anthochaera phrygia*).

Lizzie adopted the maligned stray dog, naming him Lucky. He and Maud became best buddies.

And four years later, Frank Stanmore and Lizzie Mackenzie are still together.

The Wannabe Genie

Victor Kelleher

Doug was walking on the beach one day when he found a bottle. An ancient-looking bottle, made of bubbly-green glass, with a glass stopper to match.

Doug tried peering inside, but the glass was too thick and fuzzy. So, he tugged at the stopper, which came away with a popping noise, and out through the opening gushed a cloud of purple smoke.

Something began to move in the smoke! Something alive!

A face appeared first, and after that, the body of someone about Doug's age. He was wearing a red turban, with a bright red ruby in the front; his ears and nose were pierced by heavy gold rings. He was bare-chested, except for the tattoo of a crystal ball, and for trousers, he had what looked like very silky, very baggy pyjamas.

Doug was so stunned he could hardly speak.

'Who are you?' he managed in a whisper.

The stranger bent down and pressed his forehead to Doug's feet.

'My saviour!' he cried. 'You've rescued me from the prison of the bottle.'

Doug leapt backwards as the stranger began kissing his toes.

'Hey! Cut it out!' he yelled. 'Just tell me who you are.'

The stranger stood up and fixed Doug with a grateful smile. 'I was once an apprentice genie,' he explained. 'But I couldn't get my spells just right. They were always a bit off. As a punishment, the Master Genie shrank me into that bottle and threw it into the sea. He said I wouldn't escape for a thousand years.'

That sounded like a ridiculous amount of time to Doug. A thousand years? For getting some spells wrong? He suddenly felt very sorry for the genie, and not only because of his daggy trousers.

'Is that really how long you've been locked away in the bottle?' he asked, just to be sure.

'If this is the twenty-first century,' the genie said, 'then yes, that's about it, give or take a few years. A full millennium, as they say in the scrolls.'

'That Master Genie of yours, he sounds

like a real creep,' said Doug. 'Worse than my dad, and that's saying something.'

The genie shook his turbaned head.

'Oh no, he could have locked me up forever if he'd wanted. As masters go, he's one of the best. Though not as kind and generous as you!'

And the genie made another attempt to kiss Doug's toes.

'Hey! Leave off!' Doug yelled, kicking at the sand to beat him away. 'All I did was open a bottle. It was no big deal.'

The genie rose slowly to his feet.

'It was a big deal for me. So, I'm granting you the standard three wishes. I hear that's the going rate. There's just one problem: like I said, I'm only an apprentice. My spells don't work as well as they should. In fact, they can be pretty low grade. Some might even call them useless. Worse than useless on a bad day. Anyway, you've been warned.'

Doug took no notice of the warning.

'Three wishes!' He let out a low whistle. 'You're kidding me, right?'

'I kid you not,' said the genie.

'And there's no catch? You want nothing in return?'

'Zilch,' the genie replied.

'Then count me in,' Doug told him. 'As for

all that stuff about you being a learner . . . I'll take my chances.'

'You sure about that?' the genie cautioned him.

'Tell you what,' Doug said. 'Give me a demonstration of what you can do – magic-wise, I mean – and we'll take it from there.'

'How about this . . .' the genie suggested, and disappeared in a puff of purple smoke. A few seconds later, he reappeared at Doug's side.

'That's good enough for me,' Doug said. 'So here goes with my first wish. You ready?'

'Ready as I'll ever be,' the genie said, bracing himself for what was to come.

Doug didn't even have to think about it. He knew straight off what he wanted most in the world.

'I want to be rich,' he said. 'That's it, my top wish.'

The genie gave him a tired smile, as if to say, here we go again. 'So how rich is rich?' he asked.

Doug waved one hand vaguely in the air. 'You know, rolling in it. Filthy rich. Like . . . like a movie star, with a mansion, expensive cars, pots of money, servants and anything else you can come up with.'

'That's a pretty big first wish,' the genie pointed out.

'Who cares?' Doug told him. 'It's what I want. And you're the genie, right? So, get on with it.'

The genie sighed. 'Remember what I told you. I'm on my learner plates. I can't promise to get everything spot on.'

'Never mind about that,' said Doug. 'Just give it a go.'

'You'd better stand back then,' said the genie, and closing his eyes, he muttered some magical-sounding words and waved his hands around.

For an instant, the day darkened slightly and a hot wind gusted along the beach, nearly blowing the genie's turban off. As the day brightened again, the genie opened his eyes and straightened his turban.

'I reckon I've done it,' he said with a grin. 'I've made you rich.' He rubbed his hands together, obviously very pleased with himself. 'So, what's on the agenda for wish number two?'

Doug looked around him. The beach was nearly empty, like before. He couldn't see a mansion or expensive cars anywhere.

'Hang on,' he said. 'I need to know you've delivered on the first wish before I make a second. Where's the stuff you promised? The mansion and all the rest?'

'It's right where your old house used to

be. Back in the street where you've always lived.'

'Hang on,' Doug said again. 'Why didn't you give me a place in a posh area, where the other rich people hang out?'

'Because you didn't ask for that. Or for a new piece of land. Only for the mansion and the usual trimmings. I was just obeying orders, genie style.'

'So you say,' Doug grumbled.

'Anyway, head off home,' the genie urged him, 'and check out the new place for yourself. I'll wait here.'

'No way,' said Doug suspiciously. 'You're coming with me. I'm not letting you out of my sight until I've had all my wishes.'

'Suit yourself,' the genie said. 'Your word is my command. Isn't that how it's supposed to go?'

Doug was beginning to lose faith in magic wishes. All the way home, he harboured the suspicion that this whole genie thing was some kind of trick.

But he was wrong. When they reached his street, there was the biggest mansion he'd ever seen. It had squeezed everything else out – stretching right across the road, and from one corner to the next.

'What do you reckon?' asked the genie.

'Wow, what a . . .' Doug began, and

stopped, as he noticed something weird. 'Hold on a sec. Where are the windows? And the doors? What are all those gaping holes in the walls doing there?'

'I told you my spells aren't perfect,' the genie said defensively.

'That's the understatement of the year. Take a look at the roof. It doesn't even fit. It's too small! And those side walls! They're nearly falling down!'

The mansion, so-called, was even more of a wreck inside. There were no cupboards, no carpets, no overhead lights, no ceilings in half the rooms. There were heaps of builder's rubble everywhere, and the floor (where there was any floor!) looked more rickety than the roof.

'Do you call this a mansion?' said Doug. 'I call it a dump.'

Doug's mum and dad obviously agreed.

'What's happening to us?' they muttered desperately, as they hurried from room to room. 'We can't live here, in this . . . this *tip*! Nobody could.'

Doug had never seen his parents so worried before. Even at the best of times, they weren't the happiest people in the world; but they weren't usually this miserable.

'This house is the pits,' he told the genie.

'You haven't made my life better; you've made it worse. Nothing could be as awful as this.'

But again, he was wrong. Because round about then the neighbours began crowding in through the doorless opening in the front hall.

'What have you done with our houses?' they shouted. 'And our gardens? We demand them back!'

They looked so upset that Doug and the genie made a run for it – down a dusty passage and into a windowless room. Caught in a dead-end, they could hear the angriest of the neighbours pounding along the passage after them.

'You got us into this mess,' Doug said to the genie. 'How about you get us out of it? In a hurry!'

'It'll cost you,' the genie pointed out. 'There are no freebies where I come from.'

Okay, okay. So here's my second wish. Give me a mansion in the country instead. Make sure it's a beautiful part of the country. Oh, and take us there on a magic carpet. Yeah, that should do it. But don't hang about!'

The genie frowned.

'That sounds like two wishes to me. A mansion *and* a magic carpet ride.'

The angry neighbours were getting closer. Some were yelling for blood.

'One wish or two, what does it matter?' said Doug. 'Just do it!'

'Wishes two and three coming up,' the genie said, and spun around on his heels.

Then he snapped his fingers, and the whole day dimmed again. That same hot wind blew past, stronger than before, and the last of the daylight slipped away. Doug, lost in a shadowy space, felt the ground lift beneath him and he glimpsed a starlit sky rushing past overhead.

They landed with a bump that tipped the genie's turban over his eyes, and all at once the day brightened.

'Here we are, safe and sound,' the genie declared, straightening his turban, and adding a puff of purple smoke for good measure.

When it cleared, Doug found himself standing on a country road. Beside them, in an otherwise empty paddock – with wonderful views of forested mountains – was a huge mansion.

'There it is,' said the genie proudly. 'Exactly what the client ordered: wish number three. Wish number two, of course, being the magic carpet ride – a special privilege, I might add, as carpet rides are usually reserved for genies. Anyway, I'm done here. Time I was on my way.'

'Not so fast!' Doug grabbed at the genie's baggy silk trousers and yanked him back, just as he was about to step onto his carpet. 'This mansion is worse than the last one. Check it out. It's hardly more than an untidy pile of bricks! In fact, it's the biggest wreck ever.'

A car drew up while they were standing there, and dropped off Doug's mum and dad, who stood open-mouthed, staring at their new home.

'Good heavens!' sobbed Doug's mum. 'What did we do to deserve this? Somebody up there must have it in for us!'

Doug's dad was trying hard not to cry.

'We're ruined!' they wailed together.

Doug hated seeing them so down, and was almost glad when they wandered off along the nearest lane.

'You've got to do something,' he told the genie. 'You can't leave everything like this!'

'Sorry, mate,' said the genie. 'You've had all your wishes, and a deal's a deal. Look on the bright side: you've got a lovely plot of land this time, and all this peace and quiet.' He waved a hand at the deserted countryside. 'There'll be no one out here to disturb you.'

As if to prove him wrong, there was a series of rattles and bangs and a local farmer arrived in his ancient ute.

'Hoy!' he yelled. 'What's that dump doing on my farm? Get it off or I'll have the law on you!'

'There you are,' Doug said. 'No lovely plot of land, and a dump for a house. It's not much of a wish, is it?'

'Hm . . .' said the genie. 'I see what you mean.'

'Here's the problem,' the genie said. 'When people let genies out of bottles, they get three wishes in exchange. That's the time-honoured rule, and as I'm only a learner genie, I'm not in a position to change it. What would my master say? He'd probably squeeze me back in a bottle – a smaller bottle maybe – for another thousand years. Or worse, an eternity or two. That's how masters are, believe me. Now, you wouldn't want that to happen, would you?'

Doug had to admit that he wouldn't.

'Well, there you go,' said the genie. 'I've honoured my part of the contract, so . . .'

'Wait on,' Doug interrupted him. 'If you really think about it, I've only had two half wishes.'

'What about the magic ride out here to

the country? You've got to factor that in as well.'

'All right, one whole wish and two halves. After all, you haven't made me rich like you promised. And where's the pile of cash I asked for? All I have is a pile of bricks instead, and on someone else's land.'

'Yeah, I suppose you do have a point there,' admitted the genie.

'As I see it,' Doug went on, 'you still owe me a whole wish.'

The genie pulled thoughtfully at his nose ring.

'Okay,' he said at last. 'One more wish, but that's my limit.'

'What if your spells go wrong again?' Doug asked. 'Do I get another go?'

'Not on my watch,' the genie said. 'That would mean more bottle time, for certain. Now then, let's get down to it: what do you want for your very last wish?'

Doug found that a hard question to answer. He had tried becoming rich, and failed. Though it wasn't being poor that troubled him: it was how much he missed the house and street he had grown up in.

'Get a move on,' said the genie. 'I haven't got all day. I'd like to fly off to Arabia before dark.'

Doug reached a decision.

'Here's my third and final wish. I want

my old home back. Plus my old life. I want everything the way it was . . . only better.'

'If I'm not mistaken,' said the genie, 'that's four wishes. And the last one – about making everything better than before – that's a really tough call.'

'Oh, come on,' Doug begged him. 'Think of it as a package deal. You know you won't get it all right anyway. I'll be lucky if I get one decent wish out of the whole thing.'

'You should have been a genie; do you realise that?' said the genie. 'You really know how to talk people round.'

'So, it's a deal? Even the part about making everything better?'

'It's a deal.'

Because Doug had forgotten to ask for a free ride home, and because the genie was dead set against giving away any more freebies, they had to take a train back to the city.

The genie complained all the way.

'I'll never get to Arabia at this rate,' he grumbled. 'A thousand years already, and that's still not enough for some people.'

He didn't have much to say, though, when they reached Doug's street. There was the old house, as promised. But like the mansions, it was a wreck: its iron roof nearly rusted away, its windows broken, its doors hanging off their hinges.

'Oh no!' Doug groaned. 'I'm worse off than ever!'

But for once that wasn't the whole story, because when they walked in through the front door, the inside was like a palace. And that wasn't all. There was a happy feeling in the air, as if all the problems in the world had vanished in a puff of (purple?) smoke.

It was the same with Doug's mum and dad. They still looked pretty old, but now they were brimming over with health and happiness. His mum especially couldn't wipe the grin off her face.

'Welcome home, son!' she cried, and gave him the biggest hug he could remember.

She gave the genie a big hug too. And to the neighbours, when they popped over to borrow stuff. (The neighbours, Doug noticed, were nearly as cheerful as his mum and dad.)

'I got the "better" part right, didn't I?' whispered the genie.

'Yeah, well done,' Doug said, and handed him back his bottle. 'Here, I'd smash this if I were you, to be on the safe side.'

'Ta,' said the genie. 'I might just do that.'

'I expect you'll be off to Arabia right away then,' Doug added.

All at once, however, the genie didn't seem too keen to leave.

'It's not cheerful like this at the college for genies,' he pointed out. 'And that's where I'll end up after my latest showing. In fact, I kind of like it here. I reckon I'll stick around for a bit. If that's all right with you.'

'Good idea,' Mum cut in before Doug could answer. 'Young Doug here could do with a friend. He's too much of a loner, which is a worry. Get him to show you his room. It has bunk beds, so there's already a place for you to sleep.'

The genie liked the look of the bunk beds, which hadn't been invented when he was shut up in the bottle.

'Wow, look at those!' he said. 'Any chance of me sleeping in the top bunk?'

Doug shook his head. 'No way, that's mine.'

'How about a trade?' suggested the genie.

'Depends what you're offering. And don't fob me off with another of your crummy wishes.'

'Then how about this? I stay here for a year and get to use your top bunk, and in exchange, you get to spend a year in Arabia, training to be a genie. In other words, you take my place at Genie College.'

'But I don't even look like a genie.'

'That can soon be fixed. I can cook up a few spells and supply you with all the gear – the turban, the piercings, the tattoo . . . the whole outfit. I can even toss in a free ride on a luxury magic carpet.'

'Mmmm, sounds interesting,' Doug said.

'Just think about it,' the genie went on. 'You could learn all manner of spells, such as how to create your own mansion, or get your hands on a big pile of cash.'

Doug had to admit he liked the idea, especially the big pile of cash bit, which he hadn't had much luck with so far.

'So . . . are you in?' the genie pressed him.

'I'm in,' Doug said.

'Okay, then, here we go.'

Again, the light dimmed. Again, a hot wind blew. And . . . *Poof!* Everything was enveloped in a cloud of purple smoke.

When the smoke cleared, the genie had the room completely to himself. Dressed in Doug's clothes, and with a contented smile on his face, he lay sprawled on the top bunk.

Meanwhile, far, far away, and high above the clouds, a hand-woven carpet was speeding through the air. Seated on it was Doug, though not a Doug his mum and dad would have recognised. This Doug was bare-chested and resplendent in a scarlet turban, gold piercings, and baggy silk trousers. He also had a splendid, bright blue tattoo on his chest. It consisted of three words: **Arabia or Bust**.

It looked as though the junior genie had finally got it right. Or very nearly. There was just one tiny problem . . .

Doug was speeding in the wrong direction, with Antarctica dead ahead.

Old Tom's Room

Leigh Hobbs

Angela prepared to do some light dusting in the temple of doom.

She knew it may be a mission . . .

. . . of no return.

The Story of My Life

Harry Laing

Someone is writing the story of my life
and it's not me

someone is bad-typing my life
texting me into reverse
de-instagramming, un-TikToking my life
and I'm watching it spin

because someone is writing my life
with twists and turns I don't see coming
the feeling is I have to keep running

is it you?
are you writing the story of my life?
could you let me know where we're at in the story
when you're about to plunge me
into that river, off the cliff
into that situation of maximum
embarrassment?

do you enjoy ending the chapter
with me hanging off the roof
with my hands on the gutter?

all I can hold onto
is my beginning,
I know I wrote that

so please stop writing my life
it's my story
and I don't want to know the ending.

Raid

Lorraine Marwood

In the sunset, the farmhouse
trails a skirt of fruit trees,
in need of stitching repair,
years of neglect, an uneven fanning,
like jagged spears at the outer edge of shadow.

The driveway is booby-trapped
with rocks as ammunition for catapults
and three boys come to catapult,
to shatter the window ghosts.
Bang! Explosion of tight-held breath,
hessian vespers and potpourri tears.
Such an echoing babel!

The rusted water tanks
are like rings around the eyes
of season by season of sleeplessness
and the wind saws at the edges
of the tanks, a rattling dog-chain clamour.

The boys hesitate, catapults primed.
By now the wind is in the sugar gums
then spinning the clothesline one way,
then screeching the other way.
There is an aching
a whining of years, of pegs
holding fast sheets
holding fast shirts
captive and gyrating.

The same wind whistles through
the stock yard untethering
every splinter of wool, of thorn,
of cattle hide tufts, then shooting
them out like poison darts
sharpening the gloom, just before
the proper declaration of night.

Three boys, with moon-cornered eyes,
the only illumination of fear
move closer to each other.
Catapults with crumbling ammunition
abandoned for swift moving feet
that pound dirt when the wind

begins a drumming, a sawing
of the loose sheets of iron roofing
on the house itself.

Away, away, the boys themselves
are now catapulted, pulling the smudges
of night shadows apart
with hiccoughing breath.

And so, the salting of rumour,
of ghosts, of loneliness,
of despair swirling, galloping,
patrolling the abandoned farm,
takes hold.
Two broken front windows
snarl like wolf teeth,
warding off attempts at trespass,
dust flings its grit across
the kitchen table,
still set for marmalade breakfast,
while the seasons pockmark
each memory of harvest
of growth, of family, of hope,
with its silvery powder-thick
tongue.

Waiting...

Meredith Costain

Sad silent scooter
Propping up a wall
Drowning in a river
Waiting for the call

Sliding down embankments
Hanging from the trees
Littering the pavements
Huddled in the breeze

Sad silent scooter
Hope you find a friend
Someone cool to start you up
And zoom off round the bend.

How to Catch a Shadow

Sherryl Clark

3.20am and my room is so dark
I can't see my hands,
but I can hear footsteps
on the roof.
Time to fly.
I half-unfold my wings with a rustle
like silk, open the window and
stand on the sill, waiting.

There – a quick flicker.
I have to be quicker.
I launch, fully unfold, dive and
swoop up. Where is it?
There. My silver net spreads,
its sticky threads glisten.
Whoosh! Wrap. Roll.
I clutch it close.
It's mine again.

A Tattoo

Steven Herrick

An old lady with hair like silver fairy floss
walks into a doctor's surgery,
rolls up her cream-coloured cardigan
to have her blood pressure checked,
only to reveal a tattoo
of a swallow in mid-flight on her forearm
and underneath is the name
DAVID.
The swallow is wrinkled,
its wings faded,
and when the doctor asks her who David is
she remembers
it was the first boy she kissed.
David told her he loved her,
promised he'd ink her name on his arm,
she did the same.
Their love lasted
longer than the sting of the needle
but David the boy flew away
faster than the swallow,
leaving a mark
to always remind her,
the pain of lost love
the stain of her first kiss.

Willy Wagtail

Ursula Dubosarsky

Late at night
No stars no moon
I heard a windy
Whistling tune

I heard it sing
The whole night long
I never knew
So strange a song

The notes were dreamy
Droll and deep
I closed my eyes
But could not sleep

I went outside
I heard it call
But nobody
Was there at all

And in the glaze of
Morning sun
The world was still
The song was done

Then through the web
Of branches vast
Something flittered
Fluttered past

And then I knew
What I had heard!
A shy and gentle
Little bird

Perched on high
This ancient tree
It tipped its head
And gazed at me.

'By night I will
Forever sing!
Of everything –
Of everything!'

About the Contributors

Deborah Abela

After training as a teacher, Deb travelled to Africa, where she was trapped in a desert sandstorm, harassed by monkeys and thrown in jail twice. She's since become an internationally published and awarded author of thirty books, including her climate change trilogy, *Grimsdon*, *New City* and *Final Storm*. Her latest books are *The Book of Wondrous Possibilities* and *The Kindness Project*.
www.deborahabela.com

Janeen Brian

Janeen is an award-winning children's author and poet with over 110 books published in the trade and educational markets. She writes picture books, novels, short fiction, poetry and non-fiction. One book, *Yong: the journey of an unworthy son*, was adapted into a play, performed in the Sydney Opera House and won the

Sydney Theatre Award for Best Production for Children 2023. Janeen left primary teaching in 1990 to write full time.

Sue Burzstynski

Sue is the author of fourteen books for children and teens, including fiction and non-fiction. She has written short stories for magazines and articles for the School Magazine. Her young adult novel *Wolfborn* was a CBCA Notable book. Ford Street Publishing published her history of crime in Australia, *Crime Time: Australians Behaving Badly*. Sue was a teacher librarian and now does casual teaching and writing.

Isobelle Carmody

Isobelle writes science fiction, fantasy, children's and juvenile literature. She divides her time between a home on the Great Ocean Road in Australia and her travels abroad. She began work on the highly acclaimed *Obernewtyn Chronicles* when she was just fourteen years old. She is currently editing a new young adult book titled *Comes the Night* to be published in 2024.

Sherryl Clark

Sherryl is the author of more than seventy books for young readers, from picture books to novels. Her verse novels have won several major awards. She also writes crime fiction for adults, and works part-time as an editor.

Bill Condon

Bill lives in New South Wales with his wife, the well-known children's author, Dianne (Di) Bates. He has written more than 100 books for children and young adults. In 2010 he won the Prime Minister's Literature Award for young adult fiction. Many years ago, he also used to race greyhounds – they always beat him.

Meredith Costain

Meredith is a versatile writer and editor from Melbourne whose work ranges from picture books through to poetry, series fiction and non-fiction. Her books include the quirky *Ella Diaries*, which are frequently shortlisted in children's choice awards, CBCA Honour Book *Doodledum Dancing*, *Dog Squad*, and *Musical Harriet*, which was adapted for TV by the ABC. www.meredithcostain.com

Gary Crew

Gary is Professor Emeritus (Creative Writing) at the University of the Sunshine Coast. He has written 100 novels, illustrated books and short stories which are published internationally and has won The Children's Book Council of Australia award four times. Gary is the Australian nominee (prose) for the Hans Christian Andersen medal in 2024. He lives in blissful isolation overlooking the sea on beautiful subtropical Bribie Island, Queensland.

Cecilia Dart-Thornton

Cecilia is the author of the critically acclaimed *Bitterbynde* trilogy and the forthcoming young adult historical fantasy trilogy *Madigan's Leap*. After receiving a BA in sociology, Cecilia worked as a teacher and as an editor in a publishing house. She is now a full-time writer, and her work is published internationally in a range of languages.

Justin D'Ath

Justin has written sixty books, mostly for kids and young adult. His work has been published worldwide and been translated into eighteen languages. Justin's latest title is *Banjo Tully*, a novel for eleven- to fifteen-year-olds (and adults of every age) published by Ford Street.

Ursula Dubosarsky

Ursula was born in Sydney and wanted to be a writer from age six. She is the author of over sixty books for children and young adults and has been nominated internationally for the Hans Andersen and Astrid Lindgren awards. She was the Australian Children's Laureate for 2020-21.

Michael Earp

Michael is a non-binary writer and bookseller living in Naarm. They are the editor of *Everything Under the Moon: Fairy tales in a queerer light* and *Kindred: 12 Queer #LoveOzYA Stories*. Their writing has also appeared in *Archer*, *The Age*, *PopMatters*, *The Victorian Writer*, *Aurealis* and *Underdog: #LoveOzYA Short Stories*.

Elizabeth Fensham

At six years of age, Elizabeth wrote a truly terrible, un-publishable story. Her six-year-old self would be pleased to know that she has now written ten published novels, some of them award winning or short-listed. She writes for a range of ages – from younger readers to young adults. The writing process makes her happy.

Pamela Freeman

Pamela is a multi-award winning author of more than forty books. As Pamela Freeman, she writes children's and young adult books, in a range of genres. Her most recent children's book, *Dry to Dry: The Seasons of Kakadu*, won the CBCA Eve Pownall Award. As Pamela Hart, she writes murder mysteries and historical novels. Her newest mystery is *Fatal Crossing*, the third in the *Poppy McGowan* series.

Scot Gardner

Scot came to writing down a long winding path of careers including landscape gardening, massage and counselling, professional music, teaching and driving delivery trucks. *Off the Map* is his twentieth book and his backlist includes award-winning and internationally acclaimed books such as *Burning Eddy* and *The Dead I Know*. He has a bristling fascination for the natural world.

Susanne Gervay

Planting mangroves in Kiribati, speaking in Istanbul, reaching outback Indigenous children, Susanne writes about hope. Awarded an OAM, she delves into the great issues of our time – from disability in *Butterflies*, harmony in *Elephants Have Wings*, bullying with the *I Am Jack* books, vision in *The Boy in the Big Blue Glasses*, the Holocaust with *Heroes of the Secret Underground*, to consent in *The Edge of Limits*. sgervay.com

Steven Herrick

Steven is widely recognised as a pioneer of the verse novel for young people. His books have twice won the NSW Premier's Literary Awards and been shortlisted for the CBCA Book of the Year Awards on ten occasions. In 2019, his verse novel *by the river* won the Katholischer Jugendbuchpreis, and the prestigious Deutscher Jugendliteraturpreis in Germany. His latest book is *In times of bushfires and billy buttons*.

Simon Higgins

Simon is a former police officer, prosecutor and private investigator. A long-term martial arts student and history buff, his international publishing career spans twenty-five years, fifteen novels, and several foreign language editions. He's authored screenplays for internationally-awarded

films and animated TV shows. He currently lives in China, lecturing tertiary students and writing for television.
www.simonhiggins.net

Leigh Hobbs

Leigh is an artist and author best known for the twenty-three books he has written and illustrated featuring his characters Old Tom, Mr Chicken, Horrible Harriet, Mr Badger, The FREAKS in 4F and Fiona the Pig. Leigh was the Australian Children's Laureate in 2016-17.

Ian Irvine

Ian, an Australian marine scientist, has also written thirty-five novels. His *Three Worlds* epic fantasy sequence has been published in many countries and languages. He has also written eco-thrillers set in a world undergoing catastrophic climate change, young adult fantasy, humorous fantasy for children, a role-playing game scenario and much about the art of storytelling.

George Ivanoff

George is a Melbourne author who's written over 100 books for kids and teens. His books include *Monster Island*, the *Gamers* trilogy, the interactive *You Choose* series, the non-fiction *Survival Guides*, the *RFDS Adventures* and the *Otherworlds* series; as well as a ton of school readers and education titles. He has one wife, two kids and an uncontrollable imagination. georgeivanoff.com.au

Barry Jonsberg

Barry is a multi-award-winning international author, published in twenty countries and translated into fourteen languages. His book, *My Life As An Alphabet*, was made into the award-winning film *H is for Happiness* starring Richard Roxburgh and Miriam Margolyes in 2019. Negotiations are underway for a Broadway musical based upon the same book.

Victor Kelleher

Victor grew up in London, and began his working life at sixteen in the mines of Central Africa. He then studied hard and ended up here in Australia, as an associate professor of English. He abandoned that career in order to write; eventually gave up writing in order to roam the world again; and gave up roaming in order to write again. He has published over fifty books, and won many awards.

Harry Laing

Harry is a poet and comic performer. His collections of poetry for children are *Shoctopus*, *MoonFish* and *RapperBee*. He is in demand as a guest author in schools and regularly performs his poems for hundreds of kids. Harry lives on 115 acres beside Monga National Park, near Braidwood, NSW, where the wombats give him a hard time.

John Larkin

John is a multi-award-winning author. His 2012 novel *The Shadow Girl* won the Victorian Premier's Literary Award while *The Pause* won the 2015 Queensland Literary Award and was short-listed for the CBCA Book of the Year Award for Older Readers. His last book was *Zombies Vs the Illuminati* and his current book is *The Bogan Book Club*.

Juliet Marillier

Juliet is the author of twenty-five novels and two collections of short fiction. She writes mostly for adult readers and sometimes for young adults. Her work is published internationally and has won many awards. When not writing, Juliet looks after a small pack of elderly rescue dogs.

Lorraine Marwood

Lorraine writes poetry and verse novels. She has six collections of poetry for children and four published verse novels. Her verse novels for children have won the Prime Minister's Literary and NSW Premier's Literary awards. She is currently working on a PhD in children's verse novels. She loves weaving history into fiction. Her latest book is *Footprints on the Moon*.
www.lorrainemarwood.com

David Metzenthen

David is a Melbourne-based writer who was born way before you were. He has published many books, is highly awarded, and hopes one day to write a perfect sentence. Regarding this story, David sees something fascinating in wild rabbits, and of course, interesting people. He continues to write and hope!

Sophie Masson

Born in Indonesia of French parents, Sophie is the award-winning author of over seventy books for children, young adults and adults. Her most recent titles for children are *Satin* (illustrated by Lorena Carrington) and a middle-grade historical novel, *The Key to Rome*. In 2019, Sophie received an AM award in the Order of Australia honours list for her significant service to literature.

Sean McMullen

Sean is the author of over 100 stories and thirty-two books, a dozen of which are young adult, science fiction or fantasy. He was a Hugo Award nominee in 2011, and his works have been translated into fourteen languages. During business hours he also had a career in scientific computing.

Kirsty Murray

Kirsty is a multi-award-winning author of twenty-five books for children and young adults. Her works include eleven novels as well as non-fiction, junior fiction and picture books. From historical fiction to dystopian fantasies, Kirsty's stories span genres and explore ideas about the past, present and the future.
kirstymurray.com

James Phelan

James is the author of thirty books, including non-fiction, suspense thrillers, young adult, and middle grade fiction. After studying architecture, James worked at *The Age* as a staff writer, then studied an MA in Writing, and a PhD in Literature. At twenty-six he retired to write fiction full time.

Oliver Phommavanh

Oliver is an author and comedian who uses his experience as a primary school teacher to inspire kids to write funny stories. He's also a sneaker YouTuber (find him at Virtual Oliver P) and burger fanatic. His books include *Thai-riffic!*, *Con-nerd* and *What About Thao*.

Michael Pryor

Master storyteller Michael Pryor writes fantasy and science fiction, mostly for teenagers. He has published more than thirty-five novels and fifty short stories and he is one of the co-publishers of *Aurealis*, Australia's longest running Fantasy/SF magazine. He has been shortlisted for the Aurealis Award eleven times, and nine of his books have been CBCA Notable books. www.michaelpryor.com.au.

Pamela Rushby

Pamela has worked in advertising, as a pre-school teacher, and as a writer and producer of educational television, audio

and multimedia. She currently freelances as a writer, and loves delving into history to find her stories. Her books and films have won many awards (which she is far too modest to list).
www.pamelarushby.com

Anne Ryan

Anne is an author, illustrator, artist and Visual Art educator living in Melbourne. Through school visits, artist in residence programs, workshops and teaching as a Visual Art specialist, she has enjoyed sharing her creative processes and storytelling with young children for many years.

Trinity Ryan

Trinity has never been normal. She discovered there were better things to be. Trinity played saxophone in the Olympics, became a Mental Health Consumer Peer Worker, and followed her dream to write. Trinity is a proud aunty, her longest friend was a carpet python, and a cat keeps her company. 'The Clockmaker's Cat' is her first published story.

Lucy Sussex

Lucy is a New Zealand writer living in

Australia. She has abiding interests in women's lives, history and Australiana. Her writing includes anything from fairy penguins to horror and true crime. In 2025 she will publish *The Outrageous Fortunes*, a co-written biography about crime-writer Mary Fortune and her criminal son George.

Shaun Tan

Shaun grew up in Perth and works as an artist, writer and film-maker in Melbourne. He is best known for illustrated books that deal with social and historical subjects through dream-like imagery, widely translated throughout the world and enjoyed by readers of all ages. Shaun is the recipient of an Academy Award for the short animated film *The Lost Thing*, the prestigious Astrid Lindgren Memorial Award in Sweden and the Kate Greenaway Medal in the UK.

Tony Thompson

Tony lives in the Blue Mountains. He grew up in Toronto, Canada and travelled from place to place until deciding that Australia had the magic formula of good weather, great coffee and decent pizza. He has written five books, including a novel about the early life of Mary Shelley and an exhaustive study of the music of The Doors. He plays blues harmonica with great enthusiasm.

Sean Williams

Sean is a #1 New York Times-bestselling, multi-award-winning author for readers of all ages. He is also a composer of music and scores for stage and screen. He lives and works in Kaurna Country, South Australia.

Dianne Wolfer

Dianne is an award-winning WA author of twenty-five books for children and teens. She writes across genres and her books have been translated and adapted for screen and stage. Dianne's PhD research focused on anthropomorphism and ways animal characters are used in fiction. She loves travelling and her work is inspired by nature.

More great reading from Ford Street Publishing

Rich & Rare

A COLLECTION OF AUSTRALIAN STORIES, POETRY AND ARTWORK

Edited by Paul Collins   Foreword by Sophie Masson

'An epic book. Highly recommended' – Margaret Hamilton

'This anthology is full of sparkling gems of images and stories'
– Children's Books Daily

'Chocka-block with delightfully tasty reads from a plethora of Australian authors' – Booksellers of NZ blog

'This is a book that every Library should buy, and would make an absolutely wonderful gift for the 10-14 year old reader. Highly recommended' – ReadPlus

'An exemplary collection on several levels'
– The Sydney Morning Herald

www.fordstreetpublishing.com   FORD ST

More great reading from Ford Street Publishing

THE VANILLA SLICE KID

Adam Wallace and Jack Wodhams
Illustrations by Tom Gittus

Archie Cunningham is a shy boy who has three things – incredibly mean and greedy parents, no friends, and an amazing power.

When an uploaded video shows the world what Archie can do, he suddenly becomes the main ingredient in a recipe for world domination.

And then the fun really begins!

www.fordstreetpublishing.com

FORD ST

More great reading from Ford Street Publishing

DEAD DOG IN THE STILL OF THE NIGHT

There are two wolves inside us all. One is evil.

Life is tough for Primo, and about to get even tougher. Crashing his father's prized red Bambino Fiat 500 is just the first in a series of ill-fated events – events which are inexplicably entwined with a dead dog in the still of the night.

Throw in a volatile relationship with his girlfriend, a senseless bashing, and an attempt to save his brother's flawed marriage and you begin to realise the extent of what Primo is up against.

Can he overcome such adversity to make his life sane again?

Archimede Fusillo

www.fordstreetpublishing.com

FORD ST